Eurozone Politics

The crisis of the Eurozone has had a significant impact on the politics of Europe. In many countries, the euro was largely interpreted by elites as a development that would ameliorate their nations' problems. However, recent events have proven the contrary, with the rise of radical right-wing politics and populism across the continent.

This book investigates the politics of the euro, with a primary focus on Italy, but with additional chapters on the UK and Germany. Using a range of original and secondary data, it reconstructs how the euro was interpreted by both elites and non-elites from the late nineties to 2010. By recruiting a large sample of non-elites, it examines perceptions of the euro and the ways in which these views allowed for the justification of painful austerity measures required to enter the Economic and Monetary Union. In doing so, it sheds light on the ways in which non-elites interpret complex political objects like the euro and provides a systemic comparison of the cognitive schema of non-elites and elites.

This book will be of key interest to scholars and students of the European Union, European politics, Italian politics, comparative politics, and political economy.

Philip Giurlando is Assistant Professor at Trent University, Ontario, Canada.

Routledge Advances in European Politics

1 **Russian Messianism**
Third Rome, revolution, Communism and after
Peter J.S. Duncan

2 **European Integration and the Postmodern Condition**
Governance, democracy, identity
Peter van Ham

3 **Nationalism in Italian Politics**
The stories of the Northern League, 1980–2000
Damian Tambini

4 **International Intervention in the Balkans since 1995**
Edited by Peter Siani-Davies

5 **Widening the European Union**
The politics of institutional change and reform
Edited by Bernard Steunenberg

6 **Institutional Challenges in the European Union**
Edited by Madeleine Hosli, Adrian van Deemen and Mika Widgrén

7 **Europe Unbound**
Enlarging and reshaping the boundaries of the European Union
Edited by Jan Zielonka

8 **Ethnic Cleansing in the Balkans**
Nationalism and the destruction of tradition
Cathie Carmichael

9 **Democracy and Enlargement in Post-Communist Europe**
The democratisation of the general public in fifteen Central and Eastern European countries, 1991–1998
Christian W. Haerpfer

10 **Private Sector Involvement in the Euro**
The power of ideas
Stefan Collignon and Daniela Schwarzer

11 **Europe**
A Nietzschean perspective
Stefan Elbe

12 **European Union and E-Voting**
Addressing the European Parliament's internet voting challenge
Edited by Alexander H. Trechsel and Fernando Mendez

13 **European Union Council Presidencies**
A comparative perspective
Edited by Ole Elgström

14 **European Governance and Supranational Institutions**
Making states comply
Jonas Tallberg

15 **European Union, NATO and Russia**
Martin Smith and Graham Timmins

16 **Business, The State and Economic Policy**
The case of Italy
G. Grant Amyot

17 **Europeanization and Transnational States**
Comparing Nordic central governments
Bengt Jacobsson, Per Lægreid and Ove K. Pedersen

18 **European Union Enlargement**
A comparative history
Edited by Wolfram Kaiser and Jürgen Elvert

19 **Gibraltar**
British or Spanish?
Peter Gold

20 **Gendering Spanish Democracy**
Monica Threlfall, Christine Cousins and Celia Valiente

21 **European Union Negotiations**
Processes, networks and negotiations
Edited by Ole Elgström and Christer Jönsson

22 **Evaluating Euro-Mediterranean Relations**
Stephen C. Calleya

23 **The Changing Face of European Identity**
A seven-nation study of (supra) national attachments
Edited by Richard Robyn

24 **Governing Europe**
Discourse, governmentality and European integration
William Walters and Jens Henrik Haahr

25 **Territory and Terror**
Conflicting nationalisms in the Basque country
Jan Mansvelt Beck

26 **Multilateralism, German Foreign Policy and Central Europe**
Claus Hofhansel

27 **Popular Protest in East Germany**
Gareth Dale

28 **Germany's Foreign Policy Towards Poland and the Czech Republic**
Ostpolitik revisited
Karl Cordell and Stefan Wolff

29 **Kosovo**
The politics of identity and space
Denisa Kostovicova

30 **The Politics of European Union Enlargement**
Theoretical approaches
Edited by Frank Schimmelfennig and Ulrich Sedelmeier

31 **Europeanizing Social Democracy?**
The rise of the party of European socialists
Simon Lightfoot

32 **Conflict and Change in EU Budgetary Politics**
Johannes Lindner

33 Gibraltar, Identity and Empire
E.G. Archer

34 Governance Stories
Mark Bevir and R.A.W Rhodes

35 Britain and the Balkans
1991 until the present
Carole Hodge

36 The Eastern Enlargement of the European Union
John O'Brennan

37 Values and Principles in European Union Foreign Policy
Edited by Sonia Lucarelli and Ian Manners

38 European Union and the Making of a Wider Northern Europe
Pami Aalto

39 Democracy in the European Union
Towards the emergence of a public sphere
Edited by Liana Giorgi, Ingmar Von Homeyer and Wayne Parsons

40 European Union Peacebuilding and Policing
Michael Merlingen with Rasa Ostrauskaite

41 The Conservative Party and European Integration since 1945
At the heart of Europe?
N.J. Crowson

42 E-Government in Europe
Re-booting the state
Edited by Paul G. Nixon and Vassiliki N. Koutrakou

43 EU Foreign and Interior Policies
Cross-pillar politics and the social construction of sovereignty
Stephan Stetter

44 Policy Transfer in European Union Governance
Regulating the utilities
Simon Bulmer, David Dolowitz, Peter Humphreys and Stephen Padgett

45 The Europeanization of National Political Parties
Power and organizational adaptation
Edited by Thomas Poguntke, Nicholas Aylott, Elisabeth Carter, Robert Ladrech and Kurt Richard Luther

46 Citizenship in Nordic Welfare States
Dynamics of choice, duties and participation in a changing Europe
Edited by Bjørn Hvinden and Håkan Johansson

47 National Parliaments within the Enlarged European Union
From victims of integration to competitive actors?
Edited by John O'Brennan and Tapio Raunio

48 Britain, Ireland and Northern Ireland since 1980
The totality of relationships
Eamonn O'Kane

49 The EU and the European Security Strategy
Forging a global Europe
Edited by Sven Biscop and Jan Joel Andersson

50 **European Security and Defence Policy**
An implementation perspective
Edited by Michael Merlingen and Rasa Ostrauskaitė

51 **Women and British Party Politics**
Descriptive, substantive and symbolic representation
Sarah Childs

52 **The Selection of Ministers in Europe**
Hiring and firing
Edited by Keith Dowding and Patrick Dumont

53 **Energy Security**
Europe's new foreign policy challenge
Richard Youngs

54 **Institutional Challenges in Post-Constitutional Europe**
Governing change
Edited by Catherine Moury and Luís de Sousa

55 **The Struggle for the European Constitution**
A past and future history
Michael O'Neill

56 **Transnational Labour Solidarity**
Mechanisms of commitment to cooperation within the European Trade Union Movement
Katarzyna Gajewska

57 **The Illusion of Accountability in the European Union**
Edited by Sverker Gustavsson, Christer Karlsson, and Thomas Persson

58 **The European Union and Global Social Change**
A critical geopolitical-economic analysis
József Böröcz

59 **Citizenship and Collective Identity in Europe**
Ireneusz Pawel Karolewski

60 **EU Enlargement and Socialization**
Turkey and Cyprus
Stefan Engert

61 **The Politics of EU Accession**
Turkish challenges and Central European experiences
Edited by Lucie Tunkrová and Pavel Šaradín

62 **The Political History of European Integration**
The hypocrisy of democracy-through-market
Hagen Schulz-Forberg and Bo Stråth

63 **The Spatialities of Europeanization**
Power, governance and territory in Europe
Alun Jones and Julian Clark

64 **European Union Sanctions and Foreign Policy**
When and why do they work?
Clara Portela

65 **The EU's Role in World Politics**
A retreat from Liberal Internationalism
Richard Youngs

66 Social Democracy and European Integration
The politics of preference formation
Edited by Dionyssis Dimitrakopoulos

67 The EU Presence in International Organizations
Edited by Spyros Blavoukos and Dimitris Bourantonis

68 Sustainability in European Environmental Policy
Challenge of governance and knowledge
Edited by Rob Atkinson, Georgios Terizakis and Karsten Zimmermann

69 Fifty Years of EU-Turkey Relations
A Sisyphean story
Edited by Armagan Emre Çakir

70 Europeanization and Foreign Policy
State diversity in Finland and Britain
Juha Jokela

71 EU Foreign Policy and Post-Soviet Conflicts
Stealth intervention
Nicu Popescu

72 Switzerland in Europe
Continuity and change in the Swiss political economy
Edited by Christine Trampusch and André Mach

73 The Political Economy of Noncompliance
Adjusting to the single European market
Scott Nicholas Siegel

74 National and European Foreign Policy
Towards Europeanization
Edited by Reuben Wong and Christopher Hill

75 The European Union Diplomatic Service
Ideas, preferences and identities
Caterina Carta

76 Poland within the European Union
New awkward partner or new heart of Europe?
Aleks Szczerbiak

77 A Political Theory of Identity in European Integration
Memory and policies
Catherine Guisan

78 EU Foreign Policy and the Europeanization of Neutral States
Comparing Irish and Austrian foreign policy
Nicole Alecu de Flers

79 Party System Change in Western Europe
Gemma Loomes

80 The Second Tier of Local Government in Europe
Provinces, counties, départements and Landkreise in comparison
Hubert Heinelt and Xavier Bertrana Horta

81 Learning from the EU Constitutional Treaty
Democratic constitutionalism beyond the Nation-state
Ben Crum

82 **Human Rights and Democracy in EU Foreign Policy**
The cases of Ukraine and Egypt
Rosa Balfour

83 **Europeanization, Integration and Identity**
A social constructivist fusion perspective on Norway
Gamze Tanil

84 **The Impact of European Integration on Political Parties**
Beyond the permissive consensus
Dimitri Almeida

85 **Civic Resources and the Future of the European Union**
Victoria Kaina and Ireneusz Pawel Karolewski

86 **The Europeanization of National Foreign Policies towards Latin America**
Lorena Ruano

87 **The EU and Multilateral Security Governance**
Sonia Lucarelli, Luk Van Langenhove and Jan Wouters

88 **Security Challenges in the Euro-Med Area in the 21st Century**
Mare nostrum
Stephen Calleya

89 **Society and Democracy in Europe**
Oscar W. Gabriel and Silke Keil

90 **European Union Public Health Policy**
Regional and global trends
Edited by Scott L. Greer and Paulette Kurzer

91 **The New Member States and the European Union**
Foreign policy and Europeanization
Edited by Michael Baun and Dan Marek

92 **The Politics of Ratification of EU Treaties**
Carlos Closa

93 **Europeanization and New Member States**
A comparative social network analysis
Flavia Jurje

94 **National Perspectives on Russia**
European foreign policy in the making
Maxine David, Jackie Gower and Hiski Haukkala

95 **Institutional Legacies of Communism**
Change and continuities in minority protection
Edited by Karl Cordell, Timofey Agarin and Alexander Osipov

96 **Sustainable Development and Governance in Europe**
The evolution of the discourse on sustainability
Edited by Pamela M. Barnes and Thomas C. Hoerber

97 **Social Networks and Public Support for the European Union**
Elizabeth Radziszewski

98 The EU's Democracy Promotion and the Mediterranean Neighbours
Orientation, ownership and dialogue in Jordan and Turkey
Ann-Kristin Jonasson

99 New Democracies in Crisis?
A comparative constitutional study of the Czech Republic, Hungary, Poland, Romania and Slovakia
Paul Blokker

100 Party Attitudes Towards the EU in the Member States
Parties for Europe, parties against Europe
Nicolò Conti

101 The European Union and Occupied Palestinian Territories
State-building without a state
Dimitris Bouris

102 Portugal in the European Union
Assessing twenty-five years of integration experience
Laura C. Ferreira-Pereira

103 Governance and European Civil Society
Governmentality, discourse and NGOs
Acar Kutay

104 The EU, Migration and the Politics of Administrative Detention
Edited by Michela Ceccorulli and Nicola Labanca

105 Political Representation in the European Union
Democracy in a time of crisis
Edited by Sandra Kröger

106 New Approaches to EU Foreign Policy
Edited by Maciej Wilga and Ireneusz Pawel Karolewski

107 Democracy, Law and Religious Pluralism in Europe
Secularism and post-secularism
Edited by Ferran Requejo and Camil Ungureanu

108 Contemporary Spanish Foreign Policy
Edited by David Garcia and Ramon Pacheco Pardo

109 Reframing Europe's Future
Challenges and failures of the European construction
Edited by Ferenc Miszlivetz and Jody Jensen

110 Italy's Foreign Policy in the 21st Century
A contested nature?
Edited by Ludovica Marchi, Richard Whitman and Geoffrey Edwards

111 The Challenge of Coalition Government
The Italian case
Edited by Nicolò Conti and Francesco Marangoni

112 The Nordic Countries and the European Union
Still the other European community?
Edited by Caroline Howard Grøn, Peter Nedergaard and Anders Wivel

113 Mediating Policy
Greece, Ireland, and Portugal Before the Eurozone Crisis
Kate Nicholls

114 The European Parliament and its International Relations
Edited by Stelios Stavridis and Daniela Irrera

115 Market Expansion and Social Dumping in Europe
Edited by Magdalena Bernaciak

116 The Diplomatic System of the European Union
Evolution, change and challenges
Edited by Michael Smith, Stephan Keukeleire and Sophie Vanhoonacker

117 European Union Enlargement
Material interests, community norms and anomie
Thomas Mehlhausen

118 The Moral Economy of EU Association with Africa
Mark Langan

119 European Space Policy
European integration and the final frontier
Edited by Thomas Hörber and Paul Stephenson

120 Policy Making at the Second Tier of Local Government in Europe
What is happening in Provinces, Counties, Départements and Landkreise in the on-going re-scaling of statehood?
Edited by Xavier Bertrana, Björn Egner and Hubert Heinelt

121 The Politics of Trauma and Peace-Building
Lessons from Northern Ireland
Cillian McGrattan

122 Eurozone Politics
Perception and reality in Italy, the UK, and Germany
Philip Giurlando

123 Politics of Identity in Post-Conflict States
The Bosnian and Irish experience
Edited by Éamonn Ó Ciardha and Gabriela Vojvoda

Eurozone Politics

Perception and reality in Italy, the UK, and Germany

Philip Giurlando

Routledge
Taylor & Francis Group
LONDON AND NEW YORK

First published 2016 by Routledge

2 Park Square, Milton Park, Abingdon, Oxfordshire OX14 4RN
711 Third Avenue, New York, NY 10017

Routledge is an imprint of the Taylor & Francis Group, an informa business

First issued in paperback 2017

British Library Cataloguing in Publication Data
A catalogue record for this book is available from the British Library

Library of Congress Cataloging-in-Publication Data
Giurlando, Philip, author.
Eurozone politics : perception and reality in Italy, the UK, and Germany / Philip Giurlando.
pages cm
1. Euro. 2. Eurozone. 3. European Union—Italy. 4. European Union—Great Britain. 5. European Union—Germany. I. Title.
HG925.G563 2016
332.4'94—dc23
2015021498

ISBN: 978-1-138-94190-8 (hbk)
ISBN: 978-0-8153-7107-6 (pbk)

Typeset in Times New Roman
by Apex CoVantage, LLC

For Alexia, my mirror image

Contents

List of figures xvii
List of tables xix
Acknowledgements xxi

1 Introduction 1

2 National politics and the euro: a theoretical overview 10

3 Cognition, affect, and support for the euro: the case of Italy 34

4 Diversity within the whole: how cognitive schemes are conditioned by gender, region, political ideology, and status 48

5 Perception meets reality in Italy 67

6 The euro and relative status 87

7 Splendid isolation: the UK and the euro 104

8 Germany and the future of the euro 126

9 Conclusion 141

Postscript: Greece shakes Europe to its core (again) 151

Appendix 163
Index 173

Figures

3.1	Counterarguments	41
3.2	Emotional content	44
6.1	Perceptions of relative status in Italian newspapers	93
6.2	Italy and perceptions of corruption	100
6.3	Share of national income of top 1% in Italy	100
6.4	Italian productivity	100
7.1	Number of articles on Britain and the Euro, 1998–2002	111
8.1	Current account balance	128
8.2	Unemployment rate	128
8.3	Real economic growth	128
8.4	Support for euro	130

Tables

3.1	Attitudes towards EMU	35
3.2	General reasons for support	36
3.3	Specific reasons	37
3.4	Means and ends	37
3.5	Social comparison processes	38
3.6	Link between Italy's problems and Europe as the solution	39
3.7	Knowledge of EMU	42
4.1	Gender	51
4.2	Region	53
4.3	Political orientation	56
4.4	Status	60
5.1	What is the cause of Italy's problems?	81
5.2	Link between Italy's problems and EMU as the solution	82
6.1	Should Italy copy Europe's major countries? Which ones?	92
6.2	After Italy entered EMU, how did you perceive the country?	94
6.3	After Italy entered EMU, how did you perceive the country? (Left, right, elite, non-elite)	94
6.4	Which is the most corrupt country in Europe?	99
6.5	Ease of doing business	101
6.6	Ranking in Rule of Law Index, 2014	101
7.1	Support for, and opposition to, the euro, 1998–2002	112
7.2	Counterarguments	112
7.3	General reasons for support	112
7.4	Specific reasons for support	112
7.5	Daily Express and the euro	114
7.6	Favourable attitudes towards euro	114
7.7	Reasons for support	115
7.8	Percentage who are not satisfied with their national democracy	116
XA	Distribution of sample	164

Acknowledgements

This work benefited greatly from the advice and direction of Grant Amyot, Charles Pentland, Vince Della Sala, Zsuzsa Csergo, Paul Corner, and John McGarry. I also sharpened my ideas through the many discussions and debates that took place at some of the conferences where the individual chapters were presented. In particular, I improved my ideas through the practice of teaching. As a Teaching Assistant for POL 329 (European Politics), a Teaching Fellow for POL 470 (where the politics of the euro was taught), and as an Assistant Professor at Trent University, I had to communicate my ideas on national politics and the euro to undergraduates. The inquisitive questions and feedback from students helped to sharpen the conceptual framework and arguments that are an integral part of this work. I would also like to thank the Social Sciences and Humanities Research Council of Canada (SSHRC) for financing this project. Their generous resources allowed the extensive travel that was necessary to carry out the empirical research. Ryerson University, Queen's University, Trent University, Universitá di Trento, Universitá di Siena – all were important, in their own ways, for my intellectual formation and/or the development of this project. In particular, I am grateful for the support from my colleagues at Trent, especially Devin Penner, Nadine Changfoot, Elaine Stavro, Hasmet Uluorta, and Jonathan Greene. The assistance of Fiorella Buzzi and Vittorio De Sio when recruiting interviewees was invaluable. Many thanks also to Panayotis Economopoulos, Hara Papatheodorou, and Professor Petrakis. I also want to express my gratitude to Antonio Di Marco and Rossana Apicella for their gracious and loving hospitality during my long stays in Italy. Many thanks also to my mother, Gerardina Dimarco, for her unwavering and unconditional love and support. Tom Barbiero was invaluable in so many ways – from helping to obtain data to reviewing the manuscript. I am also indebted to Chris Jacobson for creating the Eclectic Indulgence book club that I have been a member of since 2009 and that has enriched my intellectual and spiritual life. I am grateful for the kindness, generosity, and/or intellectual stimulation of Anastasia Sinkovskaia, Ian Wilson, David O'Rourke, Ron Barber, Ken Giurlando, Frank Morrison, Shalli Samah, Roger "Poom Poom" McNeil, Angelo Galuccio, Leonardo Cancellieri, Kello Rico, Michael Bryant, Kayla Marino, David Ackerman, Caroline Birks, Fotios Sarris, Omer Aziz, Brandon Tozzzo, Dru Lazon, Stuart Sheild, Michalis Fafoutis, and many others. This project also would not have been possible without the sources of evidence presented in the following pages, especially the people who kindly agreed to be interviewed.

1 Introduction

On February 7, 1992, European heads of government met in Maastricht, Netherlands to sign the Maastricht treaty. It was a pivotal moment in the history of European integration, brought to life by both external and internal pressures. Regarding the former, the collapse of Communism and the reunification of Germany helped to create the impetus for deeper integration because for some countries, especially France, this was essential to tame the power of Deutschland (Levitt & Lord 2000). Internally, the treaty, of which monetary union was only a part, aimed to complete the internal market established in the Single European Act (SEA). The main purposes of the Maastricht treaty were to establish a common foreign and security policy, develop a Community social dimension, and, most importantly, establish the European Monetary Union (EMU). The thrust of EMU was to ensure the coordination of member states' economic policies and provide multilateral surveillance to enforce financial and budgetary discipline. The main rigorous public finance rules, known as the "Maastricht criteria", were the following:

- A fiscal deficit below 3% of GDP.
- A public debt either below 60% or moving towards that level.
- Interest rates on long term bonds that are not higher than 2% of the long term average rates of the three members with the lowest inflation rates.
- An inflation rate that is below 1.5% of the average of the inflation rates of the three best performing Member-States.

These criteria were difficult to meet even for Europe's "elite" countries, and initially many doubted the capacity of Southern European countries like Italy to satisfy the criteria and make the first round. This scepticism was well founded in light of Italy's tendency to massively expand deficits and debts, its sclerotic political system with many veto points that allowed interests to block reform, and its general unwillingness or inability to respect its obligations to apply the rules of the European Union. But Italy surprised almost everyone, including itself: it found the capacity and willingness to make some of the painful reforms that were necessary to meet the Maastricht criteria. It consequently entered the first round with a sense of accomplishment, achievement, dignity, and enhanced collective self-esteem.

In order to build support for the painful reforms required to satisfy the Maastricht criteria, Italians were sold a bill goods on the euro that failed to deliver. A sample of quotes from major Italian dailies and television media from the late nineties and early part of the subsequent decade is instructive in this regard:

- The euro will improve the functioning of the economy, making Europe's economy similar to the Americans', and it will create jobs (*Repubblica* 27/12/1996).
- Our system is notoriously one of the weaker ones, and *only* [emphasis mine] by being part of Europe can we compete with the USA, Japan, and Asia (*Corriere della Sera* 11/03/1996).
- With the euro, at stake is not only Italy's entry into Europe, but also the very existence of Italy (*Repubblica* 03/10/1996).
- The euro is certainly not a panacea but it is one of the conditions for Italy's competitiveness (*Corriere della Sera* 2/02/1997).
- Countries that do not enter the euro will be underdeveloped (*Corriere della Sera* 21/01/1997).
- Staying out of the euro will mean impoverishment (*Corriere della Sera* 09/02/1997).
- Our options are either Maastricht or death (*Repubblica* 21/02/1997).
- Entering the euro means reconciling the division [in Italy] between the North and the South (Speech by Romano Prodi, aired on RAI 2/05/1998).
- The euro creates the dynamic for growth for all European nations that would be unthinkable without the euro (TG2 Dossier Oggi Euro, aired on RAI on 01/05/1998).
- Given that we have entered the euro, it is a step in the direction, I hope, towards growth and jobs (Carlo Ciampi TG2 Dossier Oggi Euro, aired on RAI 01/05/1998).
- [Romano] Prodi says that the euro will work wonders . . . it will increase economic growth by 1% a year (Entrando nell euro, aired on RAI on 09/01/2001).
- With the euro, there will be no more financial crises (Carlo Ciampi, Porta a Porta, aired on 27/11/2001).
- With the euro, we are close to the political unification of Europe (Romano Prodi, Mister Euro, aired on 4/12/2001).
- The common currency, in a certain sense has made us more civilized and responsible (*Corriere della Sera* 03/05/1998).
- Ciampi is worried about how fast that those, especially among the governing party, are expressing to their grass-roots the equation that the euro equals green valleys (*Repubblica* 27/03/1998).
- The entry into the euro will permit, according to Prodi, the Italian economy to begin to grow (*Repubblica* 26/03/1998).
- In 49 days we will have the euro . . . it is an appointment with history, a cultural revolution which will change the most deeply rooted habits of Italians (*Repubblica* 12/11/2001).
- The euro will be an instrument of economic well-being (*Repubblica* 31/12/2001).

- With the euro we will become more competitive . . . and this will provide a strong stimulus to economic growth (Frontiere, aired on RAI on 7/12/2002).
- The common currency is essential for stability and economic growth *(Repubblica* 24/01/2004).
- With the euro we dreamed of developing [in Italy] the rule-ness of the Germans (*Repubblica* 15/11/2004).

Needless to say, these sunny predictions and exaggerated claims did not come true. As subsequent chapters will show, the establishment of the common currency has coincided with an acceleration of Italy's economic decline.

It is partly for this reason that in the past seven years my views on the euro have radically changed. Initially I was a typical Europhile, believing in the intrinsic goodness of European integration and in the notion that deeper moves towards supranationalism would benefit Europeans and help to create a continental-size power that would rival China and the US. I still think that deeper ties between Europe's peoples are a good thing; despite the hodgepodge of often competing nationalities, languages, and territories, Europe does have a shared history and culture rooted in the classical world, the rise of Christianity, and modern science. But I, like many others, underestimated the primacy of the nation as a focus on loyalty, and I did not envisage that these national loyalties would re-emerge with ferocious intensity after the effects of the Eurozone crisis came to the fore.

It is not only that my predictions turned out to be wrong; witnessing first-hand the social devastation of the euro has equally impacted my views. I spent several weeks in Athens, Greece at the height of the crisis in 2012. I saw boarded up shops everywhere, and the degradation of public spaces. Informed Greeks told me that suicides, disease, crime, and hunger all rose dramatically. One evening I was in front of the Greek parliament where I saw and interviewed enraged Greeks protesting against Germany and the policies of austerity. In Italy, I have seen entire towns, once bustling with life and energy, become depopulated, as youth leave the country en masse to find work. Ditto for Spain, where I spoke to some members of the masses of unemployed youth; they expressed little hope for the future.

It is for this reason that I now have become a "eurosceptic" in the language of Europe's political discourse. Not in the sense of being against Europe or the EU. Europe is a repository of values that overall has made the world a better place, and the EU has helped to promote more trade, interaction, and peace between the peoples of the continent. Rather, I have become sceptical of the common currency. With the exception perhaps of lower interest rates and inflation, few of the benefits that were promised have come to pass. Many astute observers at the time knew this, but those influenced by ideals of European integration either ignored or minimized the criticisms of the currency. Many Italian elites, as subsequent chapters will show, were particularly prone to greatly exaggerating the supposed benefits of the euro and misleading their public. This raises a question: how could elites – many of whom are highly knowledgeable and educated about European integration and monetary union – have been so spectacularly wrong about the effects of the currency? This is one of the main puzzles that this book will attempt to answer.

The euro was never just about introducing a new unit of value and exchange. From its conception, it has been a political project driven by the political dynamics of European integration. The debate on this topic has generally been divided between neo-functionalists and realists, with the former highlighting the role that "functional spillover" has played in driving moves towards unity. Realists, on the other hand, investigate the role of power politics at the national level in driving integration forward. They give little currency to the notion, expressed by some Europhiles, that European integration would help to overcome the forces that have characterized international politics since the dawn of history: inequality, hierarchy, competition, domination, and submission.

This book focuses on the interplay between hierarchy and Eurozone politics, and in that sense it is very much a part of the realist tradition. Hierarchy is a motor in the sense that dominant states push forward and in the process are able to crystalize their preferences in the institutions that emerge, but it is also a constraint because these states can block the preferences of others. The dynamics of hierarchy also impact secondary states, which are often motivated to pursue integration precisely because they believe that it will help to equalize their position vis-à-vis dominant states. The concept of equality is multidimensional. Depending on the actor, it may refer to equal status in the international system, or convergence that raises the standards and quality of the societal model of the secondary state towards that of the dominant state.

But the realists' almost exclusive focus on the material basis of power, such as economic strength, population, territory, and military capacity, is very limited for understanding the dynamics of power politics and the euro. Hierarchy in Europe is a multilayered phenomenon. There are political, cultural, and discursive layers that influence perception, motivation, and behaviour, especially in the process of European integration. As the next chapter will show, hierarchy has *cognitive* and *emotional* dimensions that influence interpretation of political objects like the euro in ways that are divorced from the currency's substantive reality. In particular, the euro was perceived by many as a mechanism to make their countries more like Germany, and this aspiration only makes sense in the context of a hierarchy that assumes German superiority. Becoming more like Germany, for some, also meant *equalizing* their country vis-à-vis Germany in status and prestige. It is this that helps to explain why many Italian (and other) elites were so spectacularly wrong about the euro: many did not interpret it on the basis of the cold, hard facts. It was instead refracted through the lens of their aspirations. I call this phenomenon "Associative Evaluation", and it can be briefly summed up as the tendency for political actors to define themselves as members of national groups, evaluate the relative status of their group in relation to other groups, the aspiration of lower-status groups to raise their status by becoming like the higher-status group, and the performance of this hierarchy, which entails, among other things, the division of countries into "first" and "second" tier (an expanded exposition of the idea can be found in the following chapter).

Italian perceptions of Europe are conditioned by many variables; as will be shown in chapter four, ideology, gender, and socioeconomic status play important roles in influencing preferences. But international dynamics also matter. From the beginning of the European project, a main driver for Italian elites was equality with France and Germany (see next chapter). This wish for equality, as we will see, was also important in the politics of the euro. In a sense, Italy is not dissimilar from France, which also pursued European integration, at least in part, to equalize its position in relation to Germany.

Also discussed in this book are Germany and the UK. The last was selected because in the nineties it had a debate about entering the Eurozone, and ultimately decided against the proposition. At the time, many British Europhiles condemned the decision to not adopt the currency, saying that it would undermine Britain's influence in both Europe and the world at large. Many in Britain now feel a sense of vindication. By not adopting the currency, they have escaped many of the grindingly difficult decisions that many Eurozone countries are now facing, such as whether to proceed with political centralization at the EU level, which very few want but which is deemed to be essential to save the currency. Nonetheless, Britain has not escaped the poisonous political atmosphere that has afflicted many European countries. The radical right has risen in the UK just as it has elsewhere: the victory of the UKIP in the 25 May, 2014 EU elections is an indication of a groundswell of opposition to Europe that could very well result in Britain leaving the EU altogether after it holds a referendum in 2017.

This work is also very critical of the elites, in Italy and elsewhere, who sold the euro to the public. Many of them propagated beliefs with little empirical and theoretical basis, namely that the currency would lead to economic growth and increases in employment. Many among the masses who were sceptical of the currency, or who were suspicious of the sunny narratives about the euro, have been shown to be right. And they were right despite being less educated and less knowledgeable than elites. Elite views on the euro were based on sophisticated theoretical abstractions, most of which have turned out to be wrong.

Division of chapters

The second chapter will be a theoretical overview of national politics and EMU. It will be of interest mainly to scholars and theorists of human behaviour, and readers who are only interested in the actual empirical research carried out for this work may skip this chapter and proceed to the following ones, where the data and arguments will be presented. This chapter will elaborate on the concept of hierarchy. In the context of European politics, hierarchy has both material and immaterial dimensions. The former refers to the structural basis of national power, while the latter points to the intersubjective components of hierarchy that help to reinforce it, and which constitute perception, motivation, and political action. In this sense, hierarchy as it is used here has both realist and constructivist underpinnings. The chapter also addresses the closely related debate between rationalists and constructivists on the euro, and shows that the preferences for the currency, especially among Italian actors, cannot be reduced to objective calculations of interest maximization. Rather, for many, the euro was refracted through the lens of the desire for equality. This desire only makes sense in the context of a hierarchy whereby secondary states pursue the enhancement of their own status and condition in relation to dominant states.

The third chapter will focus on the structure of Italian public attitudes towards EMU during the period between 1996 and 2010. Here I will begin to present the findings of my field work in Italy, with a focus on the dominant tendencies within the sample, allowing me to construct the cognitive schemes that were collectively held by large swaths of the population, schemes that interpreted Italy-Europe relations immediately before, during, and immediately after joining EMU. Unlike other works on the euro, this book mainly relies on primary data that I collected in 2010–2012: interviews with elites and non-elites, and a large media sample that includes editorials from major dailies and TV programmes.[1] The results of the semi-structured interviews will highlight that many Italians supported the euro because they believed that it would help to equalize Italy vis-à-vis Europe's elite countries. For some, this equalizing meant that it would fix the country's infamous political problems, while for others it meant that it would improve the functioning of the economy, and for a not-insignificant minority that it would help to "civilize" Italians.

The fourth chapter will focus on the diversity of cognitive schemes in the Italian political community. My results find significant differences between the centre-left and centre-right, and I also find differences, but less significant ones, between men and women, and Northerners and Southerners. The most important focus will be on the similarities and differences between elites and non-elites. Highlighting the congruence and incongruence between elites' and non-elites' cognitive schemes will permit me to identify the extent to which elite ideas have percolated to the masses. This will fill a large gap in the identity literature that focuses only or mainly on the statements and publications of elites, and I will do this by testing the congruence of three sources: talk shows/news programmes, newspapers, and the sample of 253 individuals – 69 of whom are elites, while the rest are non-elites. There will be a particular focus on the interviews, because elites and non-elites were asked the same questions in a series of interviews that I conducted during the period from May to October 2010.

The fifth chapter will assess an aspect of the Eurozone that many Italian elites did not expect: the acceleration of Italy's decline, and a further reduction of its position in relation to the "core". In order to reverse this trend, Italy must create one of the main determinants of status and influence in Europe: an attractive societal model which includes, inter alia, a growing and dynamic economy. This is a tall order that will require fundamental changes to the organization of the polity and economy. This chapter will also address the "immaturity" thesis, which questions whether peripheral countries like Italy are to blame for their plight, or whether the causes are international in origin. The chapter argues that the macroeconomic imbalances that the euro produced are a main cause of the crisis, and hence the origin of many of the country's recent difficulties are external, but that the power structure of the euro represents a major constraint that militates against solutions that address the structural flaws of the currency. Therefore, adjustment must be internal/domestic. However, with a few notable exceptions, Italy has been resistant to fundamental and sweeping reform, and this is mainly due to the conservatism of many interest groups that are able to prevent change. The politics of the euro were not helpful in this regard, since it became an instance of Italians' collective wish to transcend their perceived national inadequacies, and their belief that an outside entity like the euro, and not they themselves, could serve this function. This was not conducive to building the political will for the necessary reforms. The chapter will also elucidate the reforms that Italy requires to ensure it remains a standing member of the common currency.

The sixth chapter further theorizes the intersubjective features of Europe's inter-state hierarchy. Many construct their nation according to the characteristics of larger social aggregates to which it belongs. For example, to many Italians, their country's perceived national inadequacies make sense only in relation to a hierarchy of nations in Europe that places Italy on the second tier of this hierarchy. Italians want to feel a sense of equality with Europe, and they hoped that belonging to Europe would be sufficient to achieve this equality; but for many this hope became transformed into the implicit theory, embedded in actors' cognitive schemes, that securing belongingness would be sufficient to achieve this desire to have equal status or condition with Europe's elite countries. And so in the period immediately after belonging to EMU was assured, many felt that Italy was "equal" to other European nations in the objective sense. This sense of equality was felt even though Europe's hierarchy remained largely unchanged, with Italy relegated to second-tier status.

The seventh chapter will systematically compare Italians' and Britons' attitudes towards EMU. The outcome observed in Britain is very much the opposite of what was observed in Italy: while the latter enthusiastically embraced the euro, the majority of Britons were opposed, which gave the winning hand to the eurosceptics in the debate on whether the country should enter EMU. Britain is a good comparative case study because hierarchy has a very different meaning in that country. Unlike Italy, Britain is often grouped with the "core" along with France and Germany, and very few in Britain look to Europe to solve their national problems. The need for "external pressure" from Brussels, which many Italians wished for, is much less salient in Britain. Nor do we see a desire for "equality". Rather, Europhiles in Britain defended their position because they believed it would give them "leadership" of Europe. This contrast between the motives of "leadership" versus "equality" speaks volumes about the different ways that Italians and Britons conceive of the relative position and status of their respective nations. The chapter also shows that, unlike in Italy, many in Britain were remarkably prescient about the eventual effects of the common currency. Rather than the creation of some political union that would rival the US and China and that would create prosperity, many in Britain predicted, correctly, that it would undermine democracy and lead to further division in Europe.

Any discussion of the interplay between Eurozone politics and international hierarchy must take account of Germany, which will be the focus of chapter eight. One of the more interesting ironies is that the euro was meant to constrain Germany. The result has been the opposite: the country has become more powerful than ever. Its power is deeply resented across Europe, and the narrative of Germany using the euro to try to dominate the continent has become part of the discourse of many political parties in periphery countries. The rise of Germany also illustrates the curious phenomenon whereby the unknowledgeable masses were correct, while the smart, highly educated, and cosmopolitan elites were not: in a poll taken in 1998, a large plurality of average French citizens believed that the euro would strengthen Germany even as French elites worked assiduously to establish the currency because they believed that supranational institutions would weaken it (Marsh 2011). The chapter will also explore the responses to the Eurozone crisis that began in 2008, and shows they can only be understood in the context of the constraints that Europe's hierarchy places on the options of policymakers. Scholars and informed commentators agree that a sustainable solution to the crisis will require a fundamental change to the structure of the currency which includes, among other things, the establishment of a fiscal authority that can help to smooth out the imbalances between surplus and deficit countries. Don't count on it: Europe's core countries, and especially Germany, are flatly against the proposition, and their consent is a necessary condition for a proposal of that scope.

The conclusion will look ahead, assessing the implications of the structural vulnerabilities of the euro. The weaknesses in the institutional architecture have been extensively discussed elsewhere, but there has been relatively less attention on the fragilities at the national level which, arguably, constitute an even greater danger to the long term stability of the euro. One is the demographic challenges in Germany: its rapidly aging population represents future liabilities which the state will struggle to pay for. By 2020, its population will begin decreasing at the same rate as Japan's. This is significant because Germany has been the largest financer of the bailouts for periphery countries, and in the event of another financial crisis – which is more likely than not – policymakers in that country will have to decide whether the needs of its own citizens trump those of distressed Eurozone countries. Another major weakness is Italy's massive debt and its related inability to arrest its seemingly interminable decline. When markets are calm, as they have been since 2013, its debt appears to be a manageable problem. But when interest rates rise, as they most likely will, it will become an existential one.

Many commentators have proposed various solutions to putting the Eurozone on a sustainable path. Most of them are unrealizable precisely because of the constraints of hierarchy. Any proposed solution, therefore, must be sensitive to these political realities. Another possibility is the dissolution of the euro. In the near term this is unlikely, and hence policymakers must work within the constraints mentioned above as well as the structural weakness that inheres in a monetary union without a common fiscal policy. This limits the options to internal adjustment, which includes austerity, and efforts to increase productivity. So far, this approach has failed in most countries, as the politics of austerity have helped to create a huge undercurrent of rage which boiled to the surface in the European elections on May 2014, when radical parties of both the left and right scored huge gains in strategically important Eurozone countries. If their support continues on its present trajectory, they could make it harder to fix the structural weakness of the euro because they mostly reject any notion of a European political union. This does not bode well for the future of the euro.

Note

1 See appendix for details about the methodology and the sample.

References

Battistini, G. "Ma Arriva L'altola di Ciampi e' Essentiale per la Stabilita'," *Repubblica* 24 January 2004: 6.

Caracciolo, L. "Il Prezzo," *Repubblica* 03 October 1996.

"D'Alema: E Ora Tocca al Lavoro," *Corriere della Sera* 3 May 1998: 7.

Di Caro, P. "Si, Tra noi c'e il Partito della Bundesbank," *Corriere della Sera* 21 February 1997: 6.

Gaggi, M. "Basta vittimismo: I Tedeschi Hanno Ragione," *Corriere della Sera* 9 February 1999: 2.

Gambarotta, G. "Fidatevi di Euro," *Corriere della Sera* 11 March 1996: 18.

Giannini, M. "Ciampi: Niente Ubriacature il Rigore Dovra Continuare," *Repubblica* 27 March 1998: 2.

Levitt, M and Lord, C. (2000) *The Political Economy of EMU*. Basingstoke: Macmillan.

Marsh, D. (2011) *The Euro: The Battle for the New Global Currency*. New Haven, CT: Yale University Press.

Mauro, E. "Un Atto di Fede Diventa Realta," *Repubblica* 31 December 2001: 1.

Polidori, E. "Il Liberalismo Fallito del Governo Berlusconi," *Repubblica* 12 November 2001: 25.

Rampini, F. "Il Cuore D'Europa non Sara' Nelle Mani Dei Banchieri," *Repubblica* 27 December 1996: 7.

Rampini, F. "Ormai solo la Politica Puo' Farci Pedere L'Euro," *Repubblica* 2 March 1998: 8.

Rampini, F. "Un Superstato Come L'America, " *Repubblica* 26 March 1998: 1.

"Rifletteva il Nostro Paese con I Suoi Vizi," *Repubblica* 15 November 2004: 27.

Tamburello, S. "Ciampi: Nessun Rinvio, Ce La Faremo," *Corriere della Sera* 2 February 1997: 3.

Taino, D. "I Politici Non Fanno le vere Riforme," *Corriere della Sera* 21 January 1997: 21.

Clips of TV segments aired on Italy's public broadcaster are available in the archives of the RAI:

Speech by Romano Prodi, aired on RAI 2/05/1998

TG2 Dossier Oggi Euro, aired on RAI on 01/05/1998

Carlo Ciampi TG2 Dossier Oggi Euro, aired on RAI 01/05/1998

Entrando nell euro, aired on RAI on 09/01/2001

Carlo Ciampi, Porta a Porta, aired on RAI on 27/11/2001

Romano Prodi, Mister Euro, aired on RAI on 4/12/2001

Frontiere, aired on RAI on 7/12/2002

2 National politics and the euro: a theoretical overview

Scholarship on the European Monetary Union usually falls into one of three camps: elite focused (Dyson & Featherstone 1999), institutionalist (Ferrera & Gualmini 1999; Giuliani 2001; Hallerberg 2004), or political economy (Della Sala 2004, p. 1055; Padoa-Schioppa 2004; Golden 2004). Others focus on the role of public opinion, which can broadly be divided into constructivist (McNamara 1998; Jabko 2006; Risse 2003, 2001; Risse et al. 1999) and rationalist (Gabel 1998; Brinegar & Jolly 2005) approaches. The rationalist literature presumes that the Eurozone was propelled by the interest maximization strategies of key actors, although scholars disagree on the character of these interests: for some they have a political character (Sanchez-Cuenca 2000) and for others, an economic character (Kaltenthaler & Anderson 2001).

This brings us to the question on what is exactly is meant by "rational". There are actually two models of rationality in the literature: the "thin" and the "thick" version (Wendt & Fearon 2002). In the former, there is no necessary assumption that the actor chooses a policy to increase her material well-being. Rather, rationality is simply a mental process characterized with instrumentality that is compatible with any desire or goal. The "thick" version objects and assumes that actors choose rationally on the basis of their material interests, which is mostly understood to mean enhancing material – political and/or economic – well-being.

The problem with the "thin" version is that, if we take it at face value, it explains almost everything and hence it does not become a theory that can be tested and refuted. Very few people would dispute that actors have goals and that they act instrumentally to achieve them. There are some exceptions where behaviour is not goal-driven, such as when actors are under extreme duress from poverty, oppression, illness, or other conditions that may "force" certain forms of behaviour (Eckstein 1991). But these exceptions are clearly not relevant to those who adopted EMU, as they are mainly rich first-world countries that had the option of accepting or refusing the common currency. Therefore, the thin version of rationality explains too much, making it in effect a tautology: since actor X desires and acts to achieve Y, actor X is rational. Seen this way, it becomes difficult to generate a real debate or to falsify the theory. Wendt and Fearon (2002, p. 60) admit as much when they say that "in order to generate a real debate [between constructivists and rationalists] it is necessary to arbitrarily restrict the rationalist position to a particular thick theory of actor preferences." I would dispute the word "arbitrarily" in that quote, for one of the purposes of theory is to generate debate and disagreement with competing theories. The "thick" version does precisely that. It generates predictions that can be tested and refuted. Indeed, the rational choice literature on public opinion and the euro presented above is the thick version, since all assume that preferences are based on the desire to maximize material well-being. But most importantly for this book, the thick version competes with the intepretivist focus on ideas and meanings that have little or no relation to interests and other material factors.

The thick version of rational choice is useful in explaining, say, preferences for relatively simpler policies like tax-cuts or spending increases, where it is relatively easy to draw links between one's interests and the policy that will maximize them; it is not as useful in explaining support or opposition to EMU, for several reasons. There is the fact that EMU was more than the introduction of a new currency. It was a policy that had political, social, and economic dimensions that even many learned and educated actors had trouble grasping. But even if one focuses strictly on the economic aspect, from an economic perspective the weight of the evidence did not support the notion that EMU would have the benefits that euro-enthusiast politicians said would accrue to their countries. It is striking that before the euro was introduced, eminent economists as ideologically diverse as Paul Krugman and Milton Friedman predicted, accurately, that the euro would not succeed (Davies 2012). Indeed, one is struck by the fact that many of the criticisms of EMU before it was adopted – that it would incentivize reckless behaviour, that it would force Germany to bail out these countries, that it would make many countries uncompetitive and hence reduce growth – have come to pass, while the arguments in favour – that the lowering of interest rates and transaction costs would produce growth, that the Stability and Growth pact would ensure discipline – have not come to pass for most of the countries, especially in the periphery. Lastly, Europe did not form an Optimum Currency Area (OCA) (McNamara 1998), which means that without the integration of fiscal policies, unifying the currency would be detrimental to weaker members. This prediction has been verified by subsequent events. The main losers from EMU have been Italy, Portugal, Ireland, Spain, Greece, and Cyprus, all of which have seen either anaemic or debt-fuelled unsustainable growth since the euro was introduced. And with the exception of Italy, all the mentioned periphery countries received humiliating bailouts that imposed limits on their political sovereignty. The reason for these outcomes, in part, is that these countries had to adapt to a currency value that was more appropriate for Europe's economic behemoth, Germany, which has been the greatest beneficiary of the euro.

Ideas, beliefs, and political reality

Constructivists focus on how discourses that are diffused in the form of symbols, ideas, and beliefs become interpretive schemes through which European integration initiatives are evaluated. These discourses make some preferences more likely than others because of the intellectual climate that they produce. Discourses legitimate some options and delegitimize others, emphasize some information and disguise other facts, define some objectives to the exclusion of others, and so on. This is the framework that McNamara (1998), Jabko (2006), and Risse (2003, 2001, Risse et al. 1999) use in their work on the adoption of the European Monetary Union. They first reject the interest-based approach, arguing that the low level of information, even among elites, precluded the kinds of rational and calculated appraisals of costs and benefits that this rational choice model depicts. Discourses were more influential, but not by themselves. For McNamara, it was German power and influence that made discourse influential. For Jabko, it was the "strategic discursiveness" of the European Commission, while Risse asserts that it was national-based elites that gave force to the discourses through which the euro was interpreted.

These accounts of EMU have much to commend. As all three point out, material economic interest-based accounts do not explain the adoption of EMU very well. But there are weaknesses. First, both McNamara and Jabko rely exclusively on elites, both theoretically and empirically. The main actors for McNamara are the epistemic communities that provided the new framework in the aftermath of the perceived failure of Keynesianism, and the high-level bureaucrats and officials, both national and supranational, who translated these ideas into policy. Her sources are elite statements, as expressed in their publications or public speaking, and interviews with selected elites. The same can be said, *mutatis mutandis*, about Jabko. The key actors for him are the Commission, which promulgated the ideas, and national public officials, who received the ideas and translated them into policy. His sources are interviews with high-level officials in the Commission and high-level national officials in strategically important countries, like Germany and France. But this approach does not shed light on the extent to which, if at all, the discourses that they focus on permeated the masses and conditioned their support or opposition, and this is not insignificant when we take account of the fact that the support of the masses was a necessary element in implementing the Maastricht criteria. In particular, it is highly doubtful that the masses, especially in Italy, supported EMU because of their belief that Keynesianism no longer worked and that a neo-liberal paradigm was the solution. My own findings, which will be presented in the following chapters, highlight that *not one* non-elite member mentioned this discourse.

Unlike McNamara and Jabko, Risse does investigate the discourses that are present among the masses. Since the narratives he identifies are embedded within national identities, he explores these national identities with two key sources: Eurobarometer polls and secondary sources that have highlighted the nationally distinct narratives that people now take for granted (i.e. Germany and its Nazi past, Britain and its distrust of the continent, France and its illusions of grandeur and leadership, Italy and its distrust of national institutions and adulation of European ones). *Apropos* the case of Italy, he cites the widely used Eurobarometer poll that shows a strong negative correlation between confidence in national institutions and European institutions, which supports the near consensus that the Italian masses were in favour of EMU to escape their perceived national inadequacies (Risse 2003, p. 497). I found substantial evidence for this in the findings that will be presented in the following chapters. But in positing that this is a function of Italian identity, as Risse does, there is the risk of excessively homogenizing the masses (which is a risk that all identity-based accounts are prone to). My findings show that there were many other reasons for support, and that these different reasons tended to correlate with different categories of individuals, in particular, those on the centre-right or centre-left, those of different genders, and, most importantly, elites and non-elites, which, as I will show, differed in both form and content in their support for EMU. Moreover, although Eurobarometer data gives us a good picture of the public's attitudes, it is less effective in probing deeper into actors' interpretive schemes (Checkel and Katzenstein 2009, p. 10). To do this often requires ethnographic research and semi-structured interviews that are time-consuming to conduct and to code; the time-consuming character of these kinds of interviews is often in tension with the generalizability that Eurobarometer polls prioritize.

Other scholars have specifically explored the role of ideas, discourses, and identities in Italy's enthusiastic adoption of the euro (Quaglia 2004, 2006; Radaelli 2002; Giuliani 2001). This book also explores the role of ideas but expands the focus to include non-elites and the intersubjective features of hierarchy.

Hierarchy and Europe

European integration was supposed to undo, or overcome, the dynamics of hierarchy, competition, and domination that characterized a large part of the continent's history and that culminated in the savagery of the 20th century's two world wars. At best, one could say that the project has helped to promote peace, but it has not undermined the inherent power inequalities between states. Recognizing this, scholars have deployed a number of concepts to understand the asymmetrical power relations that inhere in the process of European integration. A popular one is the division between "core" and "periphery". Depending on the scholar, this refers to the difference between surplus and deficit countries (Lapavitsas et al. 2010), Northern and Southern Europe (Bastasin 2012, p.157), or, more commonly, the countries that are the motors versus those that are the followers of some of the "big bangs" of European integration (Beach & Mazucelli 2007). Others focus on "leadership" in Europe (Child 2010), exploring how elite countries pursue their objectives within the context of a supranational polity that is nominally based on the equality of sovereigns. This leadership is deemed to be especially necessary when there are deep disagreements between the parties on how to move forward.

Despite these differences in approaches to understanding Europe's power asymmetries, there is wide agreement that the "core", or "leadership", of Europe is composed of Germany and France, and occasionally Britain (Mazucelli, Geurot, & Metz 2007; Hayward 2008). Italy is rarely included into this privileged group. It is sometimes referred to as one of the "bigs" (Bunse, Magnette, & Nicolaidis 2007) or part of the "big 5" (Child 2010), but so is Spain, and few would argue that the latter is part of the "core". There is also agreement that the basis of French and German leadership is primarily material: in terms of population and absolute and per capita GDP, they are on the top of the pyramid. But focusing exclusively on material variables poses several problems for the politics of European integration. First, there is the question alluded to above, namely, that Italy is not considered part of the core even though, on the basis of material variables like territory, population, and GDP, it is not dissimilar from core countries like France and the UK. Another complication is that European integration is characterized by a high degree of cooperation and institutionalization, the latter of which sometimes entails giving up sovereignty and hence the scope for national action, which does not fit well with the realist assumption of states being primarily motivated by power maximization. Accordingly, ideas matter in the constitution of Europe's hierarchy, but scholars do not agree on which kinds of ideational variables are the most important. For Pederson (1998), it is the strategies of the dominant states, while Beach and Mazucelli (2007) focus on "reputation". Child (2010) says that the moral quality of the core matters: their decisions must not be seen as egoistic.

The theoretical framework adopted here follows this tradition of conceptualizing hierarchy with both realist (or material) and constructivist (or immaterial) underpinnings. But it also expands on the latter by further developing the inter-subjective aspects of the power inequalities between European states. To do this will require an explication of some of the *cognitive* and *affective* dimensions of Europe's inter-state hierarchy.

Hierarchy and cognition

In Wendt's (1992) model, the stuff of cognition is "inter-subjective knowledge" and "theories that actors use to understand the world". These, in turn, are the result of inter-state interaction and practice. Formulaically, Wendt's causal chain starts from state practice and interaction, and goes to cognition and identity, and then to state behaviour. This book adopts Wendt's model insofar as it investigates the interplay between interstate practice, cognition, and state behaviour. In particular, the role of Europe's hierarchy in influencing the politics of the euro will be a major focus of this book.

To develop the framework on the cognitive dimension of hierarchy, I will first outline the character of inter-state relations from the perspective of social psychology, which sheds light on how actors construct their nations and give content, meaning, and substance to them. These constructions take the form of collective representations that are widely, but not universally, held and accepted, often totally uncritically. The scholar uses the word "representation" because there is an assumption that these representations do not necessarily correspond with reality. But for the actor, these representations are real and objective and, as such, they influence his attitudes, as a member of a group, towards other social aggregates.

One of the key insights of social identity theory is that these constructions are intrinsically rooted in intergroup comparisons more than objective properties of the group (Tajfel 1978; Abrams & Hogg 2004). There are many dimensions to these intergroup comparisons, but a key dimension is hierarchy of status or condition. In this dimension, a large number of actors within a group typically perceive their group as superior, equal, or inferior in relation to other key groups (Horowitz 1985).[1] Whether large numbers of actors within the group perceive themselves in one or the other of these categories depends heavily on stereotypes that are perceived as real and objective. Actors rely on stereotypes because they are simplified versions of reality that help to economize and organize information (Ross 1995). They make a complex and contradictory world comprehensible and coherent (Lippman 1998). They produce certainty and hence reduce the cognitive discomfort of uncertainty (Hale 2004). These stereotypes are generalized towards both the ingroup and other social aggregates. They are central in making groups feel like real, coherent, and substantial entities. Social psychologists have labelled this phenomenon of stereotypes making groups feel real and coherent "entatitivity" (Castano 2002; Hamilton et al. 1994, p. 224). Entatitivity is an essential condition for the perception that one's group has the status of inferior, equal, or superior to other groups. If one's group did not feel like a real, bounded, and coherent entity, it would make little sense to apply one of these labels to it.

The status that one ascribes to one's group will influence intergroup behaviour. If one's group is perceived to be on the low end of the hierarchy, there will be motivation among a large number of actors within the group to obtain the status of equality (Turner & Reynolds 2004). This need for equal status becomes activated by certain "events" that make intergroup comparisons, and ingroup construction, salient (for the role of events, see Brubaker 1996, p. 19). Certain events evoke entatitivity and hence make collective representations psychologically operative. Events can be a threat to one's relative status, or an opportunity to increase the group's relative status, or a combination of both (Sorrentino & Yamaguchi 2008). They are occasions when intergroup comparisons and the group's relative status are widely discussed in newspapers, on TV, in workplaces, in households, and at the local bar.

European integration initiatives can be understood as one of these events that make collective representations salient and psychologically operative (Berezin 2009). When integration initiatives take place, they are often interpreted through the prism of the intergroup comparison dynamics mentioned above. When one's group is on the lower end of the hierarchy of groups, integration is interpreted by many actors to be a way to secure equality with elite groups. This perception of equality is interpreted in various ways, which explains why many individuals who disagree on most things might agree that integration or inclusion is essential to achieve equality. For some, this equality principally means fixing the country's economic "backwardness", for others mainly better political and democratic institutions, and for others it is understood as a way to improve the culture and civic attitudes of the group, but these different goals *point towards the level/standards of the dominant state(s)*.

Intergroup comparisons during integration events do not emerge from cold, calculating reason; they are propelled by the affective properties of the ideas that constitute these intergroup comparisons (Baumeister et al. 2007). These associations between ideas and affect activate approach or avoid tendencies: if the event induces positive affect, actors are inclined to accept or approach it; if it induces negative affect, they reject or avoid it (Slovic et al. 2002). In addition, much research has shown that affective associations with particular stimuli induce cognitive appraisals that depart from the standard rational calculator model (Kahneman 2003). In particular, in contexts which require decisions on complex issues and where information is low, when a stimulus is associated with positive affect, we tend to emphasize the benefits and minimize the costs. When a stimulus is associated with negative affect, we emphasize the costs and minimize the benefits (Alhakami & Slovic 1994). The risks and probabilities of particular outcomes are also skewed: stimuli associated with negative affect tend to be perceived as more risky than stimuli associated with positive affect (Slovic & Leichenstein 1968). And, finally, the data-filtering function of cognition is skewed: information that has strong affective associations – whether positive or negative – becomes salient while other information with weak affective associations is minimized (Baumeister et al. 2007).

The affective dynamics of cognition are a necessary but insufficient part of the story, however. To identify the nexus between ideas and preferences, we must look at the implicit theorizing that is present in actors' cognitive schemes (Abdelal et al. 2009 p. 7; Hewstone 1986, p. 53; Wendt 1992, p. 398). The propensity for actors to possess theories with which they make sense of the world has been extensively documented by psychologists. Depending on the literature, this dynamic has been labelled "causal attribution theory" (Taylor & Fiske 1984, p. 20), or "causal schematas" (ibid, p. 34).The stereotypes mentioned above that differentiate groups, give them substance, and place them on one point in a hierarchy rely, whether the actor is aware of it or not, on implicit theorizing. The notion that "Italians are like X" and "Germans are like Y" relies on a very selective set of criteria that the actor finds important. For some, the Germans are better because of their economic system; for others, because of their largely honest political class; and for others, because German people have a strong sense of the common good. The actor may be totally unaware that his or her diagnosis of the problem rests, to paraphrase Keynes, on the suppositions of some defunct intellectual. But indeed it does. The way that intellectuals diagnose the problem, through time, percolates to some of the masses and becomes part of that taken-for-granted repository of ideas that constitutes culture.

Implicit theorizing not only takes place in the diagnoses of the problem; it also takes place when actors construct solutions to their nation's relatively lower status. In this element of cognitive processing, actors have goals vis-à-vis their groups: to increase the relative status or condition of their group vis-à-vis other, more advanced groups. These goals are instrumental, in the sense that they possess a means-end structure. For some, the change required to achieve the end of relative equality of status or condition is to change their country's culture; for others, to change or weaken their country's corrupt political class[2]; and for others, to create more opportunities for their country's firms to modernize. The ideas associated with Europe are crucial here. Europe was often associated with "modernity", "normality", "strength", "freedom" – all concepts, not coincidentally, that are associated with Europe's elite countries. For many Italians, there was the desire and hope that securing inclusion in Europe would promote these wonderful concepts in their country. But this desire and hope became the theory that securing inclusion in Europe *would* promote these concepts in their country.

Associative evaluation

The discourse that belonging to Europe would transfer European virtues to Italy suggests that belongingness influences how the nation is constructed. That is, the properties that are ascribed to the nation depend, in part, on the character of its relationship to Europe. I call this phenomenon "Associative Evaluation". This phenomenon may manifest itself in various ways. For many, joining EMU was refracted through the aspiration of equality, and this aspiration only makes sense in the context of a hierarchy that places states in "first" or "second" tiers. In the period immediately after Italy joined EMU, it was felt by many that the country was no longer "abnormal" (Chevallard 2008, p. 50), or that it obtained a dramatic increase in its relative status in relation to Europe's elite countries, and this was felt even though the socioeconomic structure of the country and its relative position did not substantively change (for the persistence of Italy's political economy despite its adoption of the euro, see De Cecco 2007; Della Sala 2004). For others, after Italy secured inclusion in the EMU, there was hope and anticipation that the desired changes would emerge with little effort required of Italians themselves. Or there is the generalized (and highly debatable) belief that exclusion from Europe would turn Italy into a third-world country. As Antonio Puri Purini recently said, "without Brussels, we [Italy] would be a larger version of Lebanon" (*Corriere della Sera*, 27/10/2012). Here, Lebanon is a metaphor for instability, division, economic backwardness, and the lack of modernity. For this commentator, evidently, only being tied to Europe can prevent Italy from having Lebanon's apparently sad condition. One economist at the Bank of Italy even told me that "outside Europe, Italy would have no value". For him, Europe is equated with dignity, esteem, and status for Italy.

The idea of Associative Evaluation derives from the work of scholars who have shown that the self-evaluation of the individual often emerges not from objective attributes but from the group to which the individual perceives herself to belong. In this regard, one of the most influential frameworks comes from sociologist Norbert Elias (1978). He recognized that the self-evaluative aspects of the individual depended on the group to which he belonged just as much as, if not more, than his individual achievements. The originator of this idea may very well have been Freud, who recognized that narcissistic tendencies were often a function, not only of individual attributes, but of the group to which the individual belonged (Freud, 1999). Social psychologists have made similar observations: that the individual's self-esteem or positive self-evaluations often derive from the perceived status of his group rather than from his own personal attributes (Billig & Tajfel 1973; Johnston & Hewstone 1990). Elias developed this idea further with the concept of "habitus", which refers to the ways in which the development of individual consciousness evolves and shifts co-extensively and co-relationally with the nation (Elias 1991; Elias 1996). Elias and Scotson (1994) then extended this framework to a widely acclaimed study that theorized the links between individual consciousness, the group, and inter-group hierarchy. In a case study that is strikingly similar to the intergroup dynamics that are observable in Europe, he looked at two groups in Scotland and how the individual members of each group internalized the belief that the "superior" group was more virtuous than the "inferior" group. Elias makes a distinction between the "I" images and the "We" images, and shows how the hierarchy between the groups was maintained because the "We" images consisted of a series of stereotypes that depicted the "inferior" groups as less virtuous. These "We" images then changed the "I" images that formed the basis of the self-evaluative aspects of the individuals who constituted the groups, which reified the intergroup hierarchy.

Scholars have applied Elias's framework to Europe's inter-state relations. Thomas Scheff, for instance, highlights that the individual's subjective "Pride-Shame" balance often derives from the changing objective fortunes of his nation vis-à-vis other nations (Scheff 1994a; Scheff 1994b). Pablo Jaruegui (1999) also applies Elias's framework to Europe. He explores the nexus between individual self-esteem and national identity, arguing that individual self-esteem often shifts, not on the basis of individual achievements, but because of the changing fortunes of the nation within which one belongs. He focuses on two countries – Spain and the UK – and explores how entering the European community had differential effects on these two nations: for Spain, it was associated with greater self-esteem because entering represented a move towards "modernity" and a distancing from the backwardness of the Franco era, while for the UK it was associated with lower self-esteem because it represented a further distancing from its role as a global empire.

The dynamics that were present when Spain entered Europe are similar to the dynamics present in Italy when this country adopted the euro: it was perceived as a raising of the nation's self-esteem. But there were important differences. In Italy, the discourse was different because Italians have a different conception of their nation's place in Europe. Italy was one of the founders of the European project; many of the greatest theorists of European unity were Italian; and in terms of territory, population, GDP, and even membership to prestigious clubs like the G7, it has some of the trappings of a "great power". For these and other reasons many Italians perceive their nation as one of Europe's great powers, and its actual relegation to second-class status in Europe is perceived as unjust.

This widespread desire for equality with Europe's elite countries strongly influenced the character of intergroup comparisons that took place before and during the adoption of the euro. Social psychologists have recognized that the desire to enhance the self-esteem of the group is universal, and that intergroup comparisons are one of the ways in which members of groups satisfy this desire. However, the manifestation of this desire is very context-dependent (Oakes, Haslam, & Turner 1998, p. 79; Hogg, Terry, & White 1995) and takes different forms among different groups. Perhaps due to their concern with the causes of intergroup prejudice and discrimination, social psychologists have mostly explored the ways that groups, in order to create a collective sense of positive self-distinction, aim to differentiate themselves from other groups (Deschamps & Devos 1998; Hogg 2000, p. 225). This creates the impetus for positive stereotypes about the ingroup and negative stereotypes about the outgroup (hence justifying prejudice). But for lower-status groups the dynamic is often different (Abrams & Hogg 1990, p. 52). Rather than differentiation, the desire to produce positive self-distinction leads to the desire for *assimilation with the higher status group* (Hogg, Terry, & White 1995). That is, for low-status groups collective self-esteem depends on the possibility of the collective Self becoming enmeshed with the higher-status Other.

For low-status groups who aim to enhance self-esteem through assimilation, the bias is upwards towards higher status groups. It is held that assimilating with the higher-status group will mean adopting the virtues of this group. The stereotypes (Wyer, Robert, & Carlston 1979, p. 17) of the outgroup are crucial. Here, "Europe" is perceived to be associated with "modernity" and "advancement". These associations derive from the fact that "Europe" is, in the minds of many, indissolubly linked to the standards that are present in Europe's elite countries, mainly Germany. This also rests on the tendency observed by social psychologists to exaggerate the homogeneity of the outgroup (Deschamps & Devos 1998, p. 8; Johnston & Hewstone 1990, p. 199).

The theory that entering Europe would produce European virtues was embedded in the discourses surrounding Italy's entering EMU. In the nineties, after the Treaty of Maastricht was signed, Italian policymakers had to build support for the significant sacrifices that had to be made to meet the stringent public finance criteria that were required to enter the monetary union. They made extravagant promises for the euro, promising that "entering Europe" would produce paradise[3] and green valleys (Cecchini 1998), or even more hyperbolically, that it would eliminate Italy's defects by creating "mature" and "modern" European citizens (Ricci 2011).

There are two reasons for the fact that, in the public sphere, these discourses were salient: the first one is "top-down", the second one is "bottom-up". Regarding the first, politicians shrewdly recognized that being completely honest about the common currency would not help them to build the political support that they needed to implement the painful sacrifices required to enter. Other politicians, meanwhile, believed their own rhetoric that the euro would make Italy "European", which was much more likely among politicians of the centre-left and the centre. But whether they believed their own rhetoric or were merely being disingenuous, politicians played a key role in constructing the dominant discourse. The second, "bottom-up", reason emerged from the fact that in the cacophony of discourses that are present during major policy events, some are more affectively charged than others. Whether a discourse is affectively charged depends on how it is perceived by its intended audience. Among political communities, certain concepts have certain affective associations that make these concepts "resonate" among the audiences. The discourse that the euro would make Italy a "European" country resonated precisely because of the deep cultural currents within the political community that depicted Europe as the saviour for the country's problems. And when a discourse resonates, it also feels more "real" than other discourses. This feeling that it is "real" militates against the necessity to have a healthy scepticism about the discourses, or to seek out disconfirming discourses.

These affectively charged discourses that resonate with audiences need to be communicated, which is why the theoretical picture presented in this section would not be complete without an analysis of the media. Scholars have recognized that the media constitute social and political reality (Altheide & Snow 1974) through the use of narrative, metaphor, myth, and drama (Eason 1981) rather than reasoned dispassionate discussion of policy alternatives (Bennet 1980). This is particularly the case during events like the birth of the euro, where front and centre of the discussion are the images of nations and the relations between them.

Concepts like nations are highly abstract, complex, and ambiguous. They cannot be touched or physically seen, because they are associated with a host of variables – territory, politics, the economy, population, culture, and language are perhaps the most important. This complexity of the reality of the nation is reduced and made manageable in the media with the use of metaphor and stereotypes. Metaphors and stereotypes have the benefit of making the world intelligible, but they also obscure as much as they illuminate. There is the tendency to exaggerate the homogeneity of the outgroup. "Europe" was associated with modernity, even though the reality of "Europe" is very differentiated. These stereotypes and metaphors lead to some interesting dynamics of cognitive dissonance. When things happen in France, the UK, and Germany that don't fit the stereotype – such as a high-profile case of corruption – they are interpreted in individualist terms, as examples of the moral failure of the individuals involved. When a similar event happens in Italy, it fits the stereotype and is interpreted in cultural terms, as in "this is Italy! That's how Italians are!" Thus stereotypes utilized by the media not only make the world intelligible, but they are also interpretive schemes through which political realities are constituted.

Scholars who focus on the nexus between public opinion, the mass media, and international relations have discovered that one of the main determinants of the actors' selection of information in the media-created political environment is the drive for cognitive consistency (Jonsson 1982, p. 3): the strong tendency for people to see what they expect or want to see and to assimilate incoming information into existing images (Jervis 1970, p. 118; Hewstone 1986). Expectations create dispositions that lead actors to notice certain things and neglect others, and that make it difficult to consider alternatives (Bloom 1990, p. 4; Jervis 1970, p. 145). Many experiments provide support for this theory that actors' expectations lead them to a kind of confirmation or verification bias in their consumption of information (Pelham & Swan 1994, p. 335; Swan, Stein-Seroussi, & Geisler 1992) not only from media sources, but also from social settings – in conversations with friends, family, even acquaintances at the local bar (Davison 1958). In fact, social settings play an important part of the construction of political reality: because it is shared, the fantasy held by the group takes on an aura of truth (Nimmo & Combs 1983, p. 11).

The influence of these cognitive dynamics is higher for highly ambiguous stimuli (Moscovici 1976, p. 25), and nations, and the relations between them, undoubtedly fall into this category. But the expectations that lead to this highly selective consumption of information on the international environment emerge from deeply sedimented currents in the culture of the community. For this case study, there was the widespread belief and desire that entering the euro would produce equality. This belief was often unarticulated, but when it was expressed it was often framed with metaphors that the common person could relate to – for example, the belief that entering would make Italy a country of "Serie A." Most Italians were not informed about the substance of the monetary union, but because soccer is part of the national culture, most know that Serie A means "premier" and "elite." This belief was felt to be real, in part because of the affectively charged discourses propagated by politicians, and in part because of the way that information is consumed from the media and from social settings, but ultimately this idea relied on the theory that entering a monetary union would help to equalize Italy's status and condition. Chapter three will present evidence in support of this assertion.

Many want equality, but this equality is interpreted in different ways by different actors. The differences between elites and non-elites are especially important because it is generally agreed among scholars of public opinion and communication that the discourses that constitute public attitudes towards political issues are largely elite constructions. Major authors such as Walter Lippman (1998) and Philip Converse (1964) recognized that very few citizens rely on independent reasoning to form opinions about political issues, especially about complex foreign policies. For Lippman, among the masses stereotypes are the cognitive devices that are used to simplify and makes sense of a complex world, but the masses do not invent them. Rather, these stereotypes come from elites and are promulgated through various channels that link elites and non-elites. In a similar vein, Converse highlighted that what he called "mass ideologies" were not invented by the masses, but were derived from elites; these elite-invented ideologies merged with the masses' pre-existing beliefs and formed the masses' distinctive attitudes towards political issues.

The focus on the differences in the cognitive schemes of elites and non-elites is important for other reasons. Elites, despite being more knowledgeable, seem more prone to the kind of thinking that is associated with the logic of identity than are non-elites. The reason can be found in the cognitive content of their respective cognitive schemes. Elites rely on highly abstract visions of European order that lead them to minimize the concrete costs and benefits of EMU. In contrast, non-elites typically rely on more concrete evaluations, which are rooted in their daily experiences at work or with the bureaucracy. One could argue that since non-elites are patently less knowledgeable than elites on European institutions, they are less able to rationally evaluate policies like EMU. In principle this is a correct argument, but in practice the knowledge problem afflicts both elites and non-elites. Non-elites tend to be completely unaware of the counterarguments for entering EMU, which suggests that their appraisals were based exclusively on discourses and stereotypes. But elites, although they were knowledgeable of counterarguments, nonetheless interpreted the euro through the prism of theoretical abstractions that militated against a rational appraisal based on only the cold, hard facts. Chapter four will explore this in more detail.

Italy, hierarchy, and the euro

This section will further develop the idea of hierarchy and Italy's place in it. This framework will be used to interpret key texts on Italian politics, highlighting the coherence and complementarities between my ideas and the observations of important Italian intellectuals.

Italian perceptions of Europe are complex and multidimensional, containing elements of both pride and shame. Regarding the former, Italians are proud of their role in the founding of Europe, and of the pivotal role of many Italian statesmen and intellectuals in uniting the continent to promote peace, prosperity, and preventing a recrudescence of the destructive nationalisms that tore Europe apart in the 20th century. However, as the literature and primary data sources will show, among Italians there also exists an idea of inferiority vis-à-vis many other European countries. In his study of Italian political discourse as expressed in key texts and elite commentary, Huysseune (2006, p. 20) discovered the salience of this perceived hierarchy and labelled it the "imaginary geography of modernity." This idea is an interpretive framework that is intrinsically relational and creates a hierarchy of nations based on relative status and socioeconomic condition. On the basis of this discourse, Britain, France, and Germany are considered the "normal" countries, while Italy is considered an "abnormal" country. This interpretive framework is highly selective: it relies on some criteria and excludes others. It exaggerates the uniformity of each nation: evidence of familism or corruption in one of the "normal" countries is ignored, while all instances of familism or corruption in Italy are accentuated. It is simultaneously analytical and normative, diagnosing the disease and constituting the wish to cure it.

Hierarchy also manifests itself at the international level. In his seminal work on Italy and Europe, Willis highlights that, in the immediate post-war era, Italians were strongly motivated to obtain international equality with Europe's "great powers" (Willis 1971, p. 16). When negotiations on the European Coal and Steel Community began, Foreign Minister Sforza "feared the establishment of Franco-German hegemony in Western Europe (Willis 1971, p. 33). Subsequently, when designing the inter-governmental institutions in the burgeoning community, "Italy's main demand was equality with France and Germany" (Willis 1971, p.61). Other students of Italy have made the same observations. Brogi (2002) highlights that Italy's main foreign policy goal in the post-war era was to be on equal terms with Europe's elite countries, and the means to do this was to secure inclusion in the burgeoning institutions that were centres of decision-making for the continent, including, but not exclusively, the European community. Brogi argues that it aimed to produce the perception that Italy was on equal terms with Europe's elite countries, which, it was felt, would produce the *reality* that it had equal status (ibid., p. 2); this is a clear instance of the implicit theorizing within actors' cognitive schemes that plays a central role in the arguments here: hoping that X will lead to Y becomes the theory that X *will* become Y. By the 1960s, this discourse of inclusion in Europe and equal status became the discourse that Europe was the solution to Italy's perceived defects, including socioeconomic "backwardness" (Conti 2009, p.133). Thus equal status transmogrified from meaning principally relatively equal status among nations in the international system to the relative equality of socioeconomic conditions between Italy and Europe's elite countries. Through the media sources that mostly reflected the positions of the Christian Democrats, this discourse then percolated to *some* of the masses and then took new forms as different actors interpreted it in different ways.

One problem with this discourse is that it did not specify any mechanisms through which belonging to Europe would make Italy like Europe. It is as if this would happen through osmosis, spontaneously, without much effort other than the effort that was required to secure inclusion in Europe (Conti 2009, p. 133). The true agent of change was perceived to be Europe, not the nation. Italian intellectuals have recognized the serious problem with this vision: it led people to believe that inclusion in Europe was *sufficient* for Italy to become like Europe, which, on the basis of any sober analysis of the facts, is untrue. Giancarlo Chevallard, an Italian bureaucrat who worked in the Commission for 25 years, chastises his fellow citizens for their exaggerated expectations of what Europe can do for Italy, pointing out that these expectations are not rooted in the reality of Europe's actual roles, functions, and capabilities (Chevallard 2008, p. 37). In a similar vein, Tullio-Altan warns his countrymen to avoid the illusion that integration into Europe will *automatically produce the sense of the common good that he and many others believe Europe can teach Italy* (Tullio-Altan 1999, p. 222. Emphasis mine). Unlike many, many of their fellow citizens, both Chevallard and Tullio-Altan were aware of a very important truth: only Italy can change itself, and integration in Europe was insufficient to give Italy the equality of status and condition that many Italians crave (although since EMU did not bring the equality that many Italians expected, more and more Italians have come to realize that only they, and not Europe, can change the country).

Other commentary from the late nineties to the present from prominent Italian intellectuals highlights the tendency to place excessive agency in the euro and Europe:

- Ciampi warned us that it would be a mistake to think that the euro will solve all our problems. The euro is a condition to resolve our problems, not the solution itself (*Corriere della Sera* 17/03/1998).
- There is the a risk that with the euro we will believe that we no longer have problems (TG2 Dossier Oggi Euro, aired on RAI on 01/05/1998).
- There is an obsession for the common currency . . . there is an air of the Fall of Constantinople, as if the Mediterranean has become a zone of religious

conflict, and instead of protecting ourselves appropriately, we put our trust in the protection of the euro (Giorgio Bocca, *Repubblica* 28/03/1997).

- In recent weeks the tone of the debate on Italy's entering the euro has become elevated because we [Italians] are uploading the responsibility for our problems onto the common currency and Germany (*Corriere della Sera* 05/02/1997).
- We thought that the euro was a life jacket that would have allowed us to preserve all our vices (Angelo Panebianco, *Corriere Della Sera* 31/10/2011).
- The paradise of the euro was artificial. In reality, the problems in Italy's political economy were present but the ruling class, blinded by the optical illusion created by the euro, avoided making the necessary reforms . . . the so-called *vincolo esterno*, which at times forced the country to implement some reforms, fundamentally made the ruling class irresponsible (Danilo Taino, *Corriere della Sera* 14/09/2011).
- As Sabino Cassese said, the so-called *vincolo esterno* constitutes an escape from the state/ourselves (Massimo Giannini, Repubblica 28/12/2011).
- We put our trust in the *vincolo esterno* to avoid the responsibility for our own rigidities (Piero Ostellino, *Corriere della Sera* 03/11/2012).
- Europeanism has become a smoke-screen . . . the crisis has reminded us that there exists something called Italy and that our well-being depends on it (*Ernesto della Loggia*, Corriere della Sera 31/01/2012).
- We need to get rid of the illusion that Europe can fix what is our responsibility to become more competitive and efficient (Michele Salvati, *Corriere della Sera* 03/05/2013).
- We trust in outsiders/foreigners, and then pursue our narrow personal interests . . . sooner or later, we believe the Germans will be forced to help us . . . we are *furbi* (cunning, manipulative, etc.) (Salvatore Bragantini, *Corriere della Sera* 24/05/2013).
- Some look at Europe as if it is a lifeguard that can save us . . . [that is] mistaken: we are the sources of our problems and only we can solve them (Alberto Alesina and Francesco Giavazzi, *Corriere della Sera* 07/09/2013).
- After the birth of the euro, we were *furbi,* thinking that we could obtain the benefits of the euro without paying the price of internal adjustment (Angelo Panebianco, Corriere della Sera 26/10/2014).

Chapter five will explore in further detail the elements of Italy's societal model that help to relegate it to secondary status in Europe's hierarchy. It will also show that this placing of excessive agency in Europe and the euro helped to disincentivize many of the reforms that the country needs if it truly wants to become a member of the "core" alongside Germany and France.

Mental maps of hierarchy

The framework outlined here raises the question: who or what is responsible for these perceptions of hierarchy? The first cause is structural: Europe's informal hierarchy is real in the sense that it is performed by political and other elites. Italy's secondary status is felt whenever it is excluded or ignored by the countries in the "core", or when it is grouped as part of the "periphery" (for example, when it is depicted as part of the "Club Med" or a member of the PIIGS). It is Italian political and intellectual elites who ultimately interpret this hierarchy of status and condition and transmit their ideas to the wider nation. This highlights that there is an important conceptual distinction between a mental map of a hierarchy that is perceived by Italians, and the hierarchy of actual status and influence that exists within Europe. The former can be measured by simply recording perceptions of Italians in the way they conceive of their nation vis-à-vis Europe's elite countries, which will be done shortly. The second is more difficult, because measuring a hierarchy of status and influence between nations requires different indicators. Chapter six will further elucidate this crucial difference between hierarchy as it is perceived and as it is practiced.

To give the reader a sense of this mental map of hierarchy that is perceived by Italian elites, here are a few expressions that were discovered in the sample of newspapers that was collected:

- In the next European summit, if our numbers are in order, we can imagine that rather than being treated like the messy and poor relative, relegated to the Seria B in Europe and nervous about others diffidence towards us, we can be the ones who are critical of others' political economy (*Repubblica* 15/04/1996).
- Veltroni is delusional: in Europe, the only ones who count when it comes to deciding are France and Germany (*Corriere della Sera* 27/08/1996).
- Anzar refused the Italian proposal for a Mediterranean axis to pressure France and Germany to delay the Maastricht criteria. It is obvious here that Italy is in the "periphery', while Anzar believes that Spain is part of the Seria A of a Europe governed by conservative governments in Bonn, Paris, and Madrid (*Corriere della Sera* 07/10/1996).
- Italians are Europeans only in words, not in behaviour (*Corriere della Sera* 05/02/1997).
- When I hear people insult Italy and Spain, when bankers describe them disdainfully as "countries of the Club Med", I am horrified. For me Italy is Dante, Spain is Cervantes (*Corriere della Sera* 24/05/1997).
- Yesterday the Financial Times raised the "Italian question" for Europe. This is a subtle way of saying that there exists a "Club Med" and that Italy is a potentially is a big problem (*Corriere della Sera* 06/02/1997).
- There are fears that the countries of "Club Med" [which includes Italy] will not participate in the monetary union (*Corriere della Sera* 25/02/1997).
- There is an attempt to exclude [from the euro] the countries of the so-called Club Med: Italy, Spain, and Portugal (*Corriere della Sera* 18/08/1997).
- Italy's dilemma is serious . . . if the German Chancellor accepts weak countries like Italy, he will lose votes (*Corriere della Sera*, 05/02/1997).
- Why is there so much diffidence [in Europe] towards Italy? Because of the many stereotypes of Italians (*Repubblica* 26/01/1998).

- The Germans are disturbed about the members of the "Club Med" entering the euro – Italy, Spain, and Portugal – three countries that benefit from Europe because of their economic backwardness (*Repubblica* 02/03/1997).
- We are notably behind other European countries which are stronger than us (TG2 Dossier Oggi Euro, aired on RAI on 01/05/1998).
- Ciampi knows well the diffidence of the Germans towards Italy's place in Europe. We [Italy] have a reputation of being happy, creative but at the same time disorganized and dishonest, not completely trustworthy and afflicted with instability, corruption, and mafia (*Repubblica* 07/01/1998).
- If in Europe we were all Germans, few would like us, because the best are never loved. But if we were all Italians, who knows where we would end up (*Repubblica* 30/01/1998).
- In our euro-enthusiasm there is the desire to be governed by the Commission or Germany. We are unique: the French, British, and Germans resist giving up sovereignty, while we desire to be protected from ourselves (*Repubblica* 09/02/1998).
- Without a doubt Italy is weaker and less influential than France and Germany (*Repubblica* 15/06/2001).
- What matters for the Italian head of state is that from Germany we see an impulse to unify Europe and that in this Italy is not excluded, breaking the old attempts to govern Europe only with France (*Corriere della Sera* 08/04/2001).
- In Europe there are rules and points of comparison, and the prejudices against Italy must be addressed with virtuous behaviour (*Repubblica* 30/06/2003).
- We are a country who is historically behind its neighbours to the North . . . we have been reminded by some of our best minds that we must strengthen our ties with our Northern neighbours, otherwise we would be associated with the South, which would bring only backwardness and stagnation (*Repubblica* 24/11/2004).

All these quotes are taken from articles about Italy and the euro. Within these quotes is embedded some variant of the idea that Italy is "behind" or "below" or "weaker" or "not up to the standards of" Europe's great powers or the ideal of "Europe". Subsequent chapters will show that this idea was widely present among the interview sample as well.

The idea of Italian "backwardness" can found among other important cultural elites. One of the defects that Italians purportedly possess is a deficient sense of the common good, the privileging of the private sphere to the detriment of the public. Local, parochial, and particularistic ties are pervasive in all sectors of society. And contrary to widely held stereotypes about the "modern" North and "backward" South, this lack of common good and pervasiveness of particularistic ties is widely diffused in the entire peninsula. What is more, this social system has deep historical roots. Tullio-Altan (1999, p. 157) cites the texts of Leon Battista Alberti, an influential intellectual in Florence during the Renaissance period who outlined a hierarchy of values that current students of Italy would easily recognize: at the top of this hierarchy resides the family, followed by the firm, and, lastly, friends and clients (it is curious that in this hierarchy friends and clients have equal status). It would be bad enough if the common good appeared at the bottom of this hierarchy, but it does not appear at all, leading Tullio-Alton to argue not implausibly that it is emblematic of total lack of civic spirit.

These sentiments are echoed by Della Loggia. His harshest indictment of Italy's "backwardness" is the lack of social mobility (Della Loggia 1998, p. 94). For him the reason for this stultifying low social mobility is the prevalence of family ties over public ones. This familism prevents the modernization of Italy, its development into a society where an individual's destiny is determined on the basis of merit and ambition rather than family ties. This state of affairs leads to the absence of a modern, functioning, efficient, in other words, Weberian, state. The absence of the common good leads many Italians to treat politics as a means to satisfy their private interests. This, somewhat paradoxically, leads to an excessively politicized society with a multiplicity of political interests that are coterminous with private interests (to be sure, this dynamic is present in other Western democracies, but seems to be much more pervasive in Italy). The state becomes an arena for the struggle and competition of these private interests, preventing the formation of the modern state. Della Loggia agrees with Tullio-Altan that this state of affairs is diffuse across the entire peninsula, not only the "backward" South. He also shares Tullio-Altan's belief in the historical roots of this social structure, citing Dante and his contemporaries, who observed Italy's inability to become a "modern" nation (Della Loggia 1998, p. 138) Many other scholars and intellectuals have made similar observations about Italy's social system (Cavalli 2001; Gentile 1999; Tullio-Altan 1986; Bedani & Haddock 2000, p. 206; Berger & Locke 2001, p. 41). Other scholars, however, have problematized this hierarchy of the modernity of Western European countries (Agnew 1997). But in public discourse the stereotypes are widely held, expressed by Italian intellectuals in books and newspapers, and by citizens in everyday conversations.

These stereotypes animated the wish to be on equal terms with Europe's "modern", "normal", and "advanced" nations, and for many it was a short conceptual leap to believe that Europe is the solution to the country's problems. This is reflected in the works of Italian intellectuals. For some, Europe is a sort of teacher that will inculcate Italians with the public spirit that they are presumably lacking. Tullio-Altan (1999, pp. 215–22) expresses this sentiment when he exhorts his country to aim for further European integration so that Europe can teach Italians the importance of following rules, and help renew the spirit of the public good. For Massimo D'Alema (1995), European integration is the solution to what appears to be all of Italy's perceived defects: the lack of modernity, low collective esteem, lack of rules and civil rights, low social mobility, lack of economic development, etc. For other Italian intellectuals, European integration is necessary primarily to ensure that Italy's economy meets European standards of economic development.

An implication of the theoretical framework outlined in this chapter is that a different mental map of hierarchy would have represented different cognitive schemes through which joining EMU would have been interpreted and led to different outcomes. For example, in the absence of the stereotypes that place the country on the low end of a hierarchy of status and condition, there would have been no need or desire to be on equal terms with others in the hierarchy. Similarly, there would have been no need for the implicit theory that belonging in the group with advanced European nations would produce this desired equality. These are some of the dynamics that were present in Britain during the run-up to EMU, which helps to explain why the majority of the public was opposed. The discourses in Britain were qualitatively different from Italy's, which partly explains why the outcome was different. In Britain, the perception is that, in the European hierarchy, it is one of the top-tier nations. Britons are not inclined to look to Europe as the solution to the country's problems; on the contrary, Europe is seen as the *source* of the country's problems, which was effectively encapsulated in Margaret Thatcher's quote that "in my lifetime all our problems have come from mainland Europe, and all the solutions have come from the English-speaking nations across the world" (*Economist,* 10/04/2010, p. 26). This comparative analysis between the UK and Italy will be the focus of chapter seven.

The euro was also supposed to help equalize Europe's power hierarchy by weakening Germany through the tying of its hands to supranational institutions. That, in any event, was the theory that motivated many of the euro's supporters, especially in France. Like most of the other narratives held by the euro's supporters, this one has collapsed under the weight of reality, namely, the enhancement of German power and the consequent widening of the inequality between it and other members. This result has revealed an uncomfortable truth: the increase in power that accrued to Germany after its unification cannot be undone or minimized by the schemes that attempt to tie its hand. It has also helped to create a poisonous political atmosphere, as parties across the continent blame their countries' problems on the policies that are decided in Berlin. Short of a return to traditional balancing, there is no easy solution to this problem. In any event, Berlin has no choice but to assume leadership, since whether the euro survives will depend more on Germany than any other Eurozone country. This will be the focus of the penultimate chapter. The conclusion will reflect on the future possibilities of the Eurozone.

Notes

1 Although Horowitz uses the relative status framework to explain group conflict in divided societies.

2 Many prominent Italians now recognize the folly of this particular aspiration. As Luigi Zingales, Professor of Economics, recently stated: "[With the euro] we dreamed of being governed by leaders of German-quality and what we got instead is German-French interests being imposed on us" [referring to the bailout of Greece which was used to save French and German banks at the expense of Greeks]. Available at: www.ilsole24ore.com/art/commenti-e-idee/2015–03–07/solo-unione-politica-permette-scelte-economiche-democratiche—094706.shtml?uuid=ABD87h5C

3 *Corriere della Sera*, 15 March 1998, p. 2.

References

Abdelal, R., Herrera, Y. M., Johnston, A. I., and McDermott, R. (2009) *Measuring Identity: A Guide for Social Scientists*. Cambridge: Cambridge University Press.

Abrams, D. and Hogg, M. (1990) *Social Identity Theory: Constructive and Critical Advances*. New York: Springer Verlag.

Abrams, D. and Hogg, M. (2004) Collective Identity: Group Membership and Self Conception. In: R. Brown and S. L. Gaertner (eds). *Self and Social Identity*. Malden, MA: Blackwell Publishing, pp. 147–181.

Agnew, J. (1997) Myth of a Backward Italy. In: B. Allen and M. J. Russo (eds). *Revisioning Italy: National Identity and Global Culture*. Minneapolis: University of Minnesota Press, pp. 23–42.

Alesina, A. and Giavazzi, F. "Prigionieri di un Illusione," *Corriere della Sera* 07 September 2013: 1.

Alhakami, A. S. and Slovic, P. (1994) A Psychological Study of the Inverse Relationship Between Perceived Risk and Perceived Benefit. *Risk Analysis*, 14(6), pp. 1085–1096.

Altheide, D & Snow, R. (1974) *Media Logic*. Beverly Hill, CA: Sage Publications.

Altichieri, A."Siete Pericolosi per L'Euro," *Corriere della Sera* 06 February 1997: 2.

Amato, G. "Non Scherziamo con L'Europa," *Repubblica* 24 November 2004: 1.

Bastasin, C. (2012) *Saving Europe*. Washington, DC: Brookings Institution.

Baumeister, R. F., Vohs, K. D., DeWall, C. N., and Zhang, L. (2007) How Emotion Shapes Behaviour: Feedback, Anticipation, and Reflection, Rather than Direct Causation. *Personality and Social Psychology Review*, 11(2), May issue, pp. 167–203.

Beach, D. and Mazucelli, C. (2007) *Leadership in the Big Bangs of European Integration*. New York: Palgrave Macmillan.

Bedani, G. and Haddock, B. (2000) *The Politics of Italian National Identity*. Cardiff: University Of Wales Press.

Bennet, L. (1980) Myth, Ritual and Political Control. *Journal of Communication*, 30, pp. 166–179.

Berezin, M. (2009) *Illiberal Politics in Neoliberal Times*. Cambridge: Cambridge University Press.

Berger, S. and Locke, R. M. (2001) Il Caso Italiano and Globalization. *Deadalus*, 130, pp 85–104.

Billig, M. and Tajfel, H. (1973) Social Categorization and Similarity in Intergroup Behaviour. *European Journal of Social Psychology*, 3(1), pp. 27–52.

Bloom, W. (1990) *Personal Identity, National Identity and International Relations*. Cambridge: Cambridge University Press.

Bocca, G. "Euro Si Euro No La Terra Promessa," *Repubblica* 28 March 1997: 13.

Bragantini, S. "Il Paese non lo Fanno Grande I Furbi," *Corriere della Sera* 24 May 2013.

Breda, M. "Ciampi: Costituzione Commune la Strada Giusta per L'Europa," *Corriere della Sera* 08 April 2001: 13.

Brinegar, A. P. and Jolly, S. K. (2005) Location, Location, Location: National Contextual Factors and Public Support for European Integration. *European Union Politics*, 6(2), pp. 155–180.

Brogi, A. (2002) *A Question of Self-Esteem*. Westport, CT: Praeger Publishers.

Brubaker, R. (1996) *Nationalism Reframed*. Cambridge: Cambridge University Press.

Bunse, S., Magnette, P., and Nicolaidis, K. (2007) Big versus Small: Shared Leadership in the EU and Power Politics in the Convention. In: Beach, D and Mazucelli, C. (eds). *Leadership in the Big Bangs of European Integration*. New York: Palgrave Macmillan, pp 134–157.

Castano, E., Yzerbyt, V., Paladino, M. P., and Sacchi, S. (2002) I Belong Therefore I Exist: Ingroup Identification, Ingroup Entatitivity, Ingroup Bias. *Personality and Social Psychology Bulletin,* 28(2), pp. 135–143.

Cavalli, A. (2001) Reflections on Political Culture and the National Character. *Daedalus*, 130(3), pp. 119–137.

Cecchini, M. "Quel'Amicizia Incrinata sul Lungo Cammino Verso L'Europa," *Corriere della Sera* 30 October 1998: 3.

Cecchini, M. "Ciampi: L'Euro? Non Sara' L'eta dell Oro," *Corriere della Sera* 17 March 1998 :4.

Checkel, J. T. and Katzenstein, P. J. (2009) *European Identity*. Cambridge: Cambridge University Press.

Chevallard, G. (2008) *L'Italia Vista dall'Europa: Testimonianza da Bruxxells*. Milan: Rubbettino.

Child. J. (2010) Mission Impossible? The Potential for Franco-German Leadership in an Enlarged EU. *Journal of Common Market Studies*, 48(5), pp. 1367–1390.

Clericetti, C. "L'Italia e la Virtu' Negata," *Repubblica* 15 April 1996: 6.

Conti, N. (2009) *Europa Vista dai Partiti*. Pisa: University of Pisa Press.

Converse, P. 1964. The Nature of Belief Systems in Mass Publics. In: D. Apter (ed.). *Ideology and Discontent*. New York: Free Press, pp. 201–261.

D'Alema, M. (1995) *Un Paese Normale*. Milan: Mondadori.

Davies, S. "The European Tragedy," 12 August 2012. See www.fee.org/the_freeman/detail/the-european-tragedy#axzz2Verg4Xhc.

Davison, P. (1958) The Public Opinion Process. *Public Opinion Quarterly*, 22(2), pp. 91–106.

De Benedetti, C. "Se L'Italia Resta Fuori Non E' Un Dramma Nazionale," *Corriere della Sera* 05 February1997: 2.

De Cecco, M. (2007) Italy's Dysfunctional Political Economy. *West European Politics*, 30(4), pp. 763–783.

Deeg, R. (2005) Remaking Italian Capitalism? *West European Politics*, 28(3), pp 521–548.

Della Loggia, E. "La Rimozione dell'Italia," *Corriere della Sera* 31 January 2012: 1.

Della Loggia, E. G. (1998) *L'identita Italiana*. Bologna: Il Mulino.

Della Sala, V. (2004) The Italian Model of Capitalism: On the Road between Globalization and Europeanization? *Journal of European Public Policy*, 11(8), pp. 1041–1057.

Deschamps, J. and Devos, T. (1998) Regarding the Relationship between Social Identity and Personal Identity. In: S. Worchel, F. Morales, D. Paez and J. Deschamps (eds). *Social Identity: International Perspectives*. London: Sage Publications, pp. 1–12.

Di Vico, Dario. "Ridiscutere L'Unione? Veltroni S'Illude," *Corriere della Sera* 27 August1996: 2.

Dyson, K. and Featherstone, K. (1999) *The Road to Maastricht*. Oxford: Oxford University Press.

Eason, D. (1981) Telling Stories and Making Sense. *Journal of Popular Culture*, 15(2), pp. 125–29.

Eckstein, H. (1991) Rationality and Frustration in Political Behaviour. In: Monroe, K. R. (ed.). *The Economic Approach to Politics: A Critical Reassessment on the Theory of Rational Action*. New York: Harper-Collins, pp. 74–93.

Elias, N. (1978) *Civilizing Process*. New York: Urizen Books.

Elias, N. (1991) *The Society of Individuals*. Oxford: Basil Blackwell.

Elias, N. (1996) *The Germans*. Cambridge, UK: Polity Press.

Elias, N. and Scotson, J. (1994) *The Established and the Outsiders*. London: Sage Publications.

Ferrera, M. and Gualmini, E. (1999) *Rescued by Europe?* Amsterdam: Amsterdam University Press.

Freud, S. (1999) *On Narcissism*. In: J. Sandler (ed.). *On Narcissism: An Introduction*. London: Yale University Press.

Gabel, M. (1998) Public Support for European Integration: An Empirical Test of Five Theories. *Journal of Politics,* 60(2), pp. 333–54.

Gaggi, M. “Il Concelliere e Noi,” *Corriere della Sera* 18 August 1997: 1.

Gentile, E. (1999) *La Grande Italia: Acesa e Declino del Mito della Nazione nel Ventesimo Secolo*. Milan: Mondador.

Giuliani, M. (2001) Europeanization and Italy: A Bottom Up Process? In: K. Featherstone and G. Kazamias (eds). *Europeanization and the Southern Periphery*. London: Routledge.

Golden, M. (2004) International Economic Sources of Regime Change: How European Economic Integration Undermined Italy’s Post-War Party System. *Comparative Political Studies*, 37, Dec issue, pp. 1238–74.

Guatelli, A. “No all’Europa Ultraliberale, la Moneta Unica Deve Includere anche Roma,” *Corriere della Sera* 24 May1997: 9.

Hale, H. (2004) Explaining Ethnicity. *Comparative Political Studies*, 37, 4, pp. 458–485.

Hallerberg, M. (2004) *Domestic Budgets in a United Europe*. Ithaca: Cornell University Press.

Hamilton, D. L., Weiczorkowska, G., and Lickel, B. (1994) Varieties of Groups and the Perception of Group Entatitivity. *Journal of Personality and Social Psychology*, 78(2), pp. 223–246.

Hayward, J. (2008) *Leaderless Europe*. Oxford: Oxford University Press.

Hewstone, M. (1986) *Understanding Attitudes to the European Community: A Social Psychological Study in Four Member States*. Cambridge: Cambridge University Press.

Hogg, M. (2000) Subjective Uncertainty Reduction through Self-Categorization: A Motivational Theory of Social Identity Processes. *European Review of Social Psychology*, 11, pp. 223–255.

Hogg, M., Terry, D., and White, K. (1995) A Taste of Two Theories: A Critical Comparison of Identity Theory with Social Identity Theory. *Social Psychology Quarterly*, 58(4), pp. 255–269.

Horowitz, D. (1985) *Ethnic Groups and Conflict*. Berkeley: University of California Press.

Huysseune, M. (2006) *Modernity and Secession*. New York: Berghan Books.

Jabko, N. (2006) *Playing the Market*. Ithaca: Cornell Univeristy Press.

Jauregui, P. (1999) National Pride and the Meaning of Europe: A Comparative Study of Britain and Spain. In: D. Smith & S. Wright (eds). *Whose Europe?* Oxford: Blackwell, pp. 257–287.

Jervis, R. (1970) *The Logic of Images in International Relations*. Princeton, NJ: Princeton University Press.

Johnston, L. and Hewstone, M. (1990) Intergroup Contact: Social Identity & Social Cognition. In: D. Abrams & M. Hogg (eds). *Social Identity Theory*. New York: Springer Verlag, pp. 185–210.

Jonsson, C. (1982) *Cognitive Dynamics of International Politics*. New York: St. Martin’s Press.

Kahneman, D. (2003) Maps of Bounded Rationality: Psychology for Behavioural Economics. *The American Economic Review,* 93(5), Dec, pp. 1449–1475.

Kaltenthaler, K. C. and Anderson, C. J. (2001) Europeans and Their Money: Explaining Public Support for the Common European Currency. *European Journal of Political Research*, 40(2), Oct, pp. 139–170.

"L'Italia di Mastricht? Un Alcolista, anzi un Pugile Stressato," *Corriere della Sera,* 15 March 1998: 2.

Lapavitsas, C., Kaltenbrunner, A., Lindo, D., Michell, J., Panceira, J. P., Pires, E., Powell, J., Stenfors, A., and Teles, N. (2010) Eurozone Crisis: Beggar Thyself and Thy Neighbour. *Journal of Balkan and Near Eastern Studies*, 12(4), pp. 321–373.

Lippman, W. (1998) *Public Opinion.* New Brunswick, NJ: Transaction Publishers.

Mauro, E. "L'Europa di Fronte al Caso Berlusconi," *Repubblica* 30 June 2003: 1.

Mazucelli, C., Geurot, U., and Metz, A. (2007) Cooperative Hegemony, Missing Engine, or Improbable Core? In: D. Beach and C. Mazucelli (eds). *Leadership in the Big Bangs of European Integration*. New York: Palgrave Macmillan, pp. 158–177.

McNamara, K. (1998) *The Currency of Ideas: Monetary Politics in the European Union.* Ithaca: Cornell University Press.

Moscovici, S. (1976) *Social Influence and Social Change*. London: Academic Press.

Nimmo, D. and Combs, J. (1983) *Mediated Political Realities*. New York: Longman.

Oakes, P. J., Haslam, S. A., and Turner, J. C. (1998) The Role of Prototypicality in Group Influence and Cohesion: Contextual Variation in the Graded Structure of Social Categories. In: S. Worchel, J. F. Morales, D. Paez, J-C. Deschamps (eds). *Social Identity: International Perspectives*. London & Thousand Oaks, CA: Sage, pp.75–92

Ostellino, P. "Politici a Romorchio dei Tecnocrati Europei," *Corriere della Sera* 3 November 2012: 35.

Padoa-Schioppa, T. (2004) *La Lunga Via Per L'euro*. Bologna: Il Mulino.

Panebianco, A. "Furbi e Ipocriti: Troppi Paraocchi," *Corriere Della Sera* 31 October 2011:1.

Panebianco, A. "Parigi e Londra, Alleati Improbabili," *Corriere della Sera* 26 October 2014.

Pederson, T. (1998) *Germany, France and the Integration of Europe: A Realist Interpretation.* London: Pinter.

Pelham, B. and Swan, W. (1994) The Juncture of Intrapersonal and Interpersonal Knowledge: Self Certainty and Interpersonal Congruence. *Personal Sociological Bulletin*, 30, pp. 349–357.

Polidori, E. "Euro, I Tedeschi lo Temono," *Repubblica* 07 Janurary1998: 31.

Polito, A. "Dal Diritto del Piu Forte al Sogno di un Continente Mite," *Repubblica* 15 June 2001: 38.

Purini, A. P. "L'Europa e' il Vincolo Inelittabile ma nei Partiti Manca la Visione," Corriere della Sera, 27 October 2012.

Quaglia, L. (2004) Italy's Policy Towards European Monetary Integration: Bringing Ideas Back In? *Journal of European Public Policy*, 11(6), Dec issue, pp. 1096–1111.

Quaglia, L. (2006) *Italy and the Economic and Monetary Union: The Politics of Ideas.* New York: Edwin Mellen Press.

Radaelli, C. (2002) The Italian State and the Euro: Institutions, Discourse, and Policy. In: K. Dyson (ed.). *European States and the Euro,* Oxford: Oxford University Press.

Rampini, F. "Se L'Italia Diventa Americana," *Repubblica* 02 March1997: 1.

Rampini, F. "Kohl Frena L'Entusiasmo di Prodi," *Repubblica* 30 January1998: 19.

Rampini, F. "L'Effetto Masstricht," *Repubblica* 9 February1998: 1.

Riccardo, O. "Eurolira? L'Ha Malata Madrid," *Corriere della Sera* 07 October 1996: 19.

Ricci, M. "I Primi Dieci Anni dell'Euro," *Repubblica* 28 December 2011.

Risse, T. (2001) A European Identity? Europeanization and the Evaluation of Nation-State Identities. In: M. G. Cowles, J. A. Caparoso, T. Risse (eds). *Transforming Europe: Europeanization and Domestic Change*. Ithaca: Cornell University Press.

Risse, T. (2003) The Euro Between National and European Identity. *Journal of European Public Policy*, 10(4), Aug issue, pp. 487–505.

Risse, T., Engelman-Martin, D., Knope, H. J., and Roscher, K. (1999) To Euro or Not to Euro? The EMU and Identity Politics in the EU. *European Journal of International Relations*, 5(2), pp. 147–187.

Rosapina, E. "L'ultima Diga Olandese Dovra Fermare Italia," *Corriere della Sella* 26 January 1998: 2.

Ross, M. (1995) Psychocultural Interpretation Theory and Peacemaking in Ethnic Conflicts. *Political Psychology*, 16(3), pp. 523–44.

Salvati, M. "Il Linguaggio della Verita'," *Corriere della Sera* 3 May 3 2013: 1.

Sanchez-Cuenca, I. (2000) The Political Basis of Support for European Integration. *European Union Politics*, 1(2), pp. 147–171.

Scheff, T. (1994a). *Bloody Revenge: Emotions, Nationalism, & War*. Boulder, CO: Westview Press.

Scheff, T. (1994b) Emotions and Identity: A Theory of Ethnic Nationalism. In: C. Calhoun (ed.). *Social Theory and the Politics of Identity*. Cambridge: Blackwell, pp. 277–304.

Slovic, P., Finucane, M., Peters, E., and MacGregor, D. G. (2002) Rational Actors or Rational Fools? Implications of the Affect Heuristic for Behavioural Economics. *Journal of Socio-Economics*, 31, pp. 329–342.

Slovic, P and Leichenstein, S. (1968) Relative Importance of Probabilities and Payoffs in Risk Taking. *Journal of Experimental Psychology Monograph*, 78(3), pp. 1–18.

Special Report: Britain 2010. *The Economist* 10 April 2010: 26.

Sorrentino, R. M. and Yamaguchi, S. (2008) *Handbook of Motivation and Cognition Across Cultures*. San Diego, CA: Academic Press/Elsevier.

Swan, W., Stein-Seroussi, A. and Giesler, B. (1992) Why People Self-Verify. *Journal of Personality and Social Psychology*. 62(3), pp. 392–401.

Taino, D. "Arthuis: Italia al Piu Presto nell'Euro," *Corriere della Sera* 25 February1997: 2.

Taino, D. "Una Classe Dirigente per Stare in Europa," *Corriere della Sera,* 14 September 2011 : 42.

Tajfel, H. (1978) *Differentiation Between Social Groups*. London: Academic Press

Taylor, S and Fiske, S. (1984) *Social Cognition*. Reading, MA: Addison-Wesley.

TG2 Dossier Oggi Euro, aired on RAI on 01/05/1998.

Tullio-Altan, C. (1986) *La Nostra Italia. Arretratezza Socioculturale, Clientismo, Trasformismo, e Ribellismo Dal Unita ad Oggi*. Milan: Feltrinelli.

Tullio-Altan, C. (1999) *Gli Italiani in Europa*. Bologna: Il Mulino.

Turner, J. C. and Reynolds, K. (2004) The Social Identity Perspective in Intergroup Relations: Theories, Themes, and Controversies. In: R. Brown and S. L. Gaertner (eds). *Self and Social Identity*. Malden, MA: Blackwell Publishing, pp. 133–152.

Willis, F. R. (1971) *Italy Chooses Europe*. New York: Oxford University Press.

Wendt, A. (1992) Anarchy is What States Make of it: The Social Construction of Power Politics. *International Organization*, 46(2), pp. 391–425.

Wendt, A. and Fearon, J. (2002) Rationalism and Constructivism: A Skeptical View. In: W. Carlsnoes, T. Risse, and B.A. Simmons (eds). *Handbook of International Relations*. London: Sage, pp. 52–72.

Wyer, J. R., Robert, S. and Carlston, D. E. (1979) *Social Cognition, Inference, and Attribution*. Hillsdale, NJ: Lawrence Erlbaum Associates.

3 Cognition, affect, and support for the euro: the case of Italy

The crisis that is currently shaking the foundations of the euro – a crisis that threatens the very foundations of the European project – was not envisaged by the vocal majority of elites who supported its establishment in the mid- to late nineties. It was, however, foreseen by many of the euro's opponents (Risse et al. 1999, p. 150). This raises an important question: did the opponents who predicted the current events simply make a lucky guess? Or were their predictions accurate because, unlike the euro's many supporters, they analyzed the establishment of the currency on the basis of only the cold, hard facts? Although hindsight is 20/20, in this case, one could persuasively argue that the opponents did not simply make a lucky guess; their analysis was indeed based on the cold hard facts of the case (Eichengreen 2012). This is in stark contrast to the majority of elites who were vocal supporters, who tended to refract the euro through the prism of their aspirations, which trumped an analysis of the actual concrete costs and benefits of joining. This suggests that when analyzing European integration events like the euro, it is important to investigate how these events are constructed by actors, but not only elites; elites rely on the support of various categories of non-elites, and hence it is important to also explore how the latter ascribe meanings to integration events. Identifying these meanings, and how they translate into preferences, is important to understanding the behaviour of political communities. This chapter aims to do precisely that.

The following graphs will only present the aggregate results of the statistical analysis. In this chapter there will be no attempt to explore different patterns among different social groups, such as between elites and non-elites; that will be the focus of the following chapter. A detailed synopsis of the sample and methodology can be found in the appendix.

Table 3.1 shows that with both the newspaper articles and interview subjects, a large majority were in favour of EMU. It also shows the close correspondence between the results from the two different samples: one that includes elites, and one that excludes elites and is weighted to adjust for eurosceptic Southerners. In addition, Table 3.1 shows the very close similarity between the results from both samples and the results from Eurobarometer data. Table 3.1 also demonstrates the relatively few articles that were critical of EMU in both of Italy's national newspapers; this highlights what Zaller (1992) called a one-sided policy climate:

Table 3.1 Attitudes towards EMU (percentages)

1) Newspaper articles (N = 430)	
Supportive/positive towards euro	78.60
Critical/negative towards euro	17.67
Opposed to euro	0.90
Miscellaneous	2.83
Total	100
2) Interview subjects[1] (N = 253)	
In favour of euro in late 1990s	84.18
Not in favour in late 1990s	11.46
Indifferent to euro in late 1990s	4.34
Total	99.98*
In favour in summer of 2010	69.96
Not in favour in summer of 2010	27.34
Indifferent in summer of 2010	2.70
Total	100
3) Interview subjects[2] (N = 184)	
In favour of euro in late 1990s	81.37
Not in favour in late 1990s	14.21
Indifferent to euro in late 1990s	4.37
Total	99.95*
In favour in summer of 2010	63.48
Not in favour in summer of 2010	32.87
Indifferent in summer of 2010	1.07
No opinion	2.58
Total	100
4) Eurobarometer	
In favour of euro in late 1990s	85[3]
In favour of euro in September 2010	65[4]

* Total does not always equal 100.00 because of rounding.
1 Self-weighted. Includes elites.
2 Weighted to adjust for over-representation of Southerners. Does not include elites.
3 Eurobarometer data, collected in 1999, cited in Radaelli (2002).
4 Eurobarometer data available at: http://ec.europa.eu/public_opinion/flash/fl_306_en.pdf

a near consensus among elites produces a media atmosphere that is dominated by a single narrative. There were critical voices, namely the Communists and the Northern League, but their narratives were trumped by the pro-euro narrative, not because of the intrinsic properties of the alternative views, but because of the characteristics of the political community, which will soon become clearer.

Table 3.2 General reasons for support (percentages)

1) Newspaper articles (N = 430)	
Economic reasons	33.25
Political reasons	56.04
Both economic and political reasons	2.5
Miscellaneous	8.21
Total	100
2) Interview subjects (N = 253)	
Economic reasons	36.36
Political reasons	36.75
Cultural reasons	5.9
Miscellaneous	20.99
Total	100
3) Interview Subjects (N = 184)	
Economic reasons	39.94
Political reasons	29.01
Cultural reasons	8.32
Miscellaneous	22.73
Total	100

Moving on to the more qualitative characteristics of support for EMU, both the newspaper articles and interview subjects highlight that, despite its monetary (and monetarist) character, a significant portion of Italians perceived EMU in political terms. Interestingly, around 6% of the sample of interview subjects perceived EMU in cultural terms – they supported EMU because they hoped that it would "civilize" Italians. This dialogue on a TV show called *TG2 Dossier Oggi Euro*, aired on 5 January, 1998, shortly after it became official that Italy would enter the euro, is illustrative of this sentiment:

Moderator: Let's go over to Mr. Toscani.

Toscani: Before, we lived in our own house, and now, we live with the French, British, and Germans [he was evidently not informed that Britain did not enter EMU], and we will see if they accept our behaviour . . . now the real sacrifice starts, *it is to become civilized* (emphasis mine).

As Table 3.3 shows, a not insignificant number of interview subjects and newspaper articles interpreted EMU principally in terms of its monetary and economic dimensions. Many were in favour because they believed that it would promote economic growth and employment, or provide protection and strength in the face of the competitive pressures that result from globalization. The data also make clear that a large majority of interview subjects interpreted EMU principally in terms of European integration.

However, as Table 3.4 shows, European integration meant different things to different people. For some, it was an end in itself, independent of the costs and benefits of joining. For others, however, it was a means to another end, and this end, for most, was for EMU to bring Italy up to European standards; for some actors "European standards" was interpreted politically and for others in economic terms.

Table 3.3 Specific reasons (percentages)

1) Newspaper articles (N = 430)	
European integration	39.53
More trade and economic growth	23.48
Stronger currency	3.48
Strength and globalization	3.48
Miscellaneous	30.03
Total	100
2) Interview subjects (N = 253)	
European integration	64.03
More trade and economic Growth	6.32
Stronger currency	6.71
Strength and globalization	2.76
Miscellaneous	20.18
Total	
3) Interview Subjects (N = 184)	
European integration	58.89
More trade and economic Growth	4.96
Stronger currency	6.51
Strength and globalization	5.65
Miscellaneous	23.99
Total	100

Table 3.4 Means and ends (percentages)

1) Newspaper articles (N = 430)	
Europe only as a means	39.06
Europe as a means *and* an end	30.69
Miscellaneous	30.25
Total	100

(*Continued*)

Table 3.4 Continued

2) Interview subjects (N = 253)	
Europe only as a means	48.22
Europe as a means *and* an end	37.54
Neither	12.64
Miscellaneous	1.6
Total	100
3) Interview Subjects (N = 184)	
Europe only as a means	51.86
Europe as a means *and* an end	26.56
Neither	16
Miscellaneous	5.58
Total	100

Table 3.5 Social comparison processes (percentages)

1) Newspaper articles (N = 430)	
Italy is behind/backwards	41.62
Italy is at the same level	23.02
Miscellaneous	35.36
Total	100
2) Interview subjects (N = 253)	
Italy is behind/backwards	18.57
Italy is at the same level	9.8
Italians are *furbetti*	18.18
Deficient politics	32.00
Italians are individualists	10
Miscellaneous	11.45
Total	100
3) Interview subjects (N = 184)	
Italy is behind/backwards	16
Italy is at the same level	7.96
Italians are *furbetti*	19.72
Deficient politics	21.95
Italians are individualists	7.95
Miscellaneous	26.42
Total	100

Many actors interpreted EMU as a means to bring Italy up to European standards, because they were in broad agreement that Italy was "backward" compared to Europe's elite countries. But different actors had different conceptions of Europe-as-equalizer. These different conceptions derived from the different ways that actors understood the character of Italian backwardness. As Table 3.5 shows, a significant plurality of interview subjects believed that the source of Italy's backwardness was the country's political class. A sizable portion, 30%, believed that Italians are backward in the cultural sense: 10% because Italians are "individualists" and 18% because Italians are *furbetti* (this word does not have an exact English equivalent, but it roughly means a willingness to take advantage of others, or circumstances, etc., for personal gain).

As the Table 3.6 highlights, sizeable numbers of both newspaper articles and interview subjects perceived EMU in terms of European integration, which would help to solve Italy's problems and bring Italy up or closer to European standards. Almost half of the articles characterized Europe as the solution to Italy's problems, while a large plurality of interview subjects posited directly and explicitly that Europe fills this role. In the interview sample, a smaller number posited an indirect link between European integration and the solution to Italy's problems,[1] while for 27% of the sample, European integration was not the solution to Italy's problems.

Table 3.6 Link between Italy's problems and Europe as the solution (percentages)

1) Newspaper articles (N = 430)	
Present	48.60
Absent	49.53
Miscellaneous	1.87
Total	100
2) Interview subjects (N = 253)	
Direct link	43.47
Indirect link	22.13
No link	27
Miscellaneous	7.4
Total	100
3) Interview subjects (N = 184)	
Direct link	35.48
Indirect link	22.50
No link	33.67
Miscellaneous	8.35
Total	100

The idea of Europe-as-equalizer was expressed in a variety of ways in all three sources – articles, interviews, and TV programmes. Often, it was expressed with metaphors that presented Italy's options as either Europe or Africa (the latter a metaphor for backwardness). The following quotes from selected interviews illustrate this. From a lawyer:

Me: Why were you in favour of EMU?
Him: For European unity.
Me: Why is European unity important for Italy?
Him: Because if we [Italy] are left alone, we would be more like North Africa than Europe.

From a store owner:

Me: . . . were you in favour of EMU in the mid to late nineties?
Reply: Yes, absolutely, it was important to make us equals, it was a desire to be a country of Serie A [the premier division of the Italian soccer league] like all the others in Europe, we knew that if we had not entered we would have been part of the third world.

From a professor of banking at Bocconi University in Milan: "Outside the euro, Italy would become closer to Africa than to Europe."

From a vice president of a large bank in the South: "Before entering the euro, we were considered a sort of North African country."

From a regional Councillor in Lombardy:

Me: If Italy was to leave the euro?
Reply: We would go to the South Mediterranean shore.

Some selected quotes from the sample of TV programmes also reveal how Europe was perceived as an equalizer of Italy's perceived backwardness. Here is a revealing exchange between the leader of the Communist Refoundation party, Fausto Bertinotti, and the Vice-President of Confindustria, Mario Cavani, on a show aired on the RAI on 21 March 1997 called *Maastricht Italia*, moderated by Alan Friedman, about whether Italy should enter in the first round:

Bertinotti: We need to think [of EMU] in terms of social policy, not in terms of the dogmas conjured up by bourgeois economists.
Vice: President: Our past does not allow us to . . . the problems that we have make it necessary for us to enter Europe, to *enter European culture and behaviour* (emphasis added).
Bertinotti: [But] we are in Europe!

In a show called *Mister Euro*, aired on 8 January 2002 and again moderated by Friedman, one of the participants says tongue-in-cheek but very enthusiastically, "for once we are like the Germans, with the same currency!" This allusion to Germany is not a coincidence: it is the country that is the ideal for most Italians when they engage in the social comparisons that reify the perceived defects of the Italian nation-state. Another TV programme, this time a news show, with a journalist interviewing people on the street:

Journalist: The euro creates a unity and makes us feel like a common people, it is a revolution in Italy.

Respondent: Yes . . . using the same currency means also *feeling that we are equal* because when we go to France and Germany . . .

This EMU/Europe-as-equalizer meme was applied in places that had little to do with the common currency. Writing in Repubblica (6 Jan 2002), on the regional differences in Italy, Mario Centorrino quotes a Sicilian who says: "Let's be frank: the entire country has the euro and it is an enormous pleasure to feel equality between Lombardy and Sicily." The comparison between Lombardy and Sicily is not a coincidence. The former is Italy's richest and most economically advanced region. Meanwhile, Sicily is associated with "backwardness" because it is part of the economically and institutionally poorer South. That the euro made this Sicilian, who is a member of the "backward" region, feel a sense of "equality" with the advanced North makes sense in light of the extra-monetary meanings that were ascribed to the euro, meanings that had little to do with the substantive content of the currency.

The amount of information that actors possess about the political object in question is another important element of the intersubjective context that is the focus of this chapter, because actors exposed to the highlighted narratives in the media are more susceptible to them if they possess a low amount of knowledge. As Figure 3.1 shows, the vast majority of newspaper articles in the sample spoke favourably about EMU and did not present or analyze counterarguments. This is reflected in the level of knowledge of the sample of interview subjects.

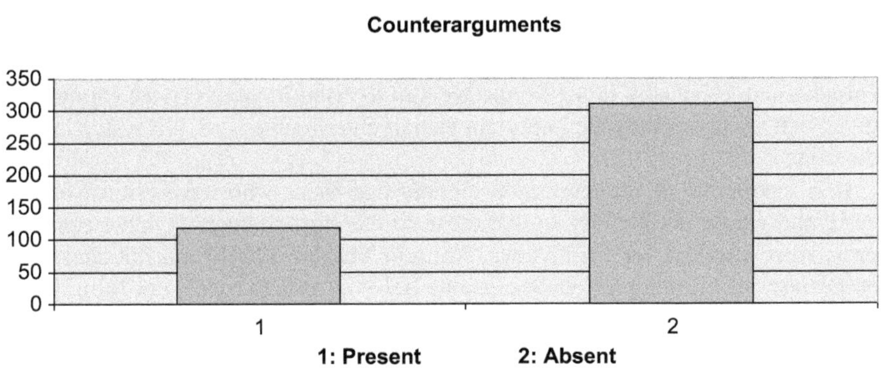

Figure 3.1 Counterarguments

Detailed information on the sample can be found in the appendix

Table 3.7 Knowledge of EMU

High	*Medium*	*Low*	*Totally uninformed*
22%	20%	38%	23%

Almost 40% displayed a low level of knowledge of EMU, and almost 25% were totally uninformed – for this latter group, the euro had little substantive meaning other than a new currency with which to go shopping; subjects in the totally uninformed category could not convey even elementary facts about the political and economic dimensions of the currency. The minority that possessed high or medium levels of knowledge were mostly elites and professionals. For the minority that could express a counterargument, almost 20% referred to the loss of sovereignty that the EMU entailed. A little over 10% said that they were concerned about the rise in prices, around 10% said that the counterarguments emerged from the political opposition,[2] 5% referred to the loss of the privilege of devaluing the currency to make the country more competitive, and around 5% expressed that they did not know any counterarguments, but whatever they were, they were unconvincing.

This low level of knowledge is instructive in light of the many unrealistic, grandiose claims conveyed in the media about what EMU could actually do for Italy, claims that had little to do with the substantive content of the actual policy. In other TV shows, the Economy Minister Ciampi suggested that the ECB would promote growth and development, even though the ECB, being modelled on the Bundesbank, had a mandate to *only* focus on price stability:

Moderator: Is there the risk that Europe will be dominated by technocrats?
Ciampi: The creation of the ECB gives certainty that monetary policy will be stable. It has the obligation to not put [price] stability at risk, but also to support growth and development.

In the same show Ciampi even claimed that the EMU would help Italy to solve its intractable Southern question: “We in the government . . . are focused on employment, especially in the South, we aim to bring in more private capital . . . given that we have made the important step of entering the euro, it is a step in this direction.”

It is instructive of the emotional climate that those who were critical of the euro, and whose predictions, unlike those of the euro-enthusiasts, have come to pass, were attacked for their views. Antonio Martino (2005) did not share the enthusiasm of his compatriots because he believed that Europe’s not forming an Optimum Currency Area would mean that sharing a common currency would produce serious imbalances between the economically strong and weak countries. For this he was dismissed as “totally senseless”, as destroying Italy’s credibility and as being the “only anti-European Italian” (Martino 2005, p.282). Another prominent and iconoclastic commentator whose predictions about the euro turned out to be true was the governor of Italy's central bank, Antonio Fazio. He warned Italians that the euro, although it could produce monetary stability, could not, in and of itself, produce growth.[3] He also warned Italians that the euro would not be "heaven" as some were framing it, that it would rather be closer to purgatory. These Catholic metaphors used to describe the euro are instructive: in a nominally Catholic country, that many believed the euro would be some sort of "heaven" obscured the true nature of the common currency, which implied radical and liberal changes to the political economy that many voters – the same voters who supported the euro – would object to. Those, like Fazio, who had legitimate (and prescient) criticisms of the euro were often labelled "eurosceptic". Being labelled eurosceptic was a way of delegitimizing voices that challenged the dominant narrative of EMU as the solution to Italy's supposed "backwardness". The attempt to delegitimize alternative narratives is itself indicative of an emotionally charged intellectual climate. This intellectual climate is made clear in a revealing comment by Professor Paolo Savona of Luiss University on the TV programme *Babele Euro*, aired in February 2002:

Moderator: What if Italy had not entered [EMU]?

Professor Savona: There are no doubts that the euro was necessary, but from an economic perspective, we must be free to discuss it and avoid creating taboos . . . in Italy there is a taboo against speaking freely about EMU . . . we need a debate [on EMU] and not to label dissenters [from the dominant narrative] as heretics.

This intellectual climate is an indication of the affective properties of the ideas that constitute the intersubjective context that is the focus of this chapter. Many Italians interpreted EMU and Italy-Europe relations in belongingness terms, and, as highlighted by Baumeister and Leary[4], belongingness implicates feelings of inclusion and exclusion: the former is associated with positive affect, and the latter with negative affect. All three sources – newspapers, interviews, and TV shows – display ample evidence for these affective properties, which were associated with EMU and Italy-Europe relations.

Figure 3.2 displays only the articles that were published before it became certain that Italy would enter EMU. To determine the emotional content, the tone of the language used to describe EMU and Italy-Europe relations was coded to identify whether EMU was associated with negative or positive affect. As Figure 3.2 shows, most articles published in the pre-EMU period were imbued with the fear of exclusion, which reflects, in part, the emotional reactions to the many statements emanating from German officials and newspapers that Italy did not belong in the exclusive club of euro countries, statements which often depicted Italy in crude terms. An instructive example of the way in which Italy was depicted by some Germans can be seen from an episode of *Maastricht Italia* that aired in March of 1997. Alan Friedman, the moderator, who wants to convey to his viewers German attitudes towards Italy's entering EMU, brings out a copy of German

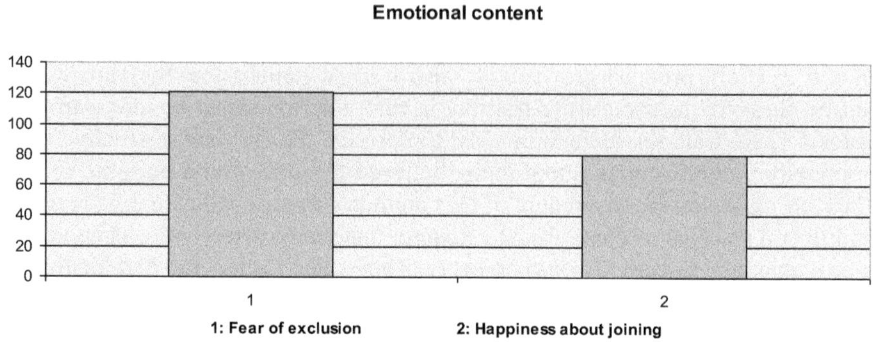

Figure 3.2 Emotional content

Detailed Information on the sample can be found in the appendix

newspaper, with an editorial that states: "For Germany to trade its mark for a currency that includes the lira *is comparable to Italians trading the lira for a currency that includes mud from the Congo*" (notice the Africa metaphor).

There are other examples that demonstrate the affective properties associated with EMU and Italy-Europe relations. On the same episode of *Maastricht Italia*, there is a revealing exchange between an Italian journalist for *Il Sole 24 Ore* (the newspaper of the Italian business community) and Lamberto Dini, Italy's Foreign Minister in 1997:

Journalist: Italy should ask itself with a certain lucidity what will really benefit it, and if Italy did, it might realize that it could be beneficial to not enter [EMU] right away.

Dini then scowls and becomes agitated.

Journalist: That kind of reaction highlights a lack of lucidity about the situation.

Dini, in an angry tone: I don't understand how someone cannot accept that Italy will be part of the first group . . . if Italy satisfies the criteria, it will enter, and that's that.

Here is another example from *Mister Euro*, of 8 January 2002. It involves an exchange between a minister in the Berlusconi government, Antonio Marzano, and Bertinotti about the price increases that emerged immediately after the euro was introduced:

Marzano: Within two months there will no longer be the circulation of both currencies . . . today people are speaking out against the euro [because of the perceived price rises], within two months they will be speaking in favour of it.

Bertinotti: *There is rather an excess of optimism*, because people are saying, once the euro arrives, all our problems will be solved (emphasis added).

A comment from an interview I conducted with a member of the Italian parliament highlights the emotional properties of ideas on Italy and Europe:

> Italy entering Europe [that is, EMU] was, like they say in Naples, a country that removed the shame from its face . . . we were always seen as a country of *furbetti*, a mess, and we entered the euro with our back straight.

Several newspaper articles published at the time also nicely capture the emotional atmosphere: "Our European partners observe our naive euro-enthusiasm with incredulity . . . this euro-euphoria underestimates the efforts required of us in EMU" (*Repubblica*, 09/02/1998). And this one: "In the country there is a climate of drunken-ness . . . there is the feeling that the euro equals green valleys" (*Repubblica*, 27/03/98). The metaphor of inebriation is very instructive, for it suggests that the reactions to Italy's entering EMU were outside the boundaries of reasonableness; this reaction bore little relationship to the substantive aspects of EMU.

Needless to say, the euro did not bring what many Italians hoped for, which was to have the status of equality with Europe's elite countries. In the period 2003–2004, it dawned on many Italians that their hopes for what the euro could do for Italy were unrealistic. Many commentators were able to see through these false hopes and wishes about what the euro could purportedly do for Italy. In an article in *Corriere della Sera* published on the 24th of October, 1998, Franco Venturini warned Italians that "the prejudices against Italy in Europe have not been eliminated with the entrance in the euro"; a year later Massimo Giannini said in *Repubblica* (06/03/99): "Antonio Fazio warned us: the common currency will bring benefits, but it will not cancel our defects . . . even if we are now better off, it is not the paradise that we believed would emerge."

Qualifier

It is important to point out that interviews paint a picture of people's perceptions when the interviews were carried out, in the Spring, Summer, and Fall of 2010. Since then, a lot has changed in Italy. In 2011 there was the palpable fear that Italy would default on its sovereign debt and be forced to leave the euro. One of the reasons is that investors lost confidence in the country's elected government to make the painful reforms that were (and are) necessary to restore the country's competitiveness. Consequently, a non-elected government of technocrats was installed to make the painful decisions that democratically elected governments had been avoiding for fear of electoral punishment. In part as a consequence of this, pro-euro attitudes have plummeted in the period since this research was conducted. In fact, polls taken in May of 2012 show that 40% of Italians want to return to the lira (Warner 2012), while all opposition parties, as of 2015, are anti-euro, a stunning and radical turnaround from the late nineties, when Eurobarometer polling data – confirmed by my own survey data – showed that 85% of Italians were in favour of the euro. Although perceptions of the euro have shifted radically since the above interviews were conducted, the arguments above are valid for the time period that is under investigation and from which the different samples were obtained, to wit: newspapers: 1996 to 2004; TV programmes: 1997 to 2002; interviews: questions were focused on perceptions in the period late-nineties to 2010.

This chapter has shown that the belief that euro would bring Italy up to the standards of Europe's elite countries was widely, but not universally, held. And even those who held this goal of equality interpreted it in different ways. The aim of the next chapter is precisely to elucidate this diversity.

Notes

1 The difference between "direct" and "indirect" link between Italy's problems and Europe as the solution is the following. Subjects were asked the "reasons" for their support for EMU. Those who responded to this question by directly and explicitly saying that they hoped that EMU would fix Italy's problems were coded as "direct link". Those who responded to the "reasons" question in a way that did not directly link their support for EMU to Italy's problems, but who, in responses to a subsequent question that asked them to compare Italy to Europe's elite countries, expressed the belief that EMU would help to make up for some perceived shortcoming that Italy possesses, were coded as "indirect link" between Europe and Italy's problems.

2 Subjects who responded by saying that the centre-right was critical or opposed to the euro were coded as "political opposition" (because it was the centre-left who brought Italy into the euro). These subjects were often unable to express the counterargument in question, but they were cognizant of the political opposition's critical attitude towards the euro, and so, in a certain sense, they were aware of counterarguments even if they could not express them precisely.

3 Porta a Porta, Interview of Antonio Fazio, aired on 27/11/2001.

4 For the role of emotional reactions to exclusion or to threats to belongingness, see Roy Baumeister and Michael Leary, "The Need to Belong: Desire for Interpersonal Attachments as a Fundamental Human Motivation," *Psychological Bulletin*, 117(3), May 1995: 497–529

References

Baumeister, R. and Leary, M. (1995) The Need to Belong: Desire for Interpersonal Attachments as a Fundamental Human Motivation. *Psychological Bulletin*, 117(3), 497–529.

Centorrino, M. "Rischi e Opportunita' della Nuova Moneta," *Repubblica* 6 Jan 2002: 15.

Eichengreen, B. (2012) European Monetary Integration with the Benefit of Hindsight. *Journal of Common Market Studies*, 50(S1), pp. 123–136.

Giannini, M. "Il Lungo Purgatorio dell Euro," *Repubblica* 6 March 1999: 1.

Giannini, M. "Ciampi: Niente Ubriacature il Rigore Dovra Continuare," *Repubblica* 27 March 1998 :2.

Martino, A. (2005) *Promises, Performance, and Prospects: Essays on Political Economy 1980–1998*. Indianapolis: Liberty Fund.

Niedermeyer, O. (1995) Trends and Contrasts. In: R. Sinnot and O. Niedermayer (eds). *Public Opinion and Internationalized Governance*. Oxford: Oxford University Press, pp. 53–72.

Radaelli, C. 2002. The Italian State and the Euro: Institutions, Discourse, and Policy. In: K. Dyson (ed.). *European States and the Euro*, Oxford: Oxford University Press.

Rampini, F. "L'Effetto Maastricht," *Repubblica*, 09 February1998: 1, pp. 212–237.

Risse, T., Engelman-Martin, D., Knope, H. J., and Roscher, K. (1999) To Euro or Not to Euro? The EMU and Identity Politics in the EU. *European Journal of International Relations*, 5(2), pp. 147–187.
Warner, J. "Only the ECB can Save the Euro Now," *The Telegraph* 30 May 30 2012.
Zaller, J. (1992) *The Nature and Origins of Mass Opinion*. Cambridge: Cambridge University Press.

4 Diversity within the whole: how cognitive schemes are conditioned by gender, region, political ideology, and status

The main purpose of this chapter is to identify the contestation, or counter-narratives, or diversity, which exists within a political community. Constructivist scholars tend to focus only on the dominant narrative or identity within the political community, an approach that is very useful for explaining dominant tendencies and practices that groups display towards certain political objects. But it also obscures the diversity that is present within the group.

This diversity takes place at multiple levels. A useful analogy is language. Just like identity, language reflects the history, peculiar circumstances, idiosyncrasies, and specific cultural attributes of a political community. And just like identity, it is not the product of design; it is the aggregate result of the evolutionary selection – in the cultural, ideational sense – of those ideas, beliefs, and practices that have been selected over long stretches of time. One of the key properties of both language and identity is that they are collectively held. But just as with identity, there is much variation in how language is expressed. In other words, different groups within a political community speak in different ways. There are not only differences between elites and non-elites, but also profession and political orientation. One could go to logical extremes and highlight the differences among families or even individuals, but that depends on the purposes of the investigator. The purpose of this chapter is to identify the differences between key groups that make up the political community: differences determined by gender, status, region, and political orientation. In so doing, it will identify the different logics that are present in the cognitive schemes of different groups.

The key findings presented here are that the fewest differences – or, the most commonalities – are present between men and women, and individuals from the South and from the North. The largest differences are present between those on the centre-left and centre-right and, most importantly, among elites and non-elites. The differences between elites and non-elites reveal some fascinating dynamics on the nexus between these two sets of actors. First, the discourses of elites only partially permeate the cognitive schemes of non-elites. Second, and consequently, there are different logics among elites and non-elites in how they approach political objects like EMU: despite the fact that elites have much higher levels of knowledge, they are less likely to display the logic of rationality than are non-elites. Lastly, in their attitudes towards EMU, many elite members looked towards Europe to protect them from the non-elites, while some non-elites looked toward Europe to protect them from the elites. That is, rather than aim to fix the country's problems through cooperation and action at the domestic level, both looked to Europe to "save" Italy from each other.

The chapter will be organized in the following way. First, there will be a discussion of the framework through which the findings from the statistical tests will be interpreted. Subsequently, the data will be presented, which will be interspersed with commentary and analysis of the results of the statistical tests, with a relatively stronger emphasis on the differences between elites and non-elites. This will be followed with a summary and conclusion.

The spectrum of identity

The semi-structured interviews consisted of a series of questions that were designed by me to extract the meanings and feelings that actors ascribed to the euro within the context of Italian-Europe relations. This allowed me to construct an "identity index", a spectrum that aims to identify the relative salience of the logic of identity versus the logic of rationality *at the level of cognition*. Reality, as always, is much more messy: most actors display both cognitive logics to some extent. The question is whether the actor's interpretations of political objects are overall relatively more consistent with stronger or weaker forms of identity. The criteria established below aim to provide a framework to identify precisely that.

The meanings and feelings that are associated with a strong logic of identity are the following: 1) Europe as a political end in itself. Viewing Europe as an end with relatively little emphasis on the costs is an indicator of the logic of appropriateness. 2) Viewing Europe in terms of political unity rather than economic utility. This is an indicator of a stronger logic of identity because it is strongly associated with visions of European order rather than economic gain, which suggests the logic of appropriateness and belonging. 3) The extent to which ideas about Europe are imbued with emotion. This is another important indicator because the emotional salience of ideas is indicative of the actor's sense of rightness or belongingness. 4) Whether the actor saw EMU as the solution to Italy's problems. This belief rests on a conception of Europe that is based more on hope than reality, and hence it indicates the extent to which the actor conceives Europe as it actually is or what he or she hopes it can do; a tendency to conceive of Europe in terms of unrealistic hopes relies on a vision of Europe that transcends an analysis of the concrete elements of this policy. 5) The overall extent to which the actors' thinking on Europe and Italy is suffused with abstraction or idealization rather than concreteness. For example, actors that responded that Europe was important because it would help bring world peace, or would make Europe a superpower, or would solve Italy's problems, were coded as subjects whose thought was characterized by abstract idealism, because these ideas are based more on hopes and dreams than on the substantive content of EMU.

The meanings and feelings that are associated with a weak sense of identity are the following: 1) Europe as a means. These actors are sensitive to the costs; that is, their support rests on whether Europe actually provides concrete benefits. 2) Europe as economic utility. For example, for many, EMU was a means towards free trade or economic growth or lower interest rates. These actors tend to evaluate European integration on the concrete costs and benefits. 3) Emotion. Actors whose support for EMU was not imbued with emotion could be said to be less likely to feel the sense of rightness and appropriateness that is associated with feelings of belongingness. 4) Whether the actor felt that Europe was not the solution to Italy's problems. For example, a sober analysis leads one to conclude that only Italy, and not Europe, can solve its own problems. Actors who recognized this can be said to have a conception that corresponds with the concrete and realistic facets of Italy-Europe relations.[1] 5) The extent to which the actor's overall thinking on Europe and Italy is suffused with concreteness rather than abstract idealization. For example, these actors supported EMU because they wanted lower interest rates, or wanted to transfer sovereignty to the ECB, or wanted low inflation – these are ideas that are rooted in the substantive content of EMU; that is, its concrete elements.

Many theorists have been critical of rational choice because actors rarely have sufficient information to objectively evaluate a policy like EMU (see chapter two). The idea is that for actors to meaningfully evaluate the costs and benefits of policy X, they have to have a sufficient level of knowledge, and when they lack that level of knowledge, it suggests that non-rational variables – like discourses and identity – better explain their behaviour. The data presented here raise questions that may qualify this proposition. What the following data suggest, rather, is *that more information is associated with a stronger logic of identity than is low information.* I discovered that those categories of individuals who were more knowledgeable about EMU were also more likely to interpret it in belongingness terms; to pay less attention to the actual costs; to think of EMU in abstract and idealistic ways rather than concretely; and to imbue their support with an emotional intensity that suggests a strong affective – that is, non-rational – attitude towards EMU.

The data

Table 4.1 highlights that pluralities of both men and women have low levels of knowledge about EMU. Those with low levels could not express even one counterargument, but in their responses on the "reasons" for support or opposition, were able to convey some elementary facts about the political/economic dimensions of EMU. Sizable numbers of both men and women are also "totally uninformed", which means that for them, the only meaning that the euro had was a new currency with which to go shopping; they could not convey even elementary facts about the institutional dimensions of EMU. Relatively more men possess "high" levels of knowledge, which means that they could convey and explain at least one counterargument; they also conveyed articulate reasons for their support. However, this relatively higher level of information about EMU does not mean that men are therefore more rational. In fact, the opposite is true, at least when it comes to Europe-Italy relations, as I shall explain.

Table 4.1 Gender

A) Knowledge of EMU (percentages)	
Men	
High	26.8
Medium	18.6
Low	33.8
Totally uninformed	20.8
Total	100
Women	
High	10.9
Medium	21
Low	41.3
Totally uninformed	26.8
Total	100
Chi-square value	7.642
Significance	.054
Degrees of freedom	3
B) Link Between Italy's problems and EMU as the solution	
Men	
Direct link	49.9
Indirect link	25.1
No link	25.1
Total	100.1
Women	
Direct link	32.8
Indirect link	28.5
No link	38.7
Total	100
Chi-square value	6.580
Significance	0.37
Degrees of freedom	2
C) Levels of Enthusiasm	
Men	
Strongly supportive	50.3
Generally supportive	37.5
Strongly opposed	5.3
Generally opposed	6.9
Total	100

(*Continued*)

Table 4.1 Continued

Women	
Strongly supportive	36
Generally supportive	46.3
Strongly opposed	12.5
Generally opposed	5.1
Total	99.9
Chi-square value	6.948
Significance	.074
Degrees of freedom	3

Detailed information on the sample can be found in the appendix

Section B of Table 4.1 highlights how higher numbers of men believe that Europe is the solution to Italy's problems. Respondents were asked to compare Italy with Europe's elite countries, and large numbers responded with some variant of the idea that Italy is "backward". Subjects were also asked what they believed the solution was, and many more men than women replied in a way that affirms a direct link between Europe and the solution to Italy's "backwardness". The notion that Europe can solve Italy's problems does not rest on a concrete analysis of what Europe actually represents. It rests on notions of Europe as the embodiment of "modernity", and the hope that by belonging to Europe, this "modernity" will somehow be transferred to Italy. Those with a more realistic and concrete conception of Italy-Europe relations recognize that only Italy can change itself, and women were more likely than men to recognize this.

Section C of Table 4.1 also highlights how women tend to approach Italy-Europe relations in a sober fashion. Subjects were asked to explain the "reasons" for their support of or opposition to EMU, and were encouraged to speak freely and openly. The tone of their voices and language was coded as levels of enthusiasm, which I contend to be a useful proxy for emotional intensity of the actor's beliefs. Those who were more strongly supportive responded with conviction, with expressions of European identity, with animation, all of which suggest that support for EMU was strongly conditioned by feelings of belongingness and rightness. Those who were generally supportive expressed their support in a more nonchalant way, without animation and conviction. Relatively more men were strongly supportive of EMU than women. This suggests that their thinking was more imbued with that sense of appropriateness and rightness that is associated with a strong sense of identity. In the previous chapter I presented data from media sources that highlights that the emotional climate that preceded EMU was such that alternative narratives about Italy and EMU were silenced, ignored, or received with anger. This response emerges, in part, from that sense of rightness and appropriateness that was also detected in actors' "reasons" for support for EMU, and men were more likely than women to perceive EMU in this manner.

These findings suggest that, at least in how the euro was perceived, women were less subject to a strong sense of identity than were men. But it is important to highlight that the statistical tests are not significant at the 3–7% level and that overall the tests showed that men and women had much in common in how they perceived the euro. The other tests that compared them on the basis of other dimensions did not demonstrate any notable differences between the two.

Table 4.2 Region

A) Levels of enthusiasm	
South	
Strongly supportive	25.3
Generally supportive	51.1
Strongly opposed	10.2
Generally opposed	13.4
Total	100
North	
Strongly supportive	48.9
Generally supportive	37.6
Strongly opposed	9.6
Generally opposed	3.9
Total	100
Chi-square value	13.887
Significance	.003
Degrees of freedom	3
B) Cognitive content	
South	
Mostly abstract benefits	23.7
Mostly concrete costs	13.2
Abstract benefits and concrete costs	27.9
Only concrete costs	19.5
Only concrete benefits	2.6
Concrete costs and concrete benefits	13.2
Total	100.1
North	
Mostly abstract benefits	46.3
Mostly concrete costs	0.5
Abstract benefits and concrete costs	20.7
Only concrete costs	17.06

(*Continued*)

Table 4.2 Continued

Only concrete benefits	4.8
Concrete costs and concrete benefits	10.1
Total	99.46
Chi-square value	21.08
Significance	.001
Degrees of freedom	5
C) Current attitudes towards EMU (summer/early Fall 2010)	
South	
In favour	50.8
Not in favour	47.6
Indifferent	1.6
Total	100
North	
In favour	72.1
Not in favour	26.3
Indifferent	1.6
Total	100
Chi-square value	9.101
Significance	.011
Degrees of freedom	2

Detailed information on the sample can be found in the appendix

There were also relatively few differences between Northerners and Southerners. Some of the differences that did emerge are statistically significant and suggest that there is a stronger sense of European identity in the North than in the South. Section A in Table 4.2, for instance, highlights that many more Northerners than Southerners were generally in favour of EMU; Northerners were much more likely to be enthusiastic supporters, meaning the tone and language of their responses to the "reasons" were imbued with animation, conviction, and praise. The graph also highlights that relatively more Southerners were likely to be opposed to EMU than Northerners.

Section B of Table 4.2 aims to measure the extent to which the actors overall thinking on EMU is suffused with abstract idealism or concreteness. For this measure, the transcribed texts were coded on the basis of the following rule: expressions of European identity, of what European unity might possibly do to Italy, to the continent, or to the world, were coded as abstract idealism.

Expressions about the concrete elements of EMU, such as the Maastricht criteria, price stability, interest rates, or the role of the ECB, were coded as concreteness. The measure also aims to divide actors by how they ascribe concreteness or abstraction to costs and benefits. Actors whose responses were dominated by the price increases that emerged after Italy joined, for example, were coded as ascribing concrete costs, while actors whose responses were dominated by the hoped-for benefits from European unity were coded as ascribing "abstract benefits". Using these rules, I found that the sample can be more or less divided on the basis of six dimensions. 1) Mostly abstract benefits. These actors fleetingly or tangentially mentioned the costs of joining, such as the reduction of the standard of living or the loss of competitiveness, but their responses were dominated by the hoped-for benefits that would, they believed, accrue from European unity. This response could be said to reflect a strong sense of identity. 2) Mostly concrete costs. These actors mentioned the hoped-for benefits that would accrue from European unity, but their thinking was dominated by the concrete costs of joining, such as the reduction in the standard of living and the loss of competitiveness. Here, the logic of identity is not as salient. 3) Both concrete costs and abstract benefits. These actors display roughly equal emphasis on abstraction and concreteness. 4) Only concrete costs. 5) Only concrete benefits. 6) Only concrete costs and concrete benefits.

As Section B of Table 4.2 highlights, Southerners are over-represented on dimensions 2, 3, and 6, while Northerners are over-represented on dimension number 1. This means that, overall, Southerners are more likely to evaluate EMU and Europe on the basis of their concrete elements, while Northerners rate them more often on the basis of abstract idealism. The content of these interpretations explains the significant differences seen in Section C. It shows that Northerners are vastly more likely to still be in favour of EMU than are Southerners, while support among Southerners for the EMU dropped dramatically from the mid-nineties to 2010. The reason for this difference is suggested in Section B of Table 4.2: Southerners are more likely to evaluate EMU and Europe based on its concrete elements. They are more sensitive to the costs of actually joining, and the costs have not been insignificant: higher prices, reduced competitiveness, and the loss of the tool of devaluation.

On the whole, Table 4.2 suggests that Northerners are more likely to evaluate EMU with a stronger logic of identity than are Southerners. The chi-square results are statistically significant, which requires reflection on some of the possible reasons for this robust relationship. One possible explanation is that the South has experienced, compared to the North, a more significant industrial and economic decline since the euro was introduced, which has created bitterness and a widespread sense that the common currency is the cause. A more likely explanation is ideology. Berlsuconi's PdL party had greater support in the South, especially in the region of Campania, where the bulk of the Southerners were selected (Salerno and Naples are both in this region), than in the North. Trento, where a sizable portion of non-elites were selected, is known to be more progressive than other cities, as is the city of Milan. As will be shown in the following pages, ideology is one of the strongest determinants of the character of actors' cognitive schemes: the centre-left is much more likely to evaluate the euro with a strong sense of identity than is the centre-right. However, it should be emphasized that Northerners and Southerners displayed differences only in these three measures outlined in Table 4.2. On the other measures, there were no significant differences.

Table 4.3 Political orientation

A) General reasons for supporting EMU	
Centre-left	
Economic	35.3
Political	58.3
Cultural	6.5
Total	100
Centre-right	
Economic	70.7
Political	26.8
Cultural	2.4
Total	100.1
Chi-square value	9.163
Significance	0.10
Degrees of freedom	2
B) Levels of enthusiasm	
Centre-left	
Strongly supportive	58.6
Generally supportive	34.9
Strongly opposed	3.3
Generally opposed	3.3
Total	100.1
Centre-right	
Strongly supportive	26
Generally supportive	50
Strongly opposed	6
Generally opposed	18
Total	100
Chi-square value	11.365
Significance	.010
Degrees of freedom	3

C) Evaluation of Italy compared to Europe's elite countries	
Centre-left	
Italians are individualists	8.34
Italy is behind	13.6
Italians are *furbetti*	21.4
Italians are creative, but . . .	16.2
Italy has terrible politics	35.7
Italy is at the same level as Europe	4.5
Total	99.74
Centre-right	
Italians are individualists	10
Italy is behind	22
Italians are *furbetti*	10
Italians are creative, but . . .	2
Italy has terrible politics	26
Italy is at the same level as Europe	30
Total	100
Chi-square value	18.897
Significance	.002
Degrees of freedom	5
D) Link between Italy's problems and Europe as the solution	
Centre-Left	
Direct link	58.4
Indirect link	22.1
No link	19.5
Total	100
Centre-Right	
Direct link	37.3
Indirect link	25.5
No link	37.3
Total	100.1
Chi-square value	4.176
Significance	.124
Degrees of freedom	2
F) Current attitudes towards EMU (summer/early fall 2010)	
Centre-Left	
In favour	86.9

(*Continued*)

Table 4.3 Continued

Not in favour	12.4
Indifferent	0.7
Total	100
Centre-Right	
In favour	54.7
Not in favour	35.8
Indifferent	9.4
Total	99.9
Chi-square value	
Significance	
Degrees of freedom	

Detailed Information on the sample can be found in the appendix

Out of 253 interview subjects, 101 were coded on the basis of ideology – 76 on the centre-left, and 25 on the centre-right. They were not asked directly what their ideology was; rather, I coded the ideological content of their responses to other questions, for example, the question of what they thought Italy's main problems were and the solutions to these problems. This helped to avoid social desirability bias, the risk of which is high, especially in Italy, where few people would be willing to openly express their true political preferences to a researcher (Sani 1989, p. 282); I discovered this phenomenon was present especially among individuals on the centre-right, many of whom would not admit to a stranger that they voted for the party of Berlusconi.[2] Subjects were only coded as either "left" or "right" if there was a high degree of clear ideological content in their responses, hence the relatively small sample: less than half were coded. Despite these numbers, meaningful comparisons between the two groups can be made. As Section A of Table 4.3 demonstrates, the political left overwhelmingly supported EMU for political reasons, while the political right supported EMU overwhelmingly for economic reasons; economic utility reasons are based more on the concrete costs and benefits, while those who supported EMU for political reasons are much more likely to express their support in terms of abstract ideals, such as the political unity of Europe. Section B also highlights differences in how EMU was perceived. Section B shows that the political left was much more likely to express enthusiastic support for EMU, which is indicative of an emotional intensity that is absent among those on the centre-right in their perceptions of Italy's entering EMU.

Section C of Table 4.3 gives a hint to why EMU was perceived differently by the two groups. This graph displays the different ways in which the two groups conceive Italy in comparison to Europe's elite countries. Subjects were asked to characterize Italy in comparison to Europe's elite countries and were encouraged to speak freely and openly, and the responses were dominated by the following six responses: 1) Italians are "individualist", which is a variant of the idea that they lack a sense of the common good, a sense of solidarity, etc. 2) Italy is behind. People who responded this way expressed the general feeling that the country is behind without specifying in what way. 3) Italians are *furbetti*. This word does not have an exact English equivalent, but roughly means the trait of exploiting others, circumstances, etc., when it is convenient or for personal gain. It connotes selfishness, intelligence, etc. 4) Italians are creative, but they also suffer from a range of defects, such as the lack of organization. 5) Italy is inferior to Europe's elite countries because of its deficient political institutions. 6) And lastly, that Italy is at the same level as Europe's elite countries.

As Section C of Table 4.3 shows, the majority of the centre-left perceives Italy's "backwardness" on the basis of the country's politics. Much of this can probably be explained by the fact that the government in 2010 was led by Berlusconi and the Forza Italia, both of which are viscerally loathed by the centre-left. Interestingly, a plurality of those on the centre-right believe that Italy is not "backward" compared to Europe's elite countries, while only a tiny minority of those on the left feel this way. The political left is also much more likely to interpret Italy's supposed backwardness in terms of the cultural traits of the Italian population, with significant numbers saying that Italians are *furbetti*, that they are individualist, and that that they are creative but also suffer from a range of defects. These differences in self-evaluation go some way in explaining the qualitatively different ways that the two groups perceived Italy's entrance into EMU. For example, as Section D of Table 4.3 shows, the centre-left is overwhelmingly more likely to posit a direct link between EMU and Europe as the solution to Italy's problems. The previous section of the Table highlighted how the political left perceives, both quantitatively and qualitatively, Italy's problems compared to Europe's elite countries differently than the political right: the left's supporters are much more pessimistic and negative about their own country, and this is a clue that helps to explain why, I surmise, they are much more enthusiastic about European integration.

Overall, the chi-square results are significant, and therefore, the findings support the proposition that the centre-left is more likely to approach Europe with a strong logic of identity than is the centre-right. This raises the question of why. Part of the explanation surely lies in the different ways that the groups perceive the Italian nation. The centre-left is much more likely to perceive Italy as a backward country than is the centre-right. The centre-left is also much more likely to idealize "Europe" as the incarnation of the social system that is present in Northern European countries. But this does not explain why the centre-left believes that European integration might somehow transfer the virtues of Northern European countries to Italy, a belief that rests on hope and wishes more than political reality. The psychological reasons for this are complex and will be explored in the conclusion of this chapter.

The groups that have up to now been compared – defined by gender, region, and political ideology – were mostly non-elites. But these non-elites did not invent the narratives that they possess about the character of Italy-Europe relations; elites did. The next section will take a closer look at the different logics embedded within their cognitive schemes.

Table 4.4 Status

A) General reasons for supporting EMU	
Non-elites	
Economic	51.2
Political	39.5
Cultural	9.3
Total	100
Elites	
Economic	28.5
Political	66.4
Cultural	5.1
Total	100
Chi-square value	13.946
Significance	.001
Degrees of freedom	2
B) Levels of enthusiasm	
Non-elites	
Strongly supportive	37
Generally supportive	44.9
Strongly opposed	9.9
Generally opposed	8.2
Total	100
Elites	
Strongly supportive	70.7
Generally supportive	26.4
Strongly opposed	0.7
Generally opposed	2.1
Total	99.9
Chi-square value	26.991
Significance	.000
Degrees of freedom	3
C) Europe as means or a means *and* an end	
Non-elites	
Means	55.1
Means and end	28.8
Neither	16.2
Total	100.1

Elites	
Means	31
Means and end	64.1
Neither	4.8
Total	99.9
Chi-square value	28.841
Significance	.000
Degrees of freedom	2
D) Cognitive content	
Non-elites	
Mostly abstract benefits	34.7
Mostly concrete costs	6.8
Abstract benefits and concrete costs	24.9
Only concrete costs	18.3
Only concrete benefits	3.6
Concrete costs and concrete benefits	11.7
Total	100
Elites	
Mostly abstract benefits	56.8
Mostly concrete costs	2.1
Abstract benefits and concrete costs	25.3
Only concrete costs	3.4
Only concrete benefits	4.8
Concrete costs and concrete benefits	7.5
Total	100
Chi-square value	19.142
Significance	.002
Degrees of freedom	5
E) Current attitudes towards EMU (summer/early fall 2010)	
Non-elites	
In favour	61
Not in favour	37.6
Indifferent	1.4
Total	100
Elites	
In favour	95.8
Not in favour	2.1

(Continued)

Table 4.4 Continued

Indifferent	2.1
Total	100
Chi-square value	33.142
Significance	.000
Degrees of freedom	2
F) Link between Italy's problems and EMU as the solution	
Non-elites	
Direct link	39.7
Indirect link	25.8
No link	34.5
Total	100
Elites	
Direct link	58.6
Indirect link	25.5
No link	15.9
Total	100
Chi-square value	10.420
Significance	.006
Degrees of freedom	2

Section A of Table 4.4 on page 54 highlights that elites are overwhelmingly more likely to have interpreted EMU in political terms, while non-elites did so in economic terms. This means that the latter are more likely to interpret EMU in terms of economic utility, while elites are more likely to interpret EMU on the basis of their visions of European order. Section B of Table 4.4 also highlights the different levels of emotional intensity that elites and non-elites ascribed to EMU. Elites were overwhelmingly more likely to express their support for EMU with a tone of conviction and praise, while non-elites were more likely to support EMU in a detached, nonchalant manner. Section C further highlights the point. Elites are overwhelmingly more likely to conceive of European integration as a means *and* an end, while non-elites are more likely to perceive it *only* as a means. This higher emphasis on instrumentality displayed by non-elites means that they are much more sensitive to the concrete costs and benefits of joining EMU than are elites. Support for this idea is found on Section D of Table 4.4. As mentioned above, this measure aims to identify the ways in which the content of the interviewee's overall responses ascribed concreteness and abstract properties to the costs and benefits of joining. The idea here is that the logic of appropriateness and belonging is more consonant with abstract idealization. The section shows that majorities of both elites and non-elites emphasized abstract benefits and minimized concrete costs, highlighting that, despite the differences between different groups, a strong sense of identity is widespread among Italians in how they perceive Italy-Europe relations. But there are also notable differences. The thinking of non-elites is much more likely to be imbued with only the concrete costs and benefits of European integration. Non-elites are overwhelmingly more likely to have expressed only the concrete costs of joining. Non-elites are also much more likely to have conveyed an equal emphasis on concrete costs and abstract benefits. Lastly, non-elites are more likely to have interpreted European integration on the basis of only concrete costs and benefits. These patterns of cognition explain some of Section E of Table 4.4. As can be seen, almost all of elites' support for EMU has remained unchanged from the mid-nineties to the summer of 2010, when the interviews were conducted. Meanwhile, although a significant majority of non-elites were in favour of EMU in the mid- to late nineties, a significant portion are no longer in favour. The reason is that EMU did not bring the benefits that were promised; it is also perceived to have lowered the standard of living of Italians through the increases in prices and from the loss of competitiveness from having a strong currency. Non-elites, being less likely to interpret EMU in terms of abstract visions of European order, interpreted it in terms of the concrete costs and benefits, and this goes some way towards explaining why significant numbers of non-elites no longer support EMU.

A number of conclusions can be inferred from these findings. First, it is clear that elites and non-elites display different cognitive logics in their interpretations of Italy-Europe relations. Elites are more likely to display a strong logic of identity than are non-elites. This highlights that assertions about the character of the identity of the political community obscure important differences between groups that constitute this community. It also counters certain stereotypes about the differences between elites and non-elites. Conventional wisdom holds that the masses are largely ignorant and hence it is they who interpret political objects on the basis of non-rational influences, such as prejudices and stereotypes (Converse 1964), while elites, who possess higher levels of knowledge, interpret political objects in more rational ways. This is one of the implications of Isernia's (2005) study, namely, that non-elites interpreted EMU on the basis of things that had little to do with the common currency, such as a possible solution to the problem of organized crime, which reflects their low levels of knowledge. It is indeed true that elites possess more knowledge of EMU than non-elites. But the data above highlight that this higher level of information did not translate into interpretations of EMU that were based on the concrete costs and benefits of joining; rather, the data highlight that elites were more likely to interpret EMU and European integration on the basis of visions of European order, belongingness, high emotional intensity, and abstract hopes – all of which are mostly non-rational in character.

It seems counterintuitive that an actor with more knowledge can be just as, if not more, non-rational in his interpretation of political objects as an actor with less knowledge. Indeed, many constructivists have argued that the lack of information is one of the reasons that meanings, beliefs, and identities are more important than material factors in explaining the behaviour of political communities (Jabko 2006;

McNamara 1998), the assumption being that more information would translate into a weaker reliance on the stuff of identity. But a closer examination reveals why more information does not necessarily translate into more rationality. Elites clearly have more knowledge of EMU, which reflects their level of education, reading habits, and experiences. This level of knowledge meant that, in their interview responses, they were cognizant of the institutional dimensions of EMU and were able to convey counterarguments. But this does not mean that this high level of knowledge played a significant role in their interpretation of EMU as a political object. For instance, as Section C in Table 4.4 shows, significantly more members of the elite than of the non-elite viewed EMU as the solution to the country's problems. But this vision of EMU, as highlighted by many sober analysts, such as Foreign Minister Antonio Martino and the governor of the Italian central bank, Antonio Fazio (both of whose predictions about the euro actually came true), did not correspond with the substance of the actual policy. Why, then, would highly knowledgeable actors hold meanings and beliefs that did not correspond with the actual policy? The answer can be found in the other sections of Table 4.4: for them, EMU was interpreted on the basis of abstract visions of European order, feelings of belongingness, and the hope – and the word "hope" needs to be emphasized here – that EMU and European integration would make Italy a "modern" and "normal" country. Meanwhile, non-elites are less likely to have interpreted EMU based on the hope that it would solve Italy's problems. For many of them, EMU was simply a new currency with which to go shopping. Other non-elite subjects supported EMU because they believed the dominant narrative that this policy would improve things. Non-elites cannot make the complex causal connections that elites can. But non-elites can identify correlations, and sometimes, *a correlation is sufficient to determine the costs and benefits of a particular policy*. Non-elites perceived that their economic situation worsened only after EMU was introduced, and although this correlation does not justify the belief that EMU caused this decline, it does justify the belief that EMU did not cause the promised improvements for the simple reason that the improvements did not occur. And this basic fact, for many non-elites, had much more cognitive salience than did abstract visions of European order, emotional intensity, and feelings of belongingness.

The differences between elites and non-elites highlight that the discourses invented by elites about European integration and Italy have only partially permeated the masses. A strong sense of identity – which is characterized by feelings of appropriateness and belongingness – is embedded in a scheme, or narrative, that constructs Italy and Europe in stereotypical ways. It constructs Europe as modernity, normality, progress, equality, and freedom; all concepts, not coincidentally, that are associated with Northern European countries, while Italy was conceived of as "backward." These ideas are imbued with feelings of belongingness and other affective associations, but they are also imbued with the implicit theory that belonging to Europe might somehow transfer these wonderful concepts to Italy. The graphs highlight that many non-elites have internalized this narrative. But they also highlight that the following categories are more likely to have internalized this narrative: men, Northerners, and the centre-left. However, overall, non-elites are relatively less likely to possess this elite-created narrative about what

Europe can do for Italy. Consequently, many non-elites perceive Italy and Europe in more concrete ways than do elites. This highlights that less knowledge of political objects does not necessarily correlate with a stronger influence of non-rational variables such as discourses and identity. In other words, the ones with the most knowledge of the euro were more likely than the less knowledgeable to interpret the euro through the prism of non-rational influences.

Analysis of results

One possible explanation for this curious finding is that more knowledgeable people are more likely to interpret political objects through the prism of ideology. An ideology, by definition, contains within it conceptions of the good society. It diagnoses the ills of the society, the causes of these ills, and the solutions to them. It contains assumptions about human agency and human nature, about the realm of the possible. It relies on simplification, abstraction, and generalization. Moreover, ideologically inclined types are often less willing or able to assess the concrete costs and benefits if this assessment conflicts with the goals, assumptions, and implications of their ideology. The individuals with a strong sense of identity display all these characteristics. They diagnosed Italian "backwardness" on the basis of cultural or political defects that prevent meaningful change. That is, there was a fatalistic sense that the Italian nation lacked the agency to solve its problems. They also have a conception of the "good society" which is incarnated in Europe because "Europe" is associated with Northern European virtues. There was the wish that Italy would become like these Northern European countries, but there was also a feeling that the country lacked the agency to make the necessary changes. Agency was therefore located in Europe, which fundamentally rested on the hope or wish that Europe could change Italy. This belief was present despite the fact, supported by common sense and a realistic assessment of the evidence, that only Italy can change itself; sovereignty, and hence agency, lies within.

If this sovereignty was not exercised in a way that promoted the desired changes, the cause is most likely the unwillingness of many politically powerful interest groups to change. There are many privileges that many groups enjoy under the current system. Although Italians have a tendency to denounce their social system, many also gain from the widespread tax evasion, the professional bodies that exclude others, the system of familial ties, *raccomandazioni*, and reciprocity that trumps merit in determining one's life's chances, clientelism, and many other myriad privileges that Italians regularly take advantage of.[3] In order to transform country, these privileges will need to be dismantled. The next chapter will address this in greater detail.

Notes

1 Many prominent Italians have chastised their fellow countrymen for their unrealistic expectations of what Europe could do for Italy. See chapter two of this book.

2 A revealing example is the following. I asked a person whom I befriended at the University of Trento who he voted for in the last election. Before replying, he looked

around apprehensively to make sure that no one could hear, and then said that he voted for Berlusconi.

3 There are many books that highlight the myriad privileges that Italians from most socioeconomic classes gain from the current system. See: Roger Abravanel and Luca D'Agnese, *Regole* (Milano: Garzanti, 2010); Roger Abravanel, *Meritocracia* (Milano: Garzanti, 2009); Marco Cobianchi, *Mani Bucate* (Milano: Chiarelettere, 2011); Roberto Ippolito, *Evasori* (Milano: Bompiani, 2008); Antonio Catricala, *Zavorre D'Italia* (Rubbettino, 2010); F. Giavazzi, *Lobby d'Italia: L'Italia dei Monopoli, delle Corporazioni e dei Privilegi* (Milano: Bur, 2008). Of course not all Italians are able to enjoy these privileged positions.

References

Converse, P. (1964) The Nature of Belief Systems in Mass Publics. In: D. Apter (ed.). *Ideology and Discontent.* New York: Free Press, pp. 201–261.

Isernia, P. (2005) L'Europa Vista dagli Italiani: Vent'Anni Dopo, In: M. Cotta, P. Isernia, and L. Verzichelli (eds). *L'Europa In Italia.* Bologna: Il Mulino, pp. 223–277

Jabko, N. (2006) *Playing the Market.* Ithaca: Cornell University Press.

McNamara, K. (1998) *The Currency of Ideas: Monetary Politics in the European Union.* Ithaca: Cornell University Press.

Sani, G. 1989. The Political Culture of Italy: Continuity and Change. In: S. Verba and G. Almond (eds). *The Civic Culture Revisited.* Newbury Park, CA: Sage Publications, pp. 273–318.

5 Perception meets reality in Italy

In August of 2011, Mario Draghi and Jean-Claude Trichet of the European Central Bank (ECB) sent a letter to the government of Silvio Berlusconi. At the time, investors were signalling their fear of a possible Italian default and driving up interest rates to an unsustainable level. The ECB, against the wishes of Germany and other "virtuous" countries, was buying Italian debt in secondary markets to push down interest rates, but was only moderately successful. The stern letter outlined what those at the ECB, including Draghi, felt Italy needed to do as a quid pro quo for the ECB's purchasing Italian bonds and for the country to get itself out of the crisis. The letter was essentially a list of suggestions of reforms deemed necessary to regain competitiveness and the confidence of investors, which included, among other things, reducing the size of the state, making it easier to sack workers by repealing or fundamentally altering article 18 of the statute of workers' rights, opening up professions to competition, reducing taxes, reducing the size of the bureaucracy, and privatizations.

This letter made the liberal character of the EMU abundantly clear (here, the word "liberal" refers to the European, not the American, meaning of the term): the reforms outlined in the letter, if taken in their entirety, would have amounted to a liberal revolution in Italy, at least in the economic sphere. But there was much resistance to the letter, unsurprisingly, from both the centre-left and the centre-right. The only party that seemed to unreservedly accept the outlines of the letter was the traditionally euro-enthusiast party of Pierferdinando Casini, the UDC, which is the offshoot of the defunct Christian Democrats. The other parties, although rhetorically pro-European, signalled their reservations and opposition to this pressure from "Europe".

The letter was also a concrete example of the attempt to "Germanize" Italy. It is no coincidence that *Der Spiegel* called Mario Draghi the most "German" Italian. His views on monetary policy were known to be strictly within the parameters of the German vision of the common currency, which included a repudiation of Keynesian macroeconomic demand management as well as the consolidation of "fiscal Protestantism" (Bellofiore, Garibaldo, & Halevi 2011) and which found concrete expression in the Maastricht criteria and the Fiscal Pact (more on the latter in chapter eight). This "Berlin Consensus" has included austerity, which has caused much social and political misery and the use of bailout money to surreptitiously save German and French banks (Zingales 2015) while resisting moves to rebalance the Eurozone economy in a way that alters the current structural advantage that accrues to German exporters.

This raises a question: was this the *vincolo esterno* (external pressure) that Italians desired when they adopted the euro? The notion that Italians (and other "periphery" countries) were motivated to enter the Eurozone because they wanted Europe's external pressure to help fix their deep-seated problems is widely expressed by scholars of and commentators on Italy. For example, Bastasin (2012) says that the Italian public supported the discipline that Europe (ostensibly) imposed, a view shared by other commentators on the country (Bardone & Reitano 2009). The evolution of the politics of the euro – what with the blatant ignoring of the fiscal rules, the decline in competitiveness of periphery countries, the social devastation of the Eurozone crisis – has rendered this narrative, like so many others used to frame the euro, highly suspect or downright naive. The pressure to *enter* the euro in the mid-nineties may have encouraged some reforms, especially in the pension system. But the adjustment required to meet the Maastricht criteria was mostly not the result of "virtuous" behaviour imposed by Europe. Rather, it was due to accounting tricks (Tanzi 2009, p. 188) and to the reduction of interest rates on Italian debt when it became clear that the country would adopt the euro (ibid). Whatever virtue Europe may have encouraged in the mid-nineties, it nonetheless remains the case that bad habits returned in 1999 (ibid) – not coincidently, the first year of the euro.

The adoption of the euro has coincided with an acceleration of Italy's decline and a lowering of its position in Europe's pecking order. The only way for Italy to truly and enduringly equalize its position in relation to the "core" countries is to transform its political economy so that it projects a societal model that attracts long-term, productivity-enhancing and employment-generating investment. This observation flows from the theoretical arguments presented in chapter two, namely, that hierarchy in Europe is determined by material and immaterial factors. Italy possesses the former, but not the latter. An attractive societal model would give the country the ideological power that, when complemented with its material assets, would likely place it in the top tier. Crucially, the adoption of the euro obscured this basic fact because many believed that entering the currency union would somehow automatically fix the country's problems. In this sense, agency was located externally rather than where it belongs: in the nation.

This raises important questions about the character of Italy's political economy. Generally, there are three positions in regards to Italy's problems: 1) that the cause is structural/geopolitical, 2) cultural variables, like "amoral familism", are the main cause, 3) the state and its occupants have been responsible for Italy's decline, because the political class enrich themselves without concern for the well-being of the electorate (the success of the Five Star Movement, which campaigns on this discourse, attests to the fact that it is widely believed). This chapter will assess these arguments and propose that the main cause is interest groups, with the complicity of the political class, who block fundamental change. These interest groups include men, tax evaders, businessmen, and public sector workers. The concluding section will argue that the euro was not conducive to tackling these fundamental problems.

Structural explanations

The arguments that focus on the international structure come in many forms. One explores the macroeconomic imbalances that the euro created (Scharpf 2011). The euro overpriced the exports of the periphery and underpriced those of the core, especially Germany. This led to deficits in the former that were financed by French and German banks, made possible by the liberalization of capital that the Maastricht treaty crystallized (Becker & Jager 2011). The institutional architecture of the euro also exacerbated these imbalances by prohibiting transfers from surplus to deficit countries and discouraging expansionary fiscal and monetary policy. Another, more cynical, strand of this argument asserts that the euro represents the fruition of Germany's policy of neomercantalism (Bellofiore, Garibaldo, & Halevi 2011), which included making itself competitive through reducing the power of labour and preventing the rise of wages of German workers, both of which were helped by a currency that underpriced its exports, increasing Germany's competitiveness at the expense of others.

There can be no doubt that the institutional architecture of the euro exacerbated the problems of the periphery countries, especially Italy. Had they retained their own currency, their exports would not have been overpriced, and in the event of a crisis, adjustment would have been procured through changes in nominal exchange rates, which would have been less politically painful than the internal devaluation and austerity that must transpire in a currency union without a political union. What is more, Germany has been the main beneficiary of the euro, and its policies have been orientated around the preservation of these benefits or at least the prevention of losses that would accrue in the event of real fiscal transfers. It is also true that Germany is structurally dominant, and that this position has been crystallized in the institutional architecture of the euro. This dominance means that any structural solution must have Germany's consent. There is little evidence that this willingness is forthcoming. Therefore, adjustment must happen internally.

Cultural explanations

Popular arguments include the theory of civic culture (Putnam 1993) and the amoral familism framework (Banfield 1958). These theories can be evaluated together because, as Putnam himself says, the existence of amoral familism is the absence of civic culture (Putnam 1993, p. 88). According to Putnam, civic culture means, among other things, that the citizen actively participates in public affairs (p. 87). The problem with this idea is that not all kinds of participation are beneficial. In fact, many lobby groups actively participate in public affairs to preserve their privileges.[1] Putnam might respond that this participation must be "enlightened" rather than "myopic" (p. 88). The problem with this is that most interests view their activities as "enlightened" and those of the other as "myopic". The firms that receive state subsidies, for example, will always justify their receipt of state largess in terms of jobs; the men who will electorally punish a party that tries to engender female equality in the marketplace will justify their vote on whatever suits their purposes; securely entrenched workers will justify their opposition to policies that aim to make the labour market more flexible in order to allow the inclusion of youth as a betrayal of "social justice" rather than a threat to their sinecures. Thus, theoretically, the concept of civic culture is too nebulous to be of value for the problems in Italy's political economy.

Regarding the theory of amoral familism, there can be no doubt that ascribing moral primacy to the family as a social and political unit can have negative consequences for the functioning of the political economy. It can prevent the formation of a Weberian bureaucracy, and lead to distrust in national institutions. But the amoral familism theory tends to unjustifiably simplify a very complex reality. It essentializes an entire population with a totalizing explanation that explains everything – and hence nothing. It ignores the fact that "familism" and a weak sense of the common good are present even in countries, like the US, that Italians tend to idealize as places that lack the shortcomings that are purportedly uniquely Italian. It also ignores the fact that familism is not necessarily correlated with backwardness: even in Italy's well-developed, "European" North, the family is a primary political, social, and moral unit. In fact, the North's high level of development and economic dynamism suggest that family forms of capitalism can produce rapid and sustained economic growth. What is more, even if we presume that familism is widespread in Italy, some polls highlight that Italians have just as high a level of civic culture as their French cousins: they are just as likely to read newspapers, have faith in their democratic institutions, and tell pollsters that "following rules is important" (Sciolla 2004, pp. 54, 106).

State-level explanations

The domestic side of the debate includes Europhile economists who, even as late as 2009, claimed that the "euro has been a great success" (Buti 2009, p. xix). For them, the main problem is the lack of structural reforms that would help Italian producers move up the export value chain. Globalization, and the rise of the emerging world, has put pressure on Italian industry because many Italian manufacturing products rely on low-level technology, putting them in direct competition with China and India. To make more technologically advanced products that do not directly compete with those emerging powers it will be necessary to invest in human capital, specifically in education that focuses on science and technology. They also endorse making labour markets more flexible in order to adapt to the fluctuating and dynamic pressures of globalization. They recognize that there is little political support for these types of reforms, and so endorse "economic pedagogy" to educate citizens on the need for these policies (Leopold 2009).

The problem with this argument is that Italian policymakers did make their labour markets more flexible and the results were hardly positive. The government of Berlusconi implemented reforms that partially liberalized labour market contracts, and these did significantly reduce unemployment. But this also created an army of low-wage, precarious jobs that rely on short-term contracts that militate against the investment in human capital that is needed to raise productivity (Boeri 2009, p. 219). It also did not protect against the scourge of unemployment that the Eurozone crisis has created and that has led to a rise in populism and an exodus of talented youth to cities like London where their job prospects are better. Recent research from the IMF has, in fact, confirmed that liberalizing labour markets is associated with *lower*, not higher, productivity (Levi 2015). Another problem is that the argument for the need of "economic pedagogy" is condescending. There are many highly educated Italians who would reject the notion that they need to be "educated" by Europhile economists, many of whom were the architects of the Eurozone debacle that the periphery has experienced.

Other domestic-level explanations are more measured. Bastasin (2012) argues that politicians misled their publics about the euro; they did not adequately inform citizens about the real nature of European integration, which entailed restructuring the political economy to make it more consistent with the reality of openness and interdependency. Politicians avoided these tough decisions because they would have been politically damaging, and now the chicken has come home to roost: the Eurozone crisis means that these tough decisions can no longer be ignored, and that the existence of the currency may very well depend on the willingness and courage of politicians to implement them.

The evidence presented in this book solidly confirms Bastasin's argument that the euro was misrepresented by many elites, and that this stemmed, at least in part, from the unfounded optimism of the supposed benefits of the euro. However, he ignores a crucial point: if elites had been completely honest about what the euro entailed, they would not have had much support for the currency. This is especially the case in Italy, where it is unlikely that most wanted the kinds of neo-liberal reforms demanded by a German-dominated currency union. And the same is true today: Bastasin applauds leaders like Mario Monti for their honesty, but the latter's resounding political failure puts paid to the notion that what countries need is a new class of leaders who speak frankly about the challenges of preserving the euro.

Others argue that the social pathologies that Italy is notorious for, such as tax evasion and clientelism, are natural or even normal responses to a rapacious political class that has abused its power (Sciolla 2003; Paci 1996). This argument depends on the assumption of a contraposition between a corrupt and parasitic state and a healthy civil society. But this is not tenable, and this can be nicely illustrated with the event that brought to light the deeply corrupt character of Italy's political class and delegitimized the post-war political system: the *Tangentopoli* scandal. Initially it was interpreted as evidence of a corrupt political class that exploited the resources of society for their own gain. This idea seemed to be supported by the widespread public support for the magistrates and their attempts to bring justice to the political system. But subsequent analysis posed a serious challenge to this framework. First, as highlighted by Tullio-Altan (1999), the widespread corruption of the political parties, especially the DC, was no secret before the magistrates took action against them. It was widely known, and yet those responsible for it did not receive electoral punishment. This suggests that for many voters, holding politicians accountable for their shady behaviour was not a priority the way that it might be in other mature democracies, and may explain why it took the magistrates and not the representative institutions of the polity to react to this state of affairs (Garrone 1996, p. 116). Others saw *Tangentopoli* as a direct consequence of Italy's form of state capitalism (Cazzaniga 1994). The active intervention of political parties and the state in the economy, by granting monopoly privileges and subsidies and acquiescing to tax evasion and other anti-competitive behaviour, led to a kind of adverse selection in the economy, whereby the parasitic rent-seekers were rewarded at the expense of the honest. The general point of these revisionists' arguments is that the system relied on the consent, either tacit or explicit, of many sub-state actors, especially businessmen and voters.

The *Tangentopoli* scandal is instructive because it highlights that, contrary to popular views, the corruption that erupted in the scandal is not reducible to a rapacious and dishonest political class. The political class is embedded in, an expression and an extension of, the country's economic relations, political parties, voter preferences, and other elements of the sub-state level (Gilbert 1998, p. 313). The next section argues that the same can be said, *mutatis mutandis*, about the following problems that undermine the attractiveness of Italy's societal model: patriarchy, an unscrupulous professional class, an undisciplined and uncompetitive class of businessmen, and a sclerotic public sector. All have served to perpetuate the status quo because of the varying forms of consent that they have given to the political class in order to preserve their privileges, large and small, at the expense of long-term sustainability.

Gender

In the World Economic Forum 2010 Global Gender Gap Report, on the gender gap index Italy was in 74th place, out of 134 countries. The report highlights that although women enjoy equal access to healthcare and education, in the labour market the glass ceiling continues to block progress. Although the country's overall rank is 74, if we look only at labour force participation, it is ranked 97, below Paraguay and Ghana. Only about half of the female working-age population actively works, while three quarters of men do, and the earned income paid to men is around double what it is for women. In Europe, Italy is ahead of only Greece and Malta in the rankings of overall female participation in the labour force.[2] Although the problem of female exclusion is higher in the South than it is in the North, the problem is nonetheless present in the North. There are many reasons for this widespread female exclusion. The first is that women in the country perform the duties that in other countries would be performed by the state: taking care of the elderly and children, for instance. The second reason, which is directly related to the first, is the continued culturally rooted attitudes towards women that relegate them to the home.[3]

This low participation has harmed competitiveness because a significant amount of human capital is not being utilized. Although women perform much of the socially valuable unpaid labour in the economy, research suggests that their contribution to economic growth would be much greater if they were more equitably included in the labour force.[4] The problem has not been completely ignored. There have been initiatives to try to tackle the problem, but it has not been a priority for policymakers in the last 10 years. As Maurizio Ferrera argues, this emerges from the fact that there is little political will to make it a priority.[5] This lack of political will fundamentally reflects a cultural conservatism: promoting gender equity does not gain as many votes as, say, changing the electoral system. But the crisis has helped to shatter illusions about the state of women in the economy and its effect on overall competitiveness. Accordingly, the technocratic government of Monti implemented policies to help to increase female labour participation in the form of tax incentives for firms who hire women. Matteo Renzi is also making efforts to increase female representation in the echelons of economic and political power. The jury is still out on whether these initiatives will be successful, but the road will be long and arduous because they will require tackling and changing some deeply held beliefs about gender relations.

Professions

Polls show that professionals are among the most pro-European groups, especially compared to the working class. Many would argue that this is a function of their relatively higher levels of education and cosmopolitanism. Others argue that this emerges from the fact that they have much to gain from European integration because they possess human capital that has value across borders. Whatever the true causes of the pro-European attitudes, in Italy the fact remains that professionals have been European in words and not in deeds. Being "European", one would think, would mean respect for the rules of the state, but professionals have displayed some of the most anarchistic attitudes towards the rules, especially in the form of tax evasion. Going to the dentist or obtaining legal services often entails two prices: one with the receipt, and one without the receipt. Paying without the receipt was normalized and practiced even by people who would call themselves "honest" (Ippolito 2008, p. 8). And while many professionals ignore the rules when it comes to taxes, they display a preference for rules that give them monopolies that limit competition and serve to transfer rents to them from consumers (Ginsborg 2003, p. 47; Abravanel & D'Agnese 2010, p. 108; Catricala 2010, p. 17). They are able to accomplish this, in part, because of the high level of representation that professionals enjoy in Parliament and the broader political system (Della Porta 1992). The harmful effects on competitiveness are manifold. First, the exclusion of outsiders limits competition, which limits innovation, and this limits the driver of real increases in standards of living: productivity. Second, it represents a tax on consumers. Some services, like dentistry, are the most expensive in Europe, and these prices reduce the real standard of living of consumers (Ginsborg 2003). Lastly, recent IMF research confirms that opening up closed professions does have a positive effect on economic output (Levi 2015).

There were attempts to address the problem, most notably by Pier Luigi Bersani, Minister of Industry under Romano Prodi from 2006 to 2008, but after significant protests he had to water down many of the measures. Although his liberalizations were an important move towards "Europeanizing" the professions, they were only a first step. The technocratic government led by Monti adopted a series of measures to help ensure that professionals pay their taxes and that introduced the discipline of competition, but not surprisingly, there was much resistance to these attempts. Initially, the legislation aimed to remove price controls and to increase the numbers of professionals that could legally practice, but due to the pressure from those who would be adversely impacted by these reforms, there were thousands of changes made to the legislation, leading some commentators to assert that they are now liberalizations in name only. The effect will be to perpetuate the status quo.

Business

Scholars have used a number of labels to describe the Italian model of capitalism, from "dysfunctional state capitalism" (Della Sala 2004) to "dysfunctional political economy" (De Cecco 2007). There are a number of traits that provide the basis for these labels. The main one, perhaps, is the concentration of ownership among Italian families, a trait which is associated with developing countries more than with developed, European nations. This family-oriented capitalism is one of the reasons for the low levels of meritocracy and social mobility in the country (Abravanel 2009). The impact on competitiveness is profound. In a globalized economy, firms must be innovative and productive, and to be so requires making the best use of the country's talent. Needless to say, a family-oriented form of capitalism makes it more difficult to make use of the country's talent, which is why the country's best and brightest are going overseas to look for work and opportunity. This family-oriented capitalism has been reproduced in part because of culture, and in part because of the actions of the state.

The state has helped to perpetuate this state of affairs through its complicity in the anti-competitive behaviour of Italian firms. The first is the clientelistic subsidy schemes that Italian businesses have relied on. A detailed study by investigative journalist Marco Cobianchi (2011) has revealed that literally millions of firms are on the public dole. In 2010, the budget contained 40 billion euros in subsidies that go to sectors such as finance, agriculture, and tourism. The inefficiencies created are profound. First, many of these funds are not allocated on the basis of projects that make good business sense. They are geared towards obtaining electoral support and other forms of consent, both implicit and explicit (Padoa-Schioppa 1990; Toci 1994, p. 132; Fotia 1997, p. 11; Sapelli 1993, p. 95). This creates many skewed incentives. Firms and entrepreneurs, rather than focussing their efforts on satisfying their customers, expend resources on lobbying the state to continue these subsidies. This has led to the development of intermediaries who specialize in helping firms to obtain public funds, which represents another wasteful and inefficient allocation of human and other forms of capital. This problem of inefficient firms dependent on the state is much more widespread in the South, but many Northern firms are equally implicated, especially the ones that obtain public funds to invest in the South, only to close up shop and end up with a handsome profit, all thanks to the taxpayer (Cobianchi 2011, p. 76). Other firms use their links with the state to ensure that they will have monopoly privileges in their sectors. It appears that not much has changed since 1964, when Joseph Lapalombara (1964) wrote his seminal work on the role of Italian industrialists who use the state to minimize competition by giving them monopoly privileges.

Given this state of affairs, it is not surprising that Italy is in 66th place on the economic freedom index, below Turkey, Madagascar, Namibia, and Mongolia (Abravanel & D'Agnese 2010, p. 78), and 56th on the World Bank's 2014 index for ease of doing business. The incentives for firms have assured a kind of adverse selection, where winners are those who have the best connections with the state, or who are lucky enough to be born in a privileged family. One of the hopes of many Europhile liberals was that European integration would help to undermine this and lead to a more open and competitive economy that was not prey to rent-seekers. But this did not transpire. And the reason is that Europe cannot fundamentally alter the behaviour of these myriad actors who benefit from the protection of the state. Although Europe has imposed many penalties on Italy for illegal subsidies and/or anti-competitive behaviour, this is has not fundamentally altered the political economy. Moreover, Europe has also accepted the legitimacy of some subsidies, and in so doing giving a European stamp of approval to them (Cobianchi 2011, p. 192).

Tax evasion

Recent data highlights that tax evasion in Italy has reached 275 billion euros.[6] In proportional terms, the problem of tax evasion is probably worse in the South than it is in the North, but it is nonetheless widespread, even normalized, in both major regions of the country (Ippolito 2008). Although tax evasion is widespread among professionals, the problem cuts across social class and region, with some experts saying that around 50% of Italians evade taxes of some sort or another (Abravanel & D'Agnese 2010, p. 225). Polls show that large majorities believe that citizens should pay their taxes (Sciolla 2004, p. 106), but what people tell pollsters does not always coincide with their actual behaviour.

Tax evasion harms competitiveness in myriad ways. First, it contributes to the large underground economy, which represents between 20% and 25% of Italian GDP. Second, it prevents firms from growing, because owners of underground, tax-evading firms might not want to become too large lest they evoke the attention of authorities. Tax evasion also disincentivizes foreign investment, because foreign investors, for whom taxes are much harder to evade, must compete with firms who do evade taxes.

Scholars have highlighted that illegal forms of behaviour, like tax evasion, are linked to the costs and benefits that rational actors experience from the activity in question. There are two kinds of costs that they must take account of. The first is the legal costs that would be imposed in the event of being caught. If the probability of being caught is low, and if the penalties on being caught are acceptable, then the rational actor will presume that the benefits of not paying taxes – higher profits, higher income, etc. – outweigh the costs. The second kind is arguably more important. This is the moral cost of evading taxes (Ippolito 2008, p. 198), which takes the form of social disapproval, ostracism, and the feelings of shame associated with an activity. If the moral costs are low – that is, if one can evade taxes and not feel shame or the disapproval of one's peers – then the incidence of illegal activity, including tax evasion, will increase, because the rational actor will presume that the benefits outweigh the costs. This model of human behaviour is necessarily stylized, but goes a long way towards explaining much of the tax evasion in Italy. If there is a general attitude such as "cosi fan tutti" (everyone does it anyway), which appears to be the case in Italy (Della Porta & Vannuci 1994), then the moral costs will be low. In a society where the moral costs are high, citizens would rationally conclude that the benefits of paying taxes exceed the benefits of evading them. In this society, citizens would also express their disapproval by reporting on those businesses and individuals who evade taxes. But in Italy, what we find is different. Indeed, very few Italians called the tax evasion hotline that was established, with some exceptions: wives reported the tax evasion of their husbands who had cheated on them (Ippolito 2008, p. 182). In other words, rather than demonstrating concern about illegal activity, reporting on tax evasion became a tool of personal revenge.

The fact that the problem is the low moral costs associated with illegal activity means that the problem is fundamentally rooted in the taken-for-granted habits and beliefs of millions of citizens, in what is deemed to be "normal" or "acceptable" behaviour in the community. The state is partly responsible, if only because it used tax evasion for electoral gain. Policymakers avoided tackling tax evasion in the South and in the Northern industrial districts because they would have been punished electorally, and the political class's unwillingness to make these politically unpopular decisions makes them complicit. After 2011, this state of affairs could no longer be sustained. In order to increase the confidence of investors, Italy had to demonstrate that it could solve the problem of tax evasion. It was also necessary to render the economy more competitive and to attract inflows of FDI. The technocratic government led by Mario Monti made addressing tax evasion one of its principal planks. There were some high-profile and politically popular tax raids in towns, like Cortina, Milan, and Naples, where tax evasion is suspected to be high. Authorities discovered that large percentages of businesses were potential evaders, but more important was the political message that the government would make the tough decisions that previous governments had been avoiding for fear of electoral punishment. The jury is still out on whether these efforts will lead to enduring changes that fundamentally alter the moral costs of evading taxes.

Public sector

In light of the previous section, it is difficult to clearly delineate the distinction between the private and the public sector. The tentacles of the state are actively present in much of the private sector, and hence it is questionable whether nominally private firms are in reality private, given that their survival depends, not primarily or exclusively on their capacity to compete in a free market, but on subsidies, tax evasion, or monopoly privileges that they enjoy from their political connections (Triglia 1995; Pizzorno 1996). Nonetheless, a discussion about Italy's lack of competitiveness, and its lack of will to address it, would be incomplete without a discussion of those corporations, institutions, organs, and other social aggregations understood to be part of the public sector. One of the key shortcomings of the Italian public sector is its excessive politicization: key positions in the Italian bureaucracy are allocated on the basis of party loyalty rather than merit (Della Porta 1992; Ginsborg 2003, p. 140). At the lower levels of the public sector, clientelism is diffuse and normalized, influencing everything from hiring to licensing decisions. The public sector includes the magistrates and the legal-institutional structure, which, in terms of efficiency and efficacy, is at the bottom of the European rankings (Abravanel 2010 & D'Agnese, p. 17), ahead of only Greece. Policymakers, both elected and non-elected, have attempted to reform the public sector, but they have encountered much resistance. The most notable attempts in recent memory were the Cassese reforms (Ginsborg 2003, p. 278), but they were largely unsuccessful.

Immaturity debate

The preceding section focused on the domestic changes that Italy needs if it wants to create an attractive societal model, and this is true regardless of whether it is in the euro. Some scholars argue that this form of analysis lends itself to reproducing the stereotypes of the "periphery", while minimizing the role of structural factors in causing the problems that they find themselves in. Even scholars like Bastasin (2012) who adopt a Europe-wide analysis tend to reproduce the narrative that the "immaturity" of the periphery is the main cause of the crisis (Dooley 2014). This chapter will not solve the puzzle of what the ultimate cause of the crisis is, but it does sustain that an attractive societal model is a *sine qua non* for truly enhancing the status and influence of countries like Italy, and that this will require politically painful domestic reforms. Structurally based solutions, like reflating the wages of German workers and/or creating a true fiscal union, are unlikely in the near term precisely because the political dynamics of the euro – namely, German hegemony – do not allow them. Therefore, change must be primarily domestic, even though the strictures of the euro make the required changes even more difficult than they might otherwise have been. But in Italy, this necessary change has been prevented by interests that have used the political process to block reform.

These interests displayed a conservative mindset in the face of reforms, but not in the common sense of the term, which refers to those on the centre-right. Rather, it refers to the simple and traditional definition of the term as resistance to change. In the way used here, conservatism is not an ideology; it is rather a general attitude that informs decisions, beliefs, and emotions. One element of the conservative attitude is the tendency to perceive changes in social relations in zero-sum terms: any gain that one set of actors may obtain comes at the expense of other actors. This greatly accentuates pessimism: since all potential social changes are viewed in zero-sum terms, there is an expectation that they will produce losses. This also leads to the tendency to perceive dark, sinister forces behind any changes that aim to alter existing social relations. These attributes lead to a kind of comfort with the status quo, even if it is increasingly evident that the status quo can no longer be sustained. The status quo not only ensures the continuance of perks and privileges that actors have become accustomed to rely on, but it also provides a sort of psychological comfort because is it associated with certainty and predictability. Uncertainty is psychologically uncomfortable for everyone, but for the conservative it is even more so because it is coupled with a fear of the loss of privileges, both big and small, and/or a zero-sum vision of the world.

The implication of this argument is that if the country wants to transform its societal model, it will have to alter the conservative attitudes of the interests that perpetuate the status quo. There were some signs that the current crisis had this effect. Mario Monti's efforts for a period enjoyed the support of a majority of Italians: when he replaced Berlusconi in November 2011 his support was above 80%, and polls in March 2012 showed that 52% approved of his efforts. One reason was that in November of 2011, there was a palpable fear that contagion would spread to Italy, causing a default and an exit from the euro. Such an event would have been psychologically traumatizing, even for those who have been critical of the common currency. This terror of leaving the euro had, it appeared, an effect on attitudes, and it seemed that for a period many interest groups recognized that the status quo needed to change and that this depended on fundamental changes in their own behaviour. But it is instructive that support for him has declined significantly since then (in the election in February 2013, Monti's party received around 10%, and in the elections of May 2014, a measly 4%). What is more, there has been an increase in support for anti-euro parties, such as the Five Star Movement. Support was high for Monti when it appeared that he could "save" the country, but then it dawned on many that for him to do this would require many painful reforms intended to change the habits of the interest groups mentioned above. This rapid decline in support for Monti's efforts to "Europeanize" Italy demonstrates why political parties have been unwilling to make the tough decisions required to change the country. It would be electoral suicide.

The euro helped to disincentivize reform

Monti's political failure is part of an enduring pattern: for the first 10 years of the euro – the period when governments were supposed to be making the necessary reforms to adapt to the common currency – the resistance to reform was present. This chapter also sustains that the euro, for the first 10 years of its existence, actually disincentivized reform. This challenges the argument of many Europhiles mentioned in the beginning, namely, that the euro was a good idea because it would impose virtuous behaviour on Italy ("*vincolo esterno*"). The actual evolution of the euro has demonstrated otherwise. To see why, it is important to outline what the euro could and could not do. It did help to stabilize inflation and provide discipline for public finance reforms. In addition, as was shown by Ferrera and Gualmini (1999), the pressure to meet the Maastricht criteria did lead to the privatizations of banks, pension and labour market reforms, and changes to the tax code that could be described as "virtuous". EMU could discipline public finance because the sovereign state was subject to the rules of the Treaty of Maastricht. But the euro could not address the private behaviours that produce high levels of tax evasion and corruption, the lack of social mobility and low levels of meritocracy due to a family-based form of capitalism, the short-termism and veto power of interest groups such as professionals, a diffuse clientelism, and a sclerotic public sector. Addressing these problems requires painful reforms that depend on the willingness of individuals to endure the short-term pain associated with fundamental changes in behaviour. This, in turn, depends on the reforms having considerable democratic legitimacy. The last 15 years have made it abundantly clear that the democratic legitimacy for these kinds of changes cannot be imposed by Europe.

Greece illustrates this further. Pressure from Europe led the government of Costas Simitis to reform the pension system. Even though the changes were minor, over a million people protested, forcing the government to withdraw the proposed changes. This showed that democratic resistance to reform trumps the pressure from Brussels. It also demonstrates that the "external pressure" is *neither* a necessary nor a sufficient condition for needed reforms. Rather, the political will to carry out changes is *both* necessary and sufficient. In other words, if the political will is absent, Europe cannot impose it, and if the political will is present, Europe's pressure is moot.

More importantly, scholars elsewhere have recognized that placing excessive agency in an external actor to fix a country's deep-seated problems is not conducive to building the democratic legitimacy that is necessary to enact politically painful reforms (Mazarr 2014). This legitimacy depends to some extent on trust that the pain of reforms will be equitably distributed and that they are in the interest of the nation, not particular interest groups. This, in turn, depends on trust that the ruling class is acting impartially and responsibly. This trust between citizens and the state is very low in Italy, and building it would require much patient and hard work that cannot be done overnight. Delegating authority to some external actor to the fix the country's problems is essentially an allocation of political capital away from that politically necessary activity.

The euro was not conducive to reform in other ways. First, the convergence of interest rates between Italy and Germany created the impression, especially in the initial post-euro period, that Italy was now part of the "virtuous" club of European nations. Students of Greece recognized a similar dynamic in that troubled nation (Prevelakis 2012). Greece, like Italy, suffered from high tax evasion, an unscrupulous professional and business class, and a sclerotic bureaucracy. But after the country entered the euro, the convergence of interest rates led to a debt-fuelled economic growth that created the false impression that Greece was now one of Europe's virtuous nations. Italy did not have the post-euro growth that was seen in Greece, but the convergence of interest rates had a similar dynamic because it created a sense of security in the status quo – not for all actors, but perhaps for most. And the reason is that interest rates are an important signal for policymakers; they convey information that helps to coordinate the behaviour between markets and governments. When interest rates are low in a highly indebted country with low prospects for growth, it reflects the belief that this country will be bailed out in the event that it is unable to repay its creditors. Markets priced in this belief because there was the impression that in the event of a crisis the country would be bailed out. In this sense, the initial effects of the euro created a false sense of security, and this weakened the incentives to make those politically unpopular decisions that are required to restore sustainable economic growth and hence prevent default.

The same dynamic played out as recently as the summer of 2011. At the time, markets were demanding higher interest rates on Italy's debt to cover the real risks of default that were previously obscured. This created the impetus for what seemed to be a flurry of reforms to be implemented by the Berlusconi government. Then the ECB intervened in secondary markets and brought interest rates down, and the pressure for reform evaporated (until November of the same year, when markets panicked again). It is for this reason that Draghi's intervention in secondary markets, announced on 6 September 2012, which would include the unlimited buying of shorter-term debt, is conditional on the country's signing of a "Memorandum of Understanding" which is thinly disguised euphemism for the imposition of reforms to restore competitiveness and economic growth. If the country starts to display reluctance, then the ECB will halt the intervention of buying unlimited short-term debt in secondary markets. This policy reflects the fear of what transpired in August 2011: as soon as interest rates go down, the pressure to restore competitiveness evaporates, and politicians hesitate to make the painful decisions for fear of the electoral consequences. It also shows how interest rates can be an important signal for governments to act decisively, as it conveys important information to policymakers. When this signal conveys false information – as the low interest rates that Italy paid on its debt did after it entered the EMU – the incentive for reform is reduced, and this is one of the reasons why Italian policymakers avoided the painful decisions in the first 10 years of the common currency.

Many of the key discourses through which the euro was interpreted were also not helpful. There was a widespread hope and belief that the euro would solve the country's deep-seated problems. This unrealistic belief is a close cousin to what has been recognized by many prominent Italian scholars and intellectuals as the widespread tendency to blame abstract entities, in generalized and simplistic ways, for the country's problems (Di Stefano 2013; Piattoni 2007; Rodota 1994; Bibee 2009). Whether it is the "political class" or the "system" or the "political parties" or the "magistrates" or even, increasingly, "Europe", many Italians display an enduring capacity to blame others for the country's problems. Underlying this tendency is the belief that the agent(s) responsible for the country's problems are outside the actor, and from here it is a short conceptual leap to the equally mistaken belief that the agent(s) that are the solution to the country's problems are also exogenous to the actor.

My own survey data illustrates how elites and non-elites tend to blame each other for the country's problems:

Subjects were asked what they thought were the causes (and solutions) to Italy's perceived backwardness, and the transcribed responses were dominated by the following five responses: 1) the political class, 2) culture, which referred to traits that Italians as a nation purportedly possess, 3) the current government, 4) the euro, and 5) institutions. As can be seen, although large numbers of non-elites blamed culture, a majority blamed the political class. Meanwhile, a significant plurality of elite members blamed culture. This can be interpreted in a variety of ways, but one plausible interpretation is that significant numbers of elites and non-elites blame each other for the country's problems. When a subject blames his country's problems on the culture of his co-citizens, for many it is a way of saying that everybody else has this trait. For instance, when a subject says that Italians are *furbetti*

Table 5.1 What is the cause of Italy's problems? (percentages)

Non-elites	
Political class	33.15
Culture	29.34
Current government (summer/fall 2010)	4.89
Euro	5.43
Institutions	5.43
Miscellaneous	21.76
Total	100
Elites	
Political class	26.08
Culture	44.92
Current government (summer/fall 2010)	0
Euro	0
Institutions	11.59
Miscellaneous	17.41
Total	100
Chi-square value	13.960
Significance	.016
Degrees of freedom	5

Detailed information on the sample can be found in the appendix

or individualist, they likely are not saying to me, the interviewer, that they too are these things; rather, other Italians are. Therefore, when elites said that "culture" was the cause of the problems, it is safe to assume that they believe themselves to be separate from these cultural deficiencies. It follows that they are locating responsibility in the masses, since they form the vast majority of the nation and hence constitute its national culture. Meanwhile, non-elites who blame the political class are referring to a belief that the political elite are deficient in a general sense.

This problem is not uniquely Italian (for an analysis of similar dynamics in the US, see Mansbridge 1997, p. 186). In countries where this trait is widespread, blaming others obscures the ways that one's own behaviour contributes to the problems in question, but in Italy there is another undesirable effect: the tendency to look for some outside entity to solve the country's problems. Evidence for this national trait was present even two centuries ago, when Italians looked to revolutionary France to solve the country's ills.[7] This trait was fertile ground for politicians and other elites who sold the euro to the population in salvation-tinged language, creating the impression that all the country's problems would be solved by entering the common currency. This too was confirmed by my survey data:

As Table 5.2 highlights, a plurality of non-elites perceive a direct link between the country's problems and Europe as the solution, while a large majority of elites perceive a direct link between the two. When this graph is understood in light of the fact that many political elites and non-elites view each other as the causes of the country's problems, it allows us to plausibly assume that large numbers of both were looking to Europe to save Italy from each other.

Table 5.2 Link between Italy's problems and EMU as the solution (percentages)

Non-elites	
Direct link	39.7
Indirect link	25.8
No link	34.5
Total	100
Elites	
Direct link	58.6
Indirect link	25.5
No link	15.9
Total	100
Chi-square value	10.420
Significance	.006
Degrees of freedom	2

Detailed information on the sample can be found in the appendix

This tendency to blame others reduced the capacity to draw logical and concrete connections between one's decisions and practices and the status quo. Living in Italy, I witnessed this phenomenon: individuals blaming others for the country's problems and then *the very same individuals* engaging in the behaviour that serves to perpetuate the problems. These observations are anecdotal, but they confirm the pattern: intelligent and well-meaning people complaining about how in Italy there is no sense of the "common good" or that the "rich" or the "political class" are the source of the country's problems – and the *very same* persons paying for services without a receipt in order to evade taxes, or benefitting from low rental costs for an apartment because the apartment they live in is "abusivo" (illegal), or ensuring favourable medical treatment for relatives because of a connection in the hospital, or bragging that they will be able to fake mental illness in order to obtain a disability pension, or buying counterfeit products in order to enhance their status without having to pay the full cost.

Part of the explanation of this trait is a very real collective action problem: challenging the status quo by changing one's behaviour will incur short-term costs (in terms of a real reduction in the standard of living), while the long-term benefits of a more attractive societal model are abstract, not in the here and now. And so the incentive is to keep engaging in the behaviours that perpetuate the status quo, while complaining about how bad things are. But the discourses through which the euro was interpreted did not help this state of affairs because they reinforced the tendency to blame others or abstract entities for the country's problems and, in so doing, reduced the capacity to draw links between one's own everyday behaviour and the unsustainable status quo. This tendency was present especially among the most pro-European. In this regard, emblematic is a pro-euro merchant whom I interviewed in the summer of 2010. In one part of the interview, she tells me that she was in favour of entering EMU because

> it was important to make us equals, it was a desire to be a country of Serie A [the premier division of the Italian soccer league] like all the others in Europe, we knew that if we would not have entered we would have been part of the third world.

This response displays much of the rhetoric that was present in the late nineties, that the alternative to the euro was "the third world". But later in this fascinating interview, in a response to my question on what she believes are the country's problems, she tells me that

> the principal problem is the "partitocrazia" [regime of parties], who use public money to intervene in the economy . . . taxes are too high, and so we all find ways to avoid paying them.

This merchant has essentially admitted to me that she and her fellow merchants engage in tax evasion, although she justifies it by the fact that taxes are too high because the country's political parties use public money to prop up firms. But she evidently does not recognize that her tax evasion is one of the reasons that Italy has remained a country of "Serie B" in Europe. Moreover, even if her belief that the source of the country's problems is the political parties is not entirely untrue, it is incomplete, because illegality is not the way to address the problem; in fact, illegality worsens the problem.

This chapter has looked at the ways in which the euro, and the discourse through which it was interpreted, helped to obscure the internal social structures that are the main cause of its lack of competitiveness and absence of economic growth. But these discourses obscured Italy's external relations, too. Italian foreign policy for the past 60 years has been motivated by the wish to be one of Europe's leading nations, alongside Germany and France, in running the continent's affairs. Entering EMU must be understood in the context of that history and in a sense is a continuation of it. But this obscured the fact that entering a prestigious monetary union could not, in and of itself, end Italy's marginalization in Europe. The next chapter will demonstrate why.

Notes

1 Putnam (1993, p.89) includes economic associations as part of his indices of "civicness".
2 Eurostat, 2011. Labour Market Participation by Sex and Age, available at: http://epp.eurostat.ec.europa.eu/statistics_explained/index.php/Labour_market_participation_by_sex_and_age
3 Italy: Education and Gender roles, available at http://family.jrank.org/pages/979/Italy-Education-Gender-Roles.html
4 L'occupazione femminile: Il Ritardo dell'Italia Rispetto all'Europa. Available at: www.politicheeuropee.it/newsletter/17076/loccupazione-femminile-il-ritardo-dellitalia-rispetto-alleuropa
5 *Corriere della Sera*, 03/06/2012.
6 "Il Fisco alla Guerra dei Trent'Anni," *Corriere della Sera*, available at: www.corriere.it/economia/11_dicembre_12/rizzo-fisco-guerra-30-anni_abafc754-2495-11e1-8d41-b588752759fb.shtml
7 *Corriere della Sera*, 13/10/2011.

References

Abravanel, R. (2009) *Meritocrazia*. Milano: Garzanti.
Abravanel, R. and D'Agnese, L. (2010) *Regole*. Milano: Garzanti.
Banfield, E.C. (1958) *The Moral Basis of a Backward Society*. Glencoe: Free Press.
Bardone, L. and Reitano, V. E. (2009) Italy in the Euro Area: The Adjustment Challenge. In: M. Buti (ed.). *Italy in EMU: The Challenges of Adjustment and* Growth. London: Palgrave, pp. 37–80.
Bastasin, C. (2012) *Saving Europe*. Washington, DC: Brookings Institution.
Becker, J. and Jager, J. (2011) European Integration in Crisis: the Centre-Periphery Divide. Paper presented at the 17th Euromemo Workshop on Alternative Economic Policy. Available at: www2.euromemorandum.eu/uploads/ws5_becker_jaeger_european_integration_in_crisis._the_centre_periphery_divide.pdf.

Bellofiore, R., Garibaldo, F., and Halevi, J. (2011) The Global Crisis and the Crisis of European Neomercantilism, *Socialist Register*, 49, pp. 120–146.
Bibee, A. (2009) The OECD View. In: M. Buti (ed.). *Italy in EMU: The Challenges of Adjustment and Growth.* London: Palgrave, pp. 195–209.
Boeri, T (2009) Comment on Chapter 3. In: M. Buti (ed.). *Italy in EMU: The Challenges of Adjustment and Growth.* London: Palgrave, pp. 117–121.
Buti, M. (ed.) (2009) *Italy in EMU: The Challenges of Adjustment and Growth.* London: Palgrave.
Catricala, A. (2010) *Zavorre D'Italia.* Milano: Rubbettino.
Cazzaniga, G. (1994) Sulle Cause Morali della Corruzione. In: L. Barca & S. Trento (eds). *L'Economia della Corruzione*. Roma-Bari: Laterza, pp. 33–47.
Cobianchi, M. (2011) *Mani Bucati*. Milano: Chiarelettere.
De Cecco, M. (2007) Italy's Dysfunctional Political Economy. *West European Politics,* 30(4), pp. 763–783.
Della Porta, D. (1992) *Lo Scambio Occulto*. Bologna: Il Mulino.
Della Porta, D. and Vanucci, A. (1994) *Corruzione Politica e Amministrazione Pubblica.* Bologna: Il Mulino.
Della Porta, D. and Vanucci, A. (1999) *Un Paese Anormale*. Roma-Bari: Laterza.
Della Sala, V. (2004) The Italian Model of Capitalism: On the Road between Globalization and Europeanization? *Journal of European Public Policy*, 11(8), pp. 1041–1057.
Di Stefano, P. "Compiacersi dei difetti: Un vezzo tutto Italiano," *Corriere della Sera* 27 December 2013.
Dooley, N. (2014) Growing Pains? Rethinking the Immaturity of the European Periphery. *Millennium Journal of International Studies* 42(3), pp. 936–946.
Ferrera, M. "Se il Fattora D Restaun Acessorio," *Corriere della Sella* 6 March 2012: 1.
Ferrera, M. and Gualmini, E. (1999) *Rescued by Europe?* Amsterdam: Amsterdam University Press.
Fotia, M. (1997) *Le Lobby in Italia*. Bari: Dedalo.
Garrone, A. G. (1996) *L'Italia Corrotta*. Roma: Riuniti.
Gilbert, M. (1998) In Search of Normality: the Political Strategy of Massimo D'Alema. *Journal of Modern Italian Studies*, 3(3), pp. 307–317.
Ginsborg, P. (2003) *Italy and its Discontents*. New York: Palgrave Macmillan.
Ippolito, R. (2008) *Evasori: Chi, Come, Quanto*. Milano: Bompiani.
Lapalombara, J. (1964) *Interest Groups in Italian Politics*. Princeton, NJ: Princeton University Press.
Leopold, A. (2009) The IMF Perspective. In: M. Buti (ed.). *Italy in EMU: The Challenges of Adjustment and* Growth. London: Palgrave, pp. 210–219.
Levi Franco, R. "I Dubbi del Fondo Monetario Sulle Riforme Strutturali," *Corriere della Sera,* 28 April 2015: 31.
Mansbridge, J. (1997) Social and Cultural Causes of Dissatisfaction with the US Government. In: J. S. Nye, P. D. Zelikow, and D. C. King (eds). *Why People Don't Trust Government*. Cambridge: Harvard University Press, pp. 133–154.
Mazarr, M. "The Rise and Fall of the Failed State Paradigm: Requiem for a Decade of Distraction," *Foreign Affairs* January/February Issue 2014.
Paci, M. (1996) Ceti Emergenti, Aree Territoriali e Mobilitazione Politica. In: N. Negri and L. Sciolla (eds). *Il Paese dei Paradossi*. Roma: La Nuova Italia Scientifica, pp. 230–245.
Padoa-Schioppa, F. (1990) *L'economia Sotto Tutela*. Bologna: Il Mulino.
Piattoni, S. (2007) *Le Virtue del Clientelismo*. Roma-Bari: Laterza.

Pizzorno, A. (1996) Vecchio e Nuovo nella Trasizione Italiana. In: N. Negri and L. Sciolla (eds). *Il Paese dei Paradossi*. Roma: La Nuova Italia Scientifica.

Prevelakis, G. (2012) Greece: the History behind the Collapse. *Eurozine,* Available at: www.eurozine.com/articles/2011-12-23-prevelakis-en.html.

Putnam, R. D. (1993) *Making Democracy Work: Civic Traditions in Modern Italy*. Princeton, NJ: Princeton University Press.

Rodota, S. (1994) Su Alcune Ragioni Istituzionale Della Corruzione. In: L. Barca and S. Trento (eds). *L'Economia della Corruzione*. Roma-Bari: Laterza, pp. 21–32.

Sapelli, G. (1993) *Sul Capitalismo Italiano*. Milano: Feltrinelli.

Scharpf, F. W. (2011) Monetary Union, Fiscal Crisis, and the Pre-emption of Democracy. Paper presented at the LEQS Annual Lecture 'Saving the Euro – at the expense of democracy in Europe?' on 12 May 2011 at the London School of Economics.

Sciolla, L. (2003) Quale Capitale Sociale? *Rassegna Italiana Di Sociologia*, 2, April-June Issue, pp. 257–282.

Sciolla, L. (2004) *La Sfida Dei Valori*. Bologna: Il Mulino.

Tamburello, S. "L'Italia Deve Salvarsi da Sola," *Corriere della Serra* 13 October 2011: 14.

Tanzi, V. (2009) Comments on Chapter 4. In M. Buti (ed.). *Italy and EMU: The Challenges of Adjustment and Growth*. London: Palgrave, pp. 185–194.

Toci, W. (1994) Partiti, Finanza e Mattone. In: L. Barca and S. Trento (eds). *L'Economia della Corruzione*. Roma-Bari: Laterza, pp. 119–134.

Triglia, C. (1995) Dinamismo Privato, Disordine Pubblico. In: N. Negri and L. Sciolla (eds). *Il Paese dei Paradossi*. Roma: La Nuova Italia Scientifica, pp. 168–187.

Tullio-Altan, C. (1999) *Gli Italiani in Europa*. Bologna: Il Mulino.

World Economic Forum 2010 Global Gender Gap Report, available at: www.weforum.org/reports/global-gender-gap-report-2010.

Zingales, L. (2015) Solo l'Unione politica permette scelte economiche democratiche. Il Sole 24 Ore. Available at: www.ilsole24ore.com/art/commenti-e-idee/2015-03-07/solo-unione-politica-permette-scelte-economiche-democratiche—094706.shtml?uuid=ABD87h5C.

6 The euro and relative status

One of the principle ways in which Europeanists have investigated the relationship between national identity and European integration is the strong/weak identity framework. The idea is that strong forms of national identity – with Britain usually the archetype – are not conducive to integration because they produce the belief that only the nation-state can legitimately exercise sovereignty. Conversely, those countries with a "weak" identity – and here, Italy is often cited as an emblematic case – are more open to integration because it is presumed that there is a more flexible and open collectively held conception of the nation-state (Berezin 2009). In this framework the causal arrow runs from the nation to the international system: the focus is on how national identity affects policies towards European integration. But comparatively fewer Europeanists explore the causal dynamics that flow in the other direction, that is, how international events like European integration impact national identity. There is a huge literature on the ways in which European integration impacts national institutions and economies, but the question of how national identities are impacted does not enjoy as much attention.

The question then becomes: how does European integration influence identity? Perhaps it depends on the country. For example, when Greece joined the European project, many Greeks perceived it as entering Western modernity and permanently leaving the "backwardness" of the Balkans. When Spain "entered Europe" it was perceived as a distancing from the backwardness of the Franco era and a move towards "modernity" in the form of democracy. A similar dynamic was certainly present when the former countries of the Soviet Union joined the EU: it was necessary to consolidate their status as Western, liberal democratic nations. "Entering Europe" had many concrete advantages and benefits, but the symbolic elements were just as important in giving a sense of psychological security and national pride, as it symbolized a move away from "backwardness" towards "modernity".

One important element of identity that is influenced by European integration is the collective perception of the relative status of the nation. Perceptions of relative status flow from the fact that one of the main features of international order is hierarchy: nations define themselves, and are defined by others, by their place on the international pecking order. Entering Europe, for many nations, is perceived as a shift upwards on this pecking order. But there is often a disjuncture between the real, objective relative status of a nation and the perceived relative status that nationalized individuals believe their country enjoys.

This distinction between real and perceived national status is important for investigating nationalized individuals' exaggerated beliefs about the impact that "entering Europe" can have on the relative status of their nation. This precisely describes the case study that will be the focus of this chapter: Italy. Specifically, Italy entering the European Monetary Union in 1999. Italians had to make many sacrifices to enter, and politicians, to build support for these sacrifices, propagated narratives that did not correspond with the actual policy. Entering the euro was framed as "entering Europe" even though Italy was one of the founders of the European project and its belongingness to Europe was not predicated on whether or not it entered the first round of euro countries. But more importantly, entering the euro, it was perceived, would upgrade Italy's second-tier status in Europe. Many Italians perceived that the relegation of their country to second-class status – compared to the first-class status enjoyed by Germany, France, and the UK – was unjust, especially in light of Italy's traditional euro-enthusiasm among both its elites and non-elites, its relative weight in terms of absolute and per-capita GDP (more on that below), and because it was one of the founders of the project. Entering the euro, it was perceived, would equalize this inequality. And so when Italy entered, there was initially a widespread sense that the country had indeed entered the league of Europe's elite countries.

But there was one problem with this perception: it was wrong. Why? Because entering EMU did not fundamentally change Italy's relative status compared to Europe's elite countries. In other words, Italians' perceptions of their relative status did not comport with the objective relative status of the nation vis-à-vis Europe's elite countries. Entering the euro was a significant achievement, but this was not sufficient to change its relative status, because in Europe, a nation's relative status depends on a host of other variables. The size of the economy is an important variable, but so is the quality of this economy: how modern it is, its levels of inequality, social mobility, and corruption. One could add technological sophistication and socio-political-bureaucratic organization. Individually, these things might not make a difference, but together they do. To change all of them in a way that raises the status of a country takes years, even decades, and, in terms of a nation's relative status, cannot be substituted by entering a monetary union.

This perception among Italians in the shift of the country's relative status was brief; it eventually became clear that the country did not really enter the club of elite nations. This raises the question: why was there a shift in perceptions that did not correspond with the objective hierarchy that remained largely unchanged in Europe? Answering that question requires an analysis of the difference between hierarchy as it is *perceived* and as it is *performed*, which will be the focus of this chapter.

Addressing this question is important because it is useful to highlight the nexus between mass perceptions and international relations. The international system is very complex, even for scholars, and most domestic actors interpret, filter, and construct it in ways that are influenced by their level of knowledge, their ideology, their circumstances, and their desires. Policymakers and politicians who conduct foreign policy have to build at least some democratic support for their decisions, and they have to appeal to the mass perceptions and desires of their constituents. In this sense, the political narratives that are propagated by elites must be strategic and selective. They must be based on culturally and psychologically compelling ideas that appeal to many citizens. But, as this chapter will show, this strategic discursiveness has a negative side effect: it obscures the real structures of power in the international system, which is characterized by hierarchy, competition, and relative gains that confer privileges to some nations and losses to others.

Discourse is the key variable that determines this misperception of relative status. A key element of discourse that will be examined is intergroup comparison. As scholars of nationalism, social psychologists, and constructivists have demonstrated, the identity of the nation relies in large part on comparisons of the collective Self with some collective Other. For instance, many Italians compare their nation (the Self) with "Europe" (the Other). "Europe" embodies the things that are perceived to be absent in Italy: normality, equality, modernity, freedom. When Italy entered EMU, this distinction became blurred for many. Many felt that this event represented a watershed for the development of the nation: it demonstrated its European credentials, it showed that it can rise up to the task, it became more "European". This blurring of the Self and Other properties transformed, at least temporarily, the construction of the national Self, as many perceived that Italy was one of Europe's top-tier nations. Social psychologists have recognized this dynamic at the nexus between the individual and the group: the individual often defines his individual status, not on the basis of his personal material achievements, but on the basis of the group to which he belongs. This chapter applies this concept to the nexus between different groups rather than between the individual and the group: how individuals define their group's status often depends on perceived assimilation with other groups.

In this case study, adopting the euro was not perceived simply as entering a monetary union. It was initially perceived to have shifted Italy's place in the European pecking order because, for many Italians, entering EMU meant that Italy was now more "European" in the sense that it was up to the standards of Europe's top-tier countries.

* * * * * *

Some elites perceived that Italy's entering the euro meant that it was no longer an "abnormal" country (Chevallard 2008, p. 50). "Abnormal", in Italy's discursive political universe, is another way of saying not normal, "normal" meaning the European ideal discussed above, which is associated with Europe's elite countries. For Chevallard and many others, the election of Berlusconi was a turning point which undermined this illusion and demonstrated that Italy was still, compared to "Europe", an "abnormal" country (ibid., p. 50), while for others the image of Italy as a country of Serie A remained.[1]

This belief was reflected in the media as well. In January 1999, right after Italy entered the euro, journalists from the RAI went out in public and interviewed citizens, asking them about their views on the new currency. For many, the meanings associated with the currency were strictly monetary, in the sense that it was simply a new medium of exchange with which to go shopping. But for many others there were extra-monetary meanings, as demonstrated by this interview:

Journalist: The euro creates a unity and makes us [Europeans] feel like a common people, it is a revolution in Italy.

Respondent: Yes . . . using the same currency means also feeling *that we are equal* because when we go to France and Germany . . .

("Entrando nell euro", aired on RAI 9 January 2001)

The key idea here is that the euro produced feelings of equality among European nations. As the data below will further show, the bias is upward, in the sense that equality is important not because it creates a sense of parity with, say, Spain, but because it does so with the euro's elite countries like France and Germany. These exaggerated beliefs about what the euro could do to impact Italy's relative status manifested itself in other ways in the media. After Italy entered the euro, Prime Minister Prodi went on the air to give a congratulatory speech to the nation where he presented the event in the following way:

> Accompanying Italians in Europe [note the conflation of EMU with Europe] means fixing the country economically, financially, and politically . . . we must look towards the South . . . the relationship between the Christian world and the Muslim world, and here, Italy has the obligation to promote peace, and if we were not in Europe, we would not be able to carry out this obligation . . . today we are stronger and with a new dignity.
>
> ("Dichiarazione di Prodi", aired on RAI May 2 1998)

The meanings associated with the euro in this speech are "strength" and "influence." This sense of new strength and influence was extended to the belief that entering "Europe" for Italy would be a harbinger of geo-political change that would help to bridge the differences between Europe and the Muslim world. Needless to say, the euro had no such effect, nor could it, because Italy's capacity to bridge the differences between the Muslim world and Europe did not rest on its capacity to enter the first round of euro countries. It strains credulity to think, for example, that leaders in Tunisia, Saudi Arabia, Iran, and Egypt would be more influenced by Italy because it was now part of a wider currency union. Rather, it is more likely that those Muslim countries would be more influenced by military power and economic strength, neither of which have much to do with the euro. But this belief in increased influence was held because of the extra-monetary meanings that were associated with the euro. It was believed that entering would increase the country's relative status and influence in the unequal inter-state pecking order.

Sentiments that equated the country's ostensible increase in relative status and condition with the adoption of the euro were discovered elsewhere. For example, Walter Veltroni, former leader of the Partito Democratico, said that "only now that Italy has the euro has the country achieved international prestige" (*Corriere della Sera* 04/05/1998). Or from Romano Prodi: "Italians understood that the euro was a great moment in history . . . it meant going with modern nations or staying behind" ("Frontiere", aired on RAI on 07/12/2002). A similar belief was expressed by some from my interview sample.

From a merchant:

Me: What are Italy's problems compared to other European countries?
Reply: There are no major differences . . . after the euro, we adapted ourselves to other European countries . . . we are equal to them.

From a surveyor:

Me: Why was entering Europe important?
Reply: Because it was important to put ourselves closer to Germany and France, which were more ahead.

From a lawyer:

Me: Did your perception of Italy change after it entered the euro?
Reply: In the beginning it was among the most important countries, behind Germany and Britain but at the same level as France.

From a regional councillor:

Me: Did your perception of Italy change after it entered the euro?
Reply: In that period there was a perception of the country as advanced.

Humour that only national audiences can understand is also a good source of those symbols that pertain to the intersubjective universe of the nation. Humour also often reveals uncomfortable truths that are made palatable because they are expressed in jests. It often penetrates the psychological defences that prevent people from saying things that many believe but that few would openly express. I found one of these jokes on "Mister Euro", moderated by Alan Friedman, aired on 8 January 2002. The show is characterized by a panel of politicians, union and business leaders, and other members of the ruling class who are interviewed by Friedman and who debate one another on the serious matters surrounding the euro. But the show aims to inject humour through one of the characters, who, in this case is the well-known Italian actress/comedian Syusy Blady. In one of her comedic skits, she goes on a tangent about the euro and then says, "*For once we are like the Germans*, with the same currency!" The euro here meant more than just a new currency with which to go shopping; it was another way of saying, "for once Italy is up to the standards of Germany". This allusion to Germany is not a coincidence: it highlights the upward bias of intergroup comparison. For lower-status groups, it is important to feel equality with higher-status groups. Germany is also the country that is the ideal for most Italians when they engage in the social comparisons that reify the perceived defects that the Italian nation-state possesses. This is confirmed by my own survey data. Out of 253 subjects, 186 responded to the open-ended question "Do you think Italy should copy Europe's major countries?" A plurality said Germany, under 10% said France, 25% responded "Europe's great powers" (which includes France and Germany), around 24% said Scandinavian countries, and under 10% said English-speaking nations.

As mentioned above, a sample of newspaper articles were collected from Italy's major newspapers to provide a quantitative idea of how perceptions of Italy's relative status changed after entering the euro. The articles were coded with a simple scheme that divided them on the basis of whether they present Italy at the "same level" as Europe's elite countries, or whether they presented Italy as "inferior" to them in some way. Regarding the latter, many articles represented Italy as a member of the "Club Med" countries, a derogatory term within which is embedded the division between the virtuous Northern European countries and the non-virtuous nations of Southern Europe. Articles that represented Italy in terms of its specific problems that other nations presumably do not have were also coded with "inferior". Conversely, articles that presented Italy as a "grande paese" of Europe (which roughly translates to "great power") were coded as "same level". Other articles that were coded in the "same level" category represented Italy as sharing the same position in Europe as Germany and France, rather than, say, Spain or Portugal. The coded articles were plotted on a graph that highlights the distribution over the time period 1996–2004, and the results can be seen in the following:

The first line highlights the numbers of articles that were published that discussed the euro or the Maastricht criteria in the context of Italy's place in Europe. There is a huge spike between late 1996 and late 1997, and then again between late 1997 and 1998. There was a flurry of articles published in these periods because at the time Italy's entering EMU was very much in doubt. Comments from Dutch and German officials raised serious questions about Italy making the first round, and many of the articles are attempts to interpret this or that comment on Italy from some German or Dutch official. The second line represents the articles that depicted Italy as one of Europe's "great powers" or that expressed the notion that Italy was at the same level of Europe's elite

Table 6.1 Should Italy copy Europe's major countries? Which ones?

Germany	*France*	*Elite Countries*	*Scandinavian Countries*	*Anglo Countries*	*Nobody*
38%	**5%**	**25%**	**24%**	**8%**	**17%**

Detailed information on the sample can be found in the appendix

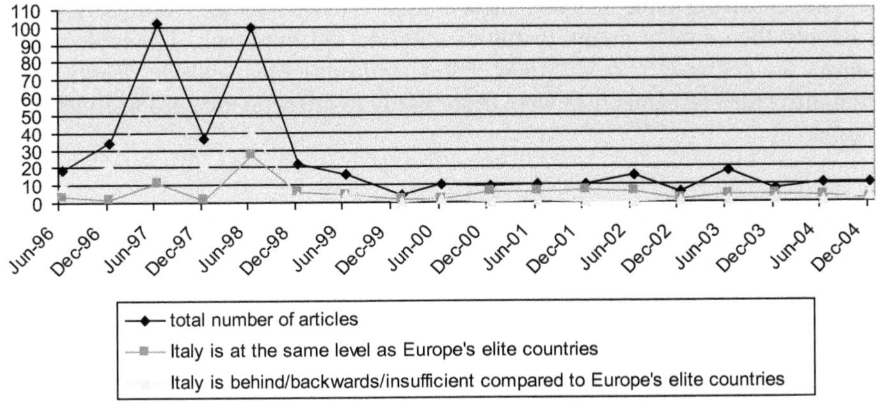

Figure 6.1 Perceptions of relative status in Italian newspapers. N: 430. *La Repubblica*: 209. *Corriere della Sera*: 221. Period: 1996–2005. Coding scheme is available upon request.

Detailed information on the sample can be found in the appendix

countries. The third line depicts the articles that represent Italy as inferior to Europe's elite countries. The graph shows a shift that begins when it became official that Italy would enter the Eurozone. By around the middle of 2000, there are slightly more articles that represent Italy as a great power at the same level of Europe's elite countries. The shift back to "inferior" starts to happen in 2004.

To get an idea of the extent to which these constructions permeated the non-elites, interview subjects were asked the question: "After Italy entered EMU, how did you perceive the country?" Like the other questions, this question was deliberately open-ended because I wanted to investigate whether, and how, perceptions of the nation-state changed after entering the common currency. The results are shown below. A plurality responded saying that they perceived the increase in prices that many Italians believe was caused by the euro. But from the perspective of this chapter, the other responses are much more interesting. Around 20% of the sample explicitly said that they perceived that Italy became equal with Germany and/or France; around 10% perceived an improvement in the quality of national institutions, while around 13% believed that "Italy improved" in a general sense (that is, without specifying exactly which way the country improved). These latter responses, which together are about 43% of the sample, perceived EMU is equalizing terms, even if they had different ideas about the way that EMU had an equalizing effect. A small portion responded saying that they felt "euphoria" after Italy entered, which attests to the emotional character for some of Italy's entering EMU, while another small portion – 10% – said that the country "worsened" but in the general sense (that is, without specifying in what way it did).

The following table aims to show which types of actors were more likely to apply the equality meme to Italy's entering the Eurozone. The table below shows the centre-left, centre-right, elites, and non-elites, and the results show that the centre-left and elites were more likely to interpret the euro in equalizing terms.

Table 6.2 After Italy entered EMU, how did you perceive the country?

Institutions improved	*Italy worsened*	*Felt Euphoria*	*Italy Improved*	*We became equals*	*Prices rose*
10%	8%	11%	13%	20%	45%

Detailed Information on the sample can be found in the appendix

Table 6.3 After Italy entered EMU, how did you perceive the country? (Left, right, elite, non-elite)

Centre-Left	
Became equals in Europe	10.66
Institutions improved	14.66
Country worsened	2.66
Euphoria	10.66
The country improved	12
We became European	10.66
Prices rose	29.33
Miscellaneous	9.37
Total	100
Centre-Right	
Became equals in Europe	0
Institutions improved	5.33
Country worsened	5.33
Euphoria	3.8
The country improved	15.38
We became European	3.84
Prices rose	46
Miscellaneous	20.32
Total	100
Elite	
Became equals in Europe	5.63
Institutions improved	22.53

Country worsened	2.81
Euphoria	12.67
The country improved	14.08
We became European	11.26
Prices rose	16.90
Miscellaneous	14.12
Total	100
Non-elite	
Became equals in Europe	7.73
Institutions improved	3.31
Country worsened	7.73
Euphoria	7.18
The country improved	9.94
We became European	6.62
Prices rose	43.64
Miscellaneous	13.85
Total	100

Detailed information on the sample can be found in the appendix

Perception and reality

The present chapter provides evidence in support of the argument that entering the Eurozone temporarily led to shifts in how Italians perceive their relative position in Europe. This section will present evidence in support of the argument that despite its adoption of the euro, Italy is objectively in the second tier in Europe's informal hierarchical structure. Before proceeding, it would be worthwhile to elaborate on the distinction between hierarchy as it is perceived and as it is performed.

In the second chapter I distinguished between 1) the hierarchy in Europe as it is perceived by many Italians, and 2) the hierarchy of status and influence in Europe. The first was identified by presenting the myriad ways in which Italians – in newspapers, TV shows, and interviews – present their nation as "behind" or "below" or "not up to the standards of" Europe. The second form, hierarchy of status and influence in Europe, is of a different species. In Europe there are several different types of hierarchy that can be analytically distinguished even if in practice they are not always mutually exclusive. 1) The influence on decisions taken in the European Union, which is a complex structure of both supranational and inter-governmental rules. In the supranational sphere, Italians have influence that is not less than others or that matches the country's actual weight relative to others. For example, members of the Eurozone each have a seat (and an equal vote) on the ECB's governing council; in the European Parliament, which allocates seats on the basis of population, Italy has as much voting power as France and the UK. Italy also has an equal vote in the Commission. However, the same cannot be said about other areas of European politics, especially the inter-governmental sphere, where Germany and France are on top and Italy is in the second tier. Establishing the relative influence of a nation in the inter-governmental sphere is difficult because bargaining takes place behind closed doors, and because policymakers keep the character of negotiations secret or obscure for reasons of domestic politics. But, as will be argued below, by exploring proxy indicators, we can infer which countries are in the first and second tier. 2) The hierarchy of material factors: population, and absolute and per-capita GDP. On this dimension, Italy is relatively close to France and thc UK. However, it does not enjoy the relative status and influence of those two nations and this may very well be the result of the next dimension. 3) The hierarchy of ideational factors that are highly valued in Europe and which are rooted in the qualitative dimensions of a country's political economy and include corruption, the credibility of the political class, economic dynamism, social equality, democratic structures, and technological sophistication. By itself this dimension may not matter much for relative influence in Europe, or Sweden would be more influential than, say, Italy or Spain. But this dimension matters for a nation's reputation and hence for its relative status when we combine it with the preceding dimension, namely, population and economic size (absolute and per-capita). In the hierarchy of the qualitative dimensions of society and economy, culture matters too, but not in the sense of the cultural treasures of the nation. In determining hierarchy, culture is important in a different sense: the beliefs and practices of its citizens which are understood to be proxies for their perceived honesty and sense of civic responsibility. The reason is that for large numbers of Europeans, the quality of nations' sociopolitical and bureaucratic organization very much depends on the national culture. This is observable in the moralistic language that is often used to describe a nation's place on Europe's pecking order. Those countries with efficient bureaucracies and credible political classes are often described as "virtuous", while those on the other end of the spectrum are often described as "lazy", "dishonest", and "irresponsible".

When Italians say that they perceive their country in the "Serie B", they may be talking about all of these dimensions, or even individual ones. For example, for many the election of Berlusconi despite all his scandals places Italy in the "Serie B"; for them, it is the political class that is determinative. For others, it is the continued exclusion by France and Germany, or the lack of social mobility, or the lack of civic culture, or some combination of these things. The general point is that this perception of inequality is real, even though inequality may mean different things to different people. This chapter argues that the perception among Italians is not without foundation, since Europe's inter-state hierarchy is objectively performed whenever Italy is excluded from the "core" or from the "leadership" of Europe.

Leaderless Europe (Hayward 2008) is a text that examines the question of hierarchy in Europe. The title of the book is misleading, because none of the contributors in the volume who explore the role of France and/or Germany in Europe actually argues that they do not possess more influence than others, including Italy. In the Preface we are told that "the reduced [but not absent] capacity of the

Franco-German tandem to offer acceptable leadership is marked by a shift in the balance of influence from French to greater German predominance *not merely in the financial sphere but more generally*" (Hayward 2008, p. vi; emphasis mine). In chapter five, we are told that "in the history of European integration, there has been both supranational and intergovernmental leadership" and that the latter "has been, to a very large extent Franco-German (Paterson 2008, p. 91). He also states that "in the years immediately following German unity" there was "an even more explicit Franco-German core" (p.104). The language of "core" suggests that others, including Italy, are part of the "periphery". This textual and discursive exclusion of Italy from being grouped together with Europe's "leaders" is present elsewhere in *Leaderless Europe* (Paterson 2008, pp. 90, 103, 107; Cole 2008, p. 161; Dimitrakopolous 2008, pp. 295, 300; Hayward 2008, p. 309). In chapter eight of *Leaderless Europe* we are reminded that "as the most significant founding fathers of the EU, France and Germany arguably count more than others" (Cole 2008, p.148), and that they dominated the agenda-setting for both the Maastricht and Amsterdam treaties (p. 152). On this basis the author makes the reasonable conclusion that France's and Germany's agreement is a necessary, but not sufficient, condition for agreement on treaties (p.153), which suggests that the consent of other states, including Italy, is neither necessary nor sufficient for these types of decisions, at least relative to the "core" countries.

Scholars disagree on the character of French and German leadership. There are two hypotheses on this question: the neorealist one (Pederson 1998), which conceives their leadership as a kind of directorate, and the weaker one, which asserts that the EU cannot progress without Franco-German cooperation. Cole (2008) provides convincing evidence that the second, weaker hypotheses is closer to reality, which would mean that their power is constrained by the other centres of power in the EU, both institutional and non-institutional.

The perceptions of scholars of Italy's relative marginalization, although important, are not the only indicators; exclusion of Italy is visible elsewhere. In 2004, it was recognized that, in the new enlarged Europe, the Franco-German couple was too restricted to provide leadership. It was proposed to the UK to join this exclusive club of "leaders". This "triumvirate" of the "Big Three" did not work out *only* because Blair was unable to secure mass support for his wish to play a leading role (Hayward 2008, p. 309). But crucially, this proposal *was not* extended to Italy even though, in terms of size, population, and economic development, Italy is comparable to the UK, and, most importantly for this chapter, *it and not the UK is part of the euro*. Italy's reaction to this attempt to produce a triumvirate is instructive. When the leaders of the "Big Three" organized meetings in Berlin in 2004 to discuss important issues like social security reform and the future of the EU, the first to sound the alarm on this exclusion of those who are not part of the "Big Three" was Italian foreign Minister Franco Frattini, who warned that "there cannot be a directorate, a divisive nucleus that would threaten European unity".[2] This sentiment was echoed by Minister of Europe Rocco Buttiglione, who after the meeting said, "Nobody in Europe is ready to be a second-class citizen".[3] Meanwhile, the leaders of Denmark, Luxembourg, and the Netherlands were not concerned at all about the "Big Three" joining to provide leadership. Poland was also sanguine about the meeting: "Better three than two," said Adam Rotfeld, undersecretary at the Polish Foreign Ministry. "These three reflect the diversity of understanding of some transatlantic problems". These disparate reactions indicate that in Italy there was a sense of insecurity about the "Big Three" meeting.

Italy was also excluded from the St. Malo process, which was an inter-governmental Franco-British initiative that was subsequently extended to include Germany (but not Italy).The debt crisis in the Eurozone has only accentuated the leadership of France and, to a greater extent, Germany. For example, the Fiscal Pact that was signed in March 2012 was essentially established by France and Germany and then presented to the other members, including Italy, as a fait accompli (Barbera & Feltri 2014). Many observers agree that to save the euro requires a banking union, Eurobonds, and a political union, and not coincidentally, a *sine qua non* for these instruments is agreement between France and Germany. It strains credulity to think that other countries' agreement or disagreement on these centralizing instruments to save the currency will be as important at France's and Germany's. Moreover, the dominant narrative of the Eurozone crisis is that it is the result of "lazy" and "corrupt" Southern European countries who lacked the willingness to make their economies more competitive and who could not control their public finances. The fact that this narrative provides the intellectual basis for the Fiscal Pact, which is intended to resolve the crisis, comes at the expense of other competing narratives. It also shows that Germany is the leader in Europe's pecking order in the economic realm, and one of the privileges of this leadership is that its narrative comes at the expense of other narratives. This hierarchy is reproduced in a multiplicity of settings, and has become even more pronounced since power has recently shifted from the Commission towards a more inter-governmentalist framework.

Italy's second-tier status can be seen elsewhere in the region's politics. The exclusion of the Italian language in Europe's patent system despite vociferous Italian opposition (patents will only be published in three languages: English, German, and French) is symbolically important for reasons of the prestige of the Italian language. But it also important indicator of Italian influence. For example, another alternative on the table, endorsed by Italy, was to make English the only language for the patent system,[4] an eminently reasonable compromise in light of the status of English as a global language of commerce and science. But France and Germany rejected this proposal for the obvious reason that it would lower the prestige of their own respective languages. Their demands became policy. Italy's did not.

Italy's exclusion can also be seen in the realm of international security. The country was excluded from the important meetings and conference calls during the recent conflicts in Libya (even though Italy played a strategically crucial part in the operations) and Ukraine (even though it has deep and influential ties to Russia), and from the "E-3" – the European nations, Germany, France, and the UK, actively working with the US and Russia to dissuade Iran from building nuclear weapons (Dimitrakopolous 2008, p. 300), even though Italy is one of Iran's most important European trading partners. This raises the question: why would Italy be excluded from these groupings? One can understand why France and the UK would be included, since both have seats on the Security Council and make significant investments in their militaries. But this cannot be said about Germany, and yet this country is invited to be a part of the "Big Three", while Italy is not.

Let's examine Italy's relative status in terms of the qualitative dimensions of its political economy. Recently, former EU Commissioner of Energy Gunther Ottinger, when asked about Italy, responded "Italians? They are like Bulgarians and Romanians" (*Corriere della Sera* 30/05/2013). Subsequently, there was the predictable ambiguous response from the German government, which said that "the German government would never express such views about Italy" (note that is not a denial of Ottinger's belief). These comments were made after Italy had chosen Enrico Letta as Prime Minister. He is a moderate, very Europeanist leader, but his premiership is the result of inconclusive elections that took place in February 2013. For many in Europe, especially in Germany, this election – where Berlusconi and a populist comedian together obtained more than half the vote – was a confirmation of the country's dysfunctional politics and/or institutions. Hence the comparison with corrupt, undeveloped countries like Bulgaria and Romania.

This image of Italy as dysfunctional is a not only held by the EU Commissioner and the German government. Majorities in Europe feel the same, as can be seen in Table 6.4:

Table 6.4 Which is the most corrupt country in Europe?

According to citizens in:	*The most corrupt European country is:*
Britain	Italy
France	Italy
Germany	Italy
Spain	Spain/Italy
Italy	Italy
Greece	Greece

Stereotypes of Europe. Available at: www.economist.com/blogs/graphicdetail/2012/05/greeks-say-they-are-hardest-working-european-nation

This coincides with other indicators which show that, despite entering the euro, Italy's political economy did not improve.

These data show that on a range of qualitative dimensions of the political economy, Italy has not improved since entering EMU, and/or it is well below its peers. Hence the beliefs expressed by the EU commissioner, the German government, and majorities in Europe are not without foundation. This likely does not matter for the country's influence in the supranational sphere of European governance; but it may help to explain the exclusions of Italy in the other areas of European politics mentioned above. This is because hierarchy in Europe is likely based on a complex interplay between material and ideational factors that have little to do with whether a country belongs to a prestigious currency union. The

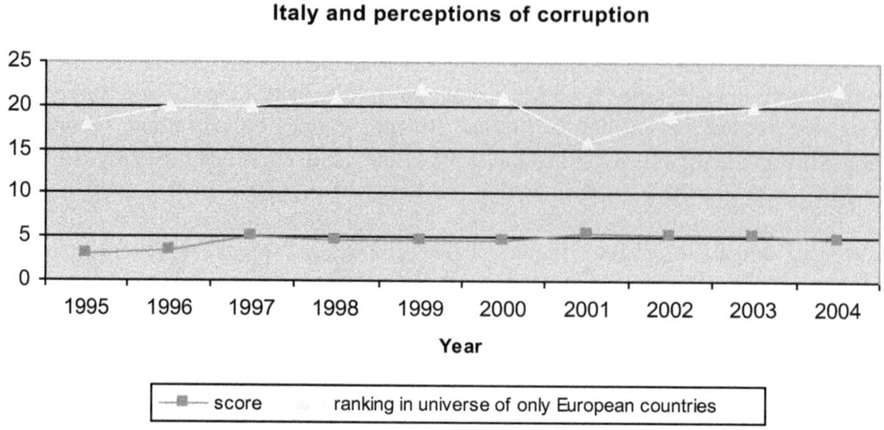

Figure 6.2 Italy and perceptions of corruption. Index survey of Italy. Score of 10 refers to least corrupt, score of 0 refers to most corrupt. Available at: Transparency International Archives. Availableat :http://archive.transparency.org/policy_research/surveys_indices/cpi

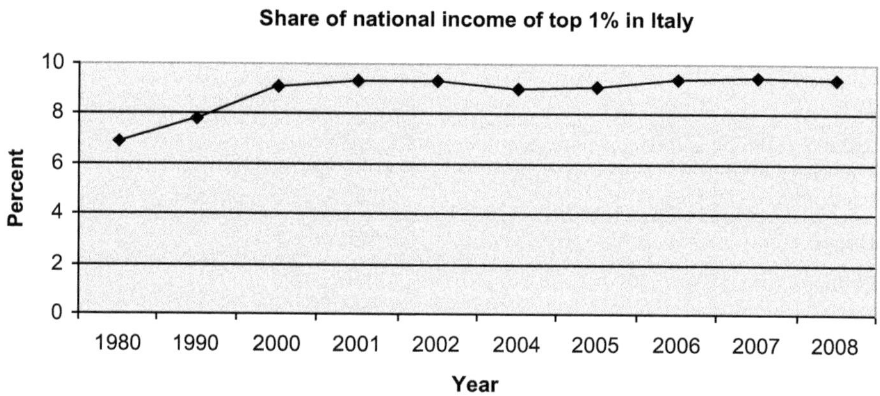

Figure 6.3 Share of national income of top 1% in Italy.

Source: OECD. Available at www.oecd.org/italy/49177743.pdf

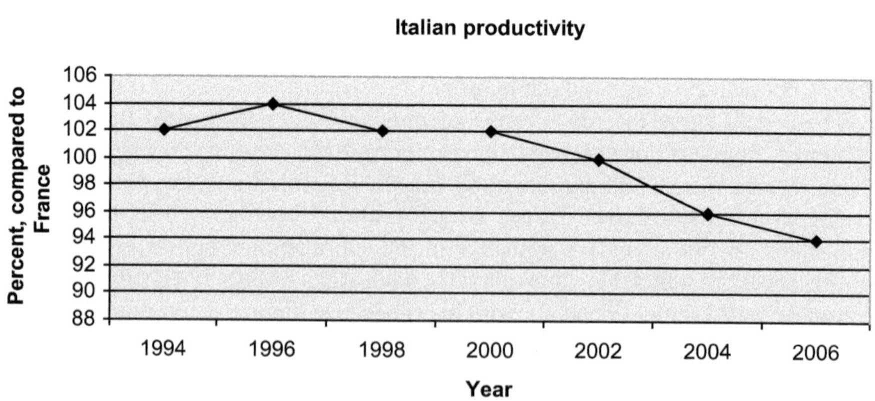

Figure 6.4 Italian productivity

Source: http://krugman.blogs.nytimes.com/2012/11/26/whats-the-matter-with-italy/

Table 6.5 Ease of doing business, ranking: 1 equals best, 189 equals worst

	Italy	*Germany*	*France*	*UK*
2013	52	13	33	9
2014	56	14	31	8

Source: World Bank. Available at: http://data.worldbank.org/indicator/IC.BUS.EASE.XQ

Table 6.6 Ranking in Rule of Law Index, 2014

Italy	*Germany*	*France*	*UK*
29	9	18	13

Source: World Justice Project. Available at http://worldjusticeproject.org/sites/default/files/files/wjp_rule_of_law_index_2014_report.pdf

material factors are mostly population and economic size (absolute and per-capita GDP). The ideational elements derive from the values that have a high priority in Europe: the quality of a nation's culture, bureaucracy, political class, economic dynamism, social mobility, equality, etc. This framework helps to explain why Italy, which has a population and GDP, in absolute and in per-capita terms, that is relatively close to France and the UK, is often relegated to second-class status. Unlike France and the UK, Italy is perceived to be part of the "Club Med" countries, with all the negative connotations that are associated with that label. It is perceived, not entirely inaccurately, to have higher levels of inequality, corruption, and general socio-bureaucratic and economic inefficiency than other nations with comparably sized economies. It is also perceived to have a corrupt and not-credible political class compared to others. These ideas often rely on simplistic stereotypes and caricatures, but they are not divorced from the facts.

One may contest the argument that there exists an informal hierarchy in Europe because of the character of the European Union, which institutionally is a polycentric consociational structure where power is diffused differently across different policy sectors and circumstances, and where different coalitions can be more or less influential depending on the character of the decision. For instance, in the Council, Hix (2005) has identified a number of coalitions, like the Nordic bloc and the Benelux coalition, that can strongly influence the Franco-German couple. Others have made a similar observation (Selck & Kaeding 2004), arguing that the UK can often be more influential than the Franco-German couple, and that France often exerts power, not with Germany, but as a leader of Mediterranean countries. Moreover, both France and Germany are constrained by the public opinion of small nations, like Denmark, which, as demonstrated by the referendum on the constitutional treaty, can have a decisive impact on Europe (Cole 2008, p.155). However, these qualifications only show that the Franco-German couple does not always exercise hegemony, and that its leadership is more contingent and intermittent, not that it is absent.

One may also challenge the argument on the grounds of complexity: there are many types of hierarchy in Europe, and it is natural that some countries would have different positions in different hierarchies. For example, militarily, France and Britain are clearly on the first tier compared to others because both have seats on the Security Council, both make significant investments in their militaries, and both have demonstrated a willingness to use force (compared to the pacifism of Germany). Meanwhile, Germany has become much more powerful in recent years because its size, population, economic weight in terms of absolute and per-capita GDP, low unemployment, technological sophistication, and social mobility has made it a first among equals, especially since the Eurozone crisis. Furthermore, a country like Italy has significant weight in the supranational sphere of governance, and one might argue that this makes up for its relative weakness in the inter-governmental sphere. These points may qualify, but they do not undermine the evidence mentioned above, for several reasons. First, despite the complexity of different types of hierarchy, the data presented in the previous chapters show that many Italians are acutely aware of their second-tier status compared to Europe's elite countries. Second, the exclusion of Italy from Europe's "core", the statistical data on corruption and indicators of economic dynamism, and the views expressed above by the EU commissioner, the German government, and majorities in Europe indicate that the perceptions held by Italians of their relative position in Europe are not without foundation.

Notes

1 Personal interview, Member of Italian Parliament, Partito Democratico, 15 Oct 2010.
2 BBC News, 18 Feb 2004. Available at http://news.bbc.co.uk/2/hi/europe/3500949.stm
3 Christian Science Monitor, 10 Feb 2004. Available at: www.csmonitor.com/2004/0210/p01s04-woeu.html
4 European Voice, 7 June 2006. See www.europeanvoice.com/article/imported/we-will-reject-white-elephant-patent-system-bosses-warn/55267.aspx

References

Barbera, A. and Feltri, N. (2014) *La Lunga Notte Dell'Euro*. Milano: Rizzoli.

Berezin, M. (2009) *Illiberal Politics in Neoliberal Times*. Cambridge: Cambridge University Press.

Chevallard, G. (2008) *L'Italia Vista dall'Europa: Testimonianza da Bruxxells*. Milan: Rubbettino.

Claudio, L and Meletti, M. "Ulivo, L'Europa Diventa Festa di Piazza," *Corriere della Sera*, 4 May 1998: 5.

Cole, A. (2008) Franco-German Relations: From Active to Reactive Cooperation. In: J. Hayward (ed.). *Leaderless Europe*. Oxford: Oxford University Press, pp. 147–166.

Dichiarazione di Prodi, aired on RAI: 2 May 1998.

Dimitrakopoulos, D. G. (2008). Collective Leadership in Leaderless Europe: A Skeptical View. In: J. Hayward (ed.). *Leaderless Europe*. Oxford: Oxford University Press, pp. 288–304.

Frontiere, aired on RAI: 07 December 2002.

Hayward, J. (2008) *Leaderless Europe*. Oxford: Oxford University Press.
Hix, S. (2005) *The Political System of the European Union*, 2nd edition. Basingstoke: Palgrave.
Lepri, P. "Il Commissario Tedescho: Siete Ingovernabili," *Corriere della Sera* 30 May 2013.
Paterson, W. E. (2008) Did France and Germany Lead Europe? A Retrospect. In: J. Hayward (ed.). *Leaderless Europe*. Oxford: Oxford University Press, pp. 89–112.
Pederson, T. (1998) *Germany, France and the Integration of Europe: A Realist Interpretation*. London: Pinter.
Selck, T. J. and Kaeding, M. (2004) Divergent Interests and Different Success Rates: France, Germany, Italy and the United Kingdom in EU Legislative Negotiations. *French Politics*, 2(2), pp. 81–94.
Venturini, F. "Crediblita' Necessaria," *Corriere Della Sera*, 04 May1998: 1

7 Splendid isolation: the UK and the euro

> Some Noble Lords . . . have always believed that the euro was a flawed project from the start which was bound to fail. Therefore, what has happened in the Eurozone over the past year or so has merely confirmed their original, brilliant judgement and there has been a certain amount of Schadenfreude going around.
>
> Lord Giles Radice, House of Lords Debate, Feb 16 2012

Many of the euro's critics in the UK did, in fact, predict with impressive accuracy what has transpired since 2010: the transfer of resources from the North to the South in the form of bailouts, higher unemployment and lower economic growth in the periphery, and the rise of xenophobic nationalism. Some would argue that this accurate prediction among many in the UK reflects certain characteristics of Britain's approach to the EU: unlike other member states, Britain has no idealistic or emotional attachment to the European project, which allows the country to evaluate integration initiatives on the basis of only the cold, hard facts (Geddes 2004, p. 4; Ludlow 2002, p. 107). On this account, Britain approaches the EU on the basis of the objective national interest and eschews the ideological, affective, and normative impulses that govern other states' relations with the EU.

This narrative has a grain of truth. Many in the UK who did predict the current crisis were able to do so, in part, because they were not blinded by the idealistic and affective attachments that were present in other countries, like Italy, which during the late nineties worked frantically to ensure that it was part of the euro's first round. But this narrative also suffers from the fallacy of composition. The accurate prediction of many eurosceptics in the UK does not mean that their approach to Europe is emblematic of most of the country. For example, many Britons, including Lord Giles Radice, were, and still are, in favour of the UK's entering the euro. Thus the views of the British towards the euro are more nuanced and complex than the above suggests.

This chapter will compare Britain with Italy. An important difference between the two is different interpretations of the relative status and condition of their respective nations, especially vis-à-vis Germany and France. Whereas in Italy there was a sense that the country is "weaker" or "below", in Britain it was (and is) widely believed that the country is "superior" or "equal" to Germany and France. Another important difference is between elites and non-elites. British elites were fiercely divided on the euro and the masses were overwhelmingly opposed. Some Conservatives, many Labourites and most Liberal Democrats were in favour, but they lost the debate, and were unable to convince the public of the merits of entering. In Italy, meanwhile, there was a consensus between elites and non-elites on the need to enter. Investigating these differences requires a comparison of the discourses in each country. Previous chapters evaluated Italian discourses, and this chapter will do the same for the UK, relying on the following sources of evidence: parliamentary debates on the euro, a media analysis of a sample of articles published in *The Guardian* and the *Daily Express*, news reports from the BBC, Eurobarometer public opinion data, and interviews I conducted with three prominent members of the British elite: Lord Howard Flight, a currency specialist and eurosceptic who is leading a campaign for the UK to leave the EU; Lord Giles Radice, a noted euro-enthusiast who has written extensively on British-EU relations and who has campaigned for establishing closer ties between them; and Philip Stephens, a cautiously pro-European columnist for the *Financial Times*, the paper that is read daily by much of the British and Brussels establishment.

The exchange rate mechanism (ERM)

An analysis of Britain's approach to the common currency should start with the ERM, the system which preceded the euro. Both Italy and the UK joined, in part, because they hoped that it would bring stability to their exchange rates and to levels of inflation. Before entering the ERM, both countries had bouts of inflation and volatile exchange rates, and it was believed that this instability could be ameliorated by tying their currencies to the Bundesbank. Politically, though, there were differences between the countries. In Italy there was wide support, not only across the political spectrum, but also among major interest groups, some of whom saw ERM as a mechanism to promote domestic interests. For example, Confindustria promoted the ERM because they hoped to constrain the macroeconomic policy management of the central government (Talani 2000, p. 33). At the societal level there was little public debate in Britain on the merits of its entering ERM (Talani 2003). But the debate among politicians was fierce and divisive; moreover, the intra-party divisions were more salient than the inter-party ones. One third of Labour voted against the ERM, while Conservatives were roughly equally divided. Opponents of ERM in both parties attacked the government's decision to enter, but the pro-ERM forces won the day.

The ERM was the precursor to full monetary union, and one of the conditions of entering the common currency was the capacity to successfully keep the country's currency within the rigorous standards established by the Bundesbank. Both countries had difficulty with the ERM, in part, because they had to increase interest rates, which increased the value of the pound and the lira relative to other currencies. The overvalued currencies and high interest rates reduced exports, lending, and economic activity in both Italy and the UK. Had the countries retained an independent monetary policy, they could have devalued and restored competitiveness. But the ERM precluded this option. When the value of the lira and the pound threatened to go below the parameters established by the ERM, the Italian and British central banks marshalled their foreign reserves to intervene in bond markets to try to increase the value of their respective currencies. They failed, forcing a humiliating exit from the ERM. But after leaving, the values of the pound and lira plummeted, leading to an export boom and reduction in unemployment in both countries.

What is striking for the purposes of this chapter is that these similar experiences were interpreted differently in each country. Both the UK and Italy benefited economically from leaving the ERM, which could lead one to conclude that both would have interpreted the event positively. But that is not the case. In Italy it was seen as a humiliating display of its lack of European credentials. It did not reduce the country's resolve to re-enter when it could so that it could be part of the first round of countries in the common currency.

In Britain, in contrast, leaving the ERM created fierce divisions within both the Labour and Conservative parties. The effect for the Conservatives was fatal: as the party who took Britain into the ERM, their support plummeted (personal Interview, Lord Flight). And whereas Conservatives were roughly equally divided on Europe before the ERM debacle, subsequently the majority, in both the party and the grassroots, became opposed, and euroscepticism strengthened further (Personal Interview, Lord Flight). The shift in public opinion was even more marked. Whereas before Black Wednesday the British were roughly equally divided on the merits of the idea of a European common currency, after the event support plummeted to a level from which it never recovered (Geddes 2004, p. 216; Buller 2006, p. 210).

Britain and the European monetary union (EMU)

Elites

The following section will assess views at the elite level in Britain and show that, despite the divisions, there were some discernible patterns. One is that the Europhiles endorsed the euro on the basis of either economic benefits or Britain's "leadership" of Europe. Another is, unlike in Italy, Britain had an actual debate on the substantive merits of the currency. Sources of evidence for the elite level in Britain will be parliamentary debates, a sample of articles in *The Guardian*, news reports from the BBC, and interviews with elites.

First the debates that took place in the House of Commons will be examined. On 27 October 1997, Gordon Brown conveyed a statement about the government's policy on the EMU. In this statement, he states "that the essential decision on whether to enter is economic" (Gordon Brown, House of Commons Debate, 27 Oct 1997). The phrases "British economic interest" and "economic benefits" are mentioned four times in the speech. The substantive political dimensions are not mentioned even once. The only political aspect mentioned in the debate is the ambiguous condition on "whether there are constitutional objections on the grounds of sovereignty". The opposition Conservatives, who were more in tune with British public opinion, saw right through Mr. Brown's attempt to obscure or ignore the real, political dimension of the EMU. In their response to Mr. Brown, they cite Treasury documents that say that "membership of the single currency would mean centralization of financial markets" (which is exactly what is happening) and the "centralization of taxing and borrowing powers" (the latter of which is happening), as well as the "transfer of resources from prosperous countries to those that are handicapped by joining the single currency" (again, a prediction that has come to pass). Mr. Brown evaded answering these points. Rather than responding directly, Mr. Brown accused the Conservatives of being divided on the question of whether "there is a constitutional bar to membership to the common currency", and repeated his inaccurate statement that the decision on whether Britain should join was essentially economic.

In the same debate, Gordon Brown defended the government's position on the basis of the "five tests" that needed to be met if the UK was to join the common currency, which were the following:

- Whether there can be sustainable convergence between Britain and the economies of the single currency.
- Whether there is sufficient flexibility to cope with economic change.
- Whether the single currency will lead to an increase in investment.
- Whether the single currency will have a positive impact on our financial services generally.
- Lastly, whether it will lead to increases in employment.

The five tests were an attempt to frame the possibility of entering the euro in a way that would be palatable to the British public, which polls showed was overwhelmingly opposed to the single currency. This strategy was evident in another debate that took place in the House of Commons on 13 January 1999. Here, supporters of the euro justified their arguments on the basis of the "British national economic interest". Indeed, in the entire debate, this argument was expressed six times; the centralizing implications of the EMU were deliberately ignored. As in the previous debate, the opposition attacked the pro-euro MP's for ignoring these implications. And the evasiveness of the responses from some pro-euro MP's is instructive. Rather than directly responding to a question on the centralizing implications of the euro, MP Louise Ellman replied that "the government has put jobs at the top of its agenda", "that European funding has supported 1100 jobs in Britain", and that Britain's "active participation in Europe will enable us to shape policies for the benefit of the people, jobs, and the generation of wealth" (House of Commons debate, 13 January 1999).

In the same debate, other pro-euro MP's say that "it is our belief that the euro could be a huge advantage to Britain economically" and that the euro "will be acceptable to the British people only in the context of a Europe which is seen to be open, accountable, democratic, and decentralized" (MP Malcolm Bruce – Liberal Democrat). When we unpack this statement, we notice many of the patterns mentioned above. First, there is the usual emphasis on the supposed economic advantages of the euro. Then this is qualified with the proviso that the euro will be acceptable in a Europe that must be open, accountable, democratic, and decentralized. The main problem with this statement is that the EMU implied *centralization, not decentralization.*

While for Italy entering Europe was associated with equality, for many in Britain it was associated with "leadership". Malcolm Bruce, for example, lamenting the government's decision to not be part of the first round of Eurozone countries, said that the "government's failure to come to terms with the euro will undermine the prospects for exercising British leadership in Europe" (House of Commons debate, 28 Jan 1999). This was echoed in the 1997 election manifesto, where Labour explicitly says "we will give Britain leadership in Europe" (Deighton 2001, p. 311). Other political arguments expressed by Europhiles were that the currency would give Britain influence. In a House of Commons debate (27 Oct 1997), Sir Edward Heath, defending the government's pro-euro position, states that the opposition's "refusal to accept the common currency immediately" means that Britain "will lose all influence in the European Union." This "influence" argument sometimes took on a different hue, suggesting that, by integrating into Europe, Britain's power would increase vis-à-vis other, non-European great powers. Mr. Stephens told me that at the White House he was told that "Britain was a much more useful ally [to the US] in Europe than out . . . and that China pays more attention to the UK than it otherwise would because it sees Britain as a free trade voice in Europe". Radice voiced similar arguments in my interview with him, but with a much stronger focus on the increased influence with the US (Personal Interview, Lord Radice).

To get the other side of the story, I posed this influence argument to the eurosceptic Lord Howard Flight. He was particularly cynical about the idea that by establishing closer ties to Europe the UK can increase its influence in the US: "There has been pressure from the US for the UK to be a member of the EU and remain a member *on the grounds that we can help argue the US's case in Europe* (emphasis mine) . . . it is clear that America will always act in its interest whether it is in our interest or not." Real influence, eurosceptics believe, comes from having a dynamic and growing economy. In this sense, they argue, the EU reduces the UK's influence, because "being part of the EU is damaging this economy . . . it is increasingly expensive, not only our own contributions but also the extra cost of food [which results from the CAP] . . . and we import damaging regulatory constraints on our economy from Europe . . . mature economies [like the UK] if they want to compete, must remove these regulations". In order to increase the UK's influence, therefore, Lord Flight believes that it would be better to establish free trade relationships and closer ties with the Commonwealth countries, because they have better growth prospects than does Europe. Lord Flight also told me that the vast majority of Britons agree with him, because, in his words, "they can see what a f*****ng mess Europe is".

The BBC

This section will compare Britain's public broadcaster (the BBC) with Italy's (the RAI). The sample is comprised of 26 news reports from the former and 19 from the latter, all of which aired during the late-nineties and early the next century and that discussed the merits of the euro for their respective countries. These sources provide a window into the beliefs of each country's cultural and other elites, and of the messages that the TV-watching public – a huge segment of the population – heard about the common currency.

The first notable difference between the two is that in the sample of the RAI, *not one* depicted any opposition to the currency. There were several segments that criticized the euro, correctly, as being based on the monetarist philosophy that constrained the government's hand to stimulate demand, but this did not translate into a principled objection to the euro. In Italy there was a consensus among major actors that the country had to join. The BBC, on this standard, was radically different. Although generally it was favourable, it also presented balanced debates that depicted both sides of the argument, which included intellectually principled opposition to the euro. Emblematic is a debate between Neil Kinnock and John Redwood on 23 April 23 2003, with the former defending the euro on the basis of the need to have a seat at the European Central Bank, while Redwood argues (presciently) against the euro because it would be irrational for very different countries to share the same interest rate (Source – BBC News). Compare that debate with this quote found in Italy's public broadcaster from Professor of Political Economy at Luiss University, Paolo Savona, who, during an interview on the RAI on 2 September 2002, says: "The Maastricht criteria, especially that of balanced budgets, interferes in a nation-state's capacity to stimulate growth during recession . . . criticizing these parameters incurs one being labelled 'anti-European', *and this prevents real debate* about these criteria" [emphasis mine]. Despite this criticism, though, Professor Savona expresses support for Italy's adoption of currency.

Further analysis of the samples reveals that the character of the dialogue was different in other ways. In Britain, among many elites the debate was sensible, moderate, and practical. Many who defended the euro did so in a way that was based mainly on the concrete features of the currency. In Italy, in contrast, the euro was often expressed hyperbolically, or ascribed with causal powers that were not really rooted in the substantive content of the currency. For example, in a debate on the BBC on 12 December 2002, which included both supporters and those opposed to the euro, even the former side admitted that the euro is not really associated with increased investment and more financial opportunities (Source – BBC News). Compare that to Italy, where proponents argued that the euro would fix Italy's economic "backwardness" (see chapter two), enhance national dignity (see chapter six), and augment international prestige. The prescience of many in Britain was also remarkable. On 28 December 2002 The BBC presented the views of union leaders in Britain who predicted, accurately, that the euro would harm workers by constraining the hands of government to regulate labour markets and stimulate demand (Source – BBC News). Compare that with a quote from an Italian union leader being interviewed on the RAI, who said that "I always thought that the euro was the right objective . . . had we been left outside, the damage for workers and pensioners would have been enormous" (TG2 Dossier Oggi Euro 01/05/1998). Another striking difference was the fear of exclusion in Italy, the kind of which I did not detect in the BBC sample. For example, in a show aired on 21 March 1997, called *Maastricht Italia* and moderated by Allen Friedman, there is a discussion about the euro among Italy's foreign minister, and business and union representatives. Around midway into the segment, the then-German Deputy, Wolfgang Schäuble, is queried, with a tone of anxiety, on whether Germany will allow Italy to enter the euro:

Friedman:	Will Italy be allowed to enter the first round?
Schäuble:	I hope that Italy satisfies the Maastricht criteria because that is the only way to be part of the first group.
Friedman:	What about the many Germans who do not want Italy to enter the first round?
Schäuble:	I don't think that is true . . . we would be very happy if Italy met the criteria and entered.
Journalist from Il Sole 24 Ore:	There is a feeling in Germany that Italy is an obstacle to EMU going ahead.
Lamberto:	Dini [angry tone]: Just as the German deputy said, Italy will enter if it satisfies the Maastricht criteria.
Bertinotti:	[sarcastic tone]: And if Germany does not satisfy the criteria?
Dini:	We cannot allow ourselves to be excluded.
Bertinotti:	But Germany cannot be excluded, right?

This conversation is pregnant with meanings, but the main ones are Italy's fear of being excluded, as well as the recognition that the currency was determined more by German dominance rather than the Maastricht criteria. Italy's sensitivity to how Germans feel also is very revealing; it is as if the country's esteem depends on German acceptance. I found nothing remotely similar in the BBC sample. Most of the debates were on whether Gordon Brown's five tests were actually met, because it was assumed that if these tests were satisfied, Britain could enter.

Overall, the sample of the two countries' public broadcasters reveal that in Italy there was a consensus and a pressing need to enter, while Britain was divided and had an *actual* debate about the euro. It also highlights that in Italy there was anxiety about being excluded, and specifically about what Germans thought about Italians. Nothing similar was found in the BBC sample.

The Guardian

The Parliamentary debates, TV media, and interviews highlight the fierce divisions among the British elite. *The Guardian*, in contrast, is a good source for the views of British Europhile elites. Accordingly, a sample of 48 articles that were published in *The Guardian* between May 1998 and December 2002 was collected. The criterion for selection was that the article discussed the Eurozone in the context of Britain; any article that discussed any dimension of the Eurozone in a way that was divorced from British-EU relations was excluded. They were coded with a simple scheme to detect the presence and frequency of the following meanings: support or opposition for Britain's entry into the euro, reasons for support, and whether there were counterarguments present. This sample of *The Guardian* will be compared with a sample of 48 articles that were published in *La Repubblica* in Italy in the same period. *La Repubblica* was selected because it is broadly similar to *The Guardian*, in the sense that it is of the centre-left and relatively highbrow. As will be shown below, an analysis of the differences between these two papers will shed more light on the character of the elite-level pro-euro narratives that took place in Britain in the period 1998–2002.

Figure 7.1 shows that *The Guardian* was a very pro-euro paper, as the vast majority of articles were in favour of British entry. Only five articles were opposed, and many of these articles were written by Labourites who were opposed for technical reasons rather than the generalized eurosceptic sentiments that many Conservatives are known to possess. Around seven articles were balanced, in the sense that they provided both sides of the argument without giving extra space or salience to either the pro or anti side of the debate.

Table 7.1 shows that *The Guardian* and *La Repubblica* were broadly similar in their positions on the euro vis-à-vis their home countries. In the same period, most of the articles published in *La Repubblica* endorsed Italy's entry into the common currency. A similar number of articles were evenly balanced. Interestingly, *not one* article in *La Repubblica* in that period was opposed. The reason is that in Italy, unlike the UK, in the late nineties and even in the immediate post-euro period there was a consensus – among both the centre-left and centre-right, elites and non-elites – that the country belonged in the euro. There were some critical voices, but they were found on the extremes of the ideological spectrum. Most main-stream

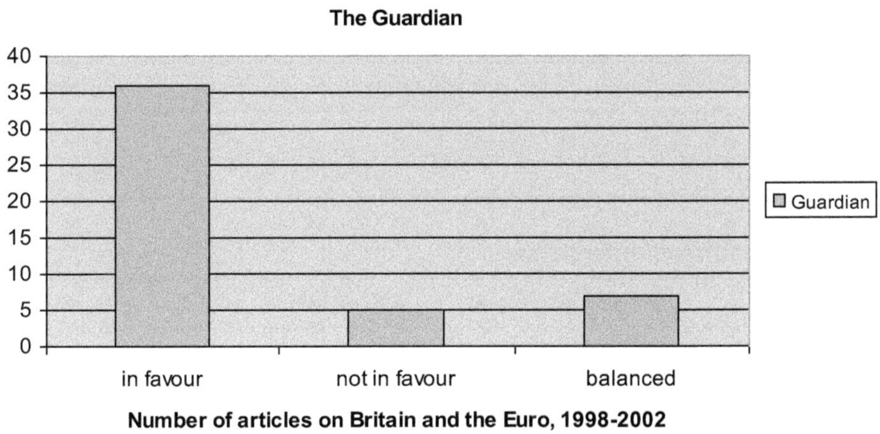

Figure 7.1 Number of articles on Britain and the Euro, 1998–2002.

political forces, and especially those on the centre-left, were unambiguously and often uncritically in favour of entering. This can be seen in Table 7.2.

All the articles were coded for the absence or presence of counterarguments, and Table 7.2 shows that the differences between the two papers are significant. Most of the pieces in *The Guardian* presented at least one counterargument, even if the writer was in favour of the euro. The reverse is true for *La Repubblica*: the vast majority were uncritically in favour of Italy's entering the common currency. This difference reflects, at least in part, some of the political dynamics of the two countries. It was the centre-left government led by Romano Prodi which brought Italy into the EMU, and *La Repubblica* was solidly in favour of both the Prodi government and the euro. Meanwhile, although the Labour government was in principle in favour of entering, there were divisions within the party, and many were opposed. Indeed, a few of the anti-euro pieces published in *The Guardian* displayed in Tables 7.3 and 7.4 were written by Labour MPs. One can imagine that these divisions played themselves out in the media in the form of more balanced arguments.

Tables 7.3 and 7.4 look at some of the reasons for support for the euro. The results of Table 7.3 show that the majority of arguments in favour of the euro

Table 7.1 Support for, and opposition to, the euro, 1998–2002

	In favour	*Not in favour*	*Balanced*
The Guardian	36	5	7
La Repubblica	38	0	10

Table 7.2 Counterarguments

	Present	*Absent*
The Guardian	31	12
La Repubblica	14	30

Table 7.3 General reasons for support

	Political	*Economic*
The Guardian	12	24
La Repubblica	17	20

Table 7.4 Specific reasons for support

	European integration	*Jobs and trade*	*Influence/Leadership*
The Guardian	0	18	12
La Repubblica	17	16	0

published in *The Guardian* were in favour for economic reasons. This follows the pattern that was found in the House of Commons debates on the euro, where economic arguments dominated over political ones. The opposite is true in Italy, where most of the arguments in favour were political in character. Table 7.4 shows the kinds of economic and political arguments that were presented. For both, economic reasons mostly referred to more jobs and trading opportunities. But their political arguments were very different. Most of the political arguments in *La Repubblica* were in favour for reasons of European integration. In contrast, in *The Guardian*, the word "integration" was rarely used, even though that is precisely what the Eurozone was. When referring to this dimension of the Eurozone, more anodyne words like "closer ties" and "partnership" and "co-operation" were used. And, as Table 7.4 shows, their political arguments were mostly about increasing Britain's influence in the international system, not only in Europe but with great powers like the US and China. This fits the pattern that was observed in the parliamentary debates, namely, wilfully ignoring the centralizing implications of the euro. Curious about this pattern, I asked Lord Radice, who, as a pro-Europe Labourite, shares many of the positions of the editorial staff of *The Guardian*:

Me: Were the pro-euro media dishonest about the [political dimensions of] euro?

Radice: They were sceptical of political union. The Dutch and French referendums showed scepticism towards political union and so I did not believe that it [the euro] would lead to political union . . . political union, especially from Germany, was mostly high-blown talk. For me it means a Stability and Growth Pact that works and is respected. It does not mean federalism, and I would not endorse federalism.

Lord Radice is one of Britain's most enthusiastic supporters of Europe. He has written many pro-Europe books, campaigned for pro-Europe causes, and defended the pro-euro case in the British Parliament. And yet his conception of political union is simply a "Stability and Growth Pact that works and is respected". This represents a significant difference with Italy, where much of the pro-euro forces were in favour because they endorsed the euro as a step towards a federal union.

The mass level

In Italy, the masses were initially overwhelmingly in favour of the currency (see chapter three). In Britain, in contrast, they were opposed. What is more, the interpretative schemes among the masses in the two countries were very different. In Britain when the euro was discussed the metaphor of war, and of being Europe's best country, were salient. Consequently, the British, unlike many Italians, do not see Brussels as the solution to their problems, nor do they see the need to have their hands tied by Europe. The sources of evidence for mass views in Britain will be the *Daily Express*, and Eurobarometer data.

The Daily Express

This tabloid is a good source for illustrating the complexities of British views at the mass level. Accordingly, a sample of 39 articles on the euro that were published between 1996 and 2004 was collected and coded to get a picture of the qualitative character of mass views towards the euro. In the late nineties the official editorial position towards the euro could be summed up as "cautious" – a "wait and see" position, or not entering unless there was clear evidence that the British economic cycle was in harmony with Europe's. The pages of the broadsheet, however, displayed fierce divisions, with some, like Andrew Marr, openly arguing in favour, while others, like Peter Hitchens and Jimmy Young, argued against.

Despite these fierce divisions, Table 7.5 shows that the majority of articles were against British entry, which parallels the distribution of attitudes towards the euro.

Table 7.5 *Daily Express* and the euro

Positive/in favour	12
Negative/against	22
Balanced	5

Table 7.6 shows that the overwhelming majority in Britain were against the euro, which is almost the exact opposite of Italy. For the purposes of this chapter, however, the qualitative portrayals of the currency were more important. For instance, the metaphors of "conflict", or the related "domination/submission" were very pronounced – out of the sample, a total of 14 articles contained a variant of it. Some examples illustrate:

- In a powerful warning to European leaders, he [John Major] condemned moves to bully countries like Britain (*The Express*, 14/12/1996).

Table 7.6 Percentage of favourable attitudes towards the euro, Britain and Italy

	Britain	*Italy*
1995	32	66
1996	31	73
1997	29	78
1998	36	88
1999	25	85
2000	21	79
2001	27	79
2002	28	76
2003	23	70

Source: Eurobarometer

- MAJOR's RAGE AT EURO PLOT (headline) . . . Premier attacks arrogant Brussels (*The Express*, 30/04/1997).
- Dark threats from Eurocrats (*The Express*, 02/12/1996).
- The Prime Minister's righteous wrath against our European partners and would be rulers (*Daily Express*, 22 April 1996).
- Europe's past lends itself to a German dominated future . . . Britain is almost alone in having survived with its honour intact (*Daily Express*, 22/04/1996).
- Euro bullies (headline): Britain vows to block the federalists (*Daily Express*, 28/05/2003).

This conception of Brussels and/or Europe as the villain and Britain as the hero is a dominant theme in other British tabloids (Deighton 2001), which have a much larger readership than do the high-brow dailies. Here, the sense of British superiority is moral in character, based as it is on its honourable history of being the only European nation to have not surrendered or capitulated to Nazi Germany. This framing of Britain's role in Europe, with all the themes of a good narrative – good, evil, conflict, struggle, victory, etc. – is given emotional salience by conveying the idea of a Manichean struggle between the British and the Continent. In this regard the selective invocation of Churchill is a particularly powerful narrative device, as is demonstrated in the following headline that appeared in the tabloids (Gowland, Turner, & Wright 2010, p. 242): "Never have so few decided so much for so many" (which is a skilful invocation of Churchill's comment, referring to the British fighter pilots who resisted the German bombing raids, that "never have so many owed so much to so few). The pro-euro press, especially high-brow publications like *The Guardian* and the *Financial Times*, could not evoke such affectively charged historical memories in their arguments in favour of the euro. They appealed to economic interest and increased influence, but this was not enough to sway the public.

Although less than half of the articles in the *Daily Express* displayed favourable views, the content of the pro-euro arguments is very revealing. Table 7.7 shows that economic benefits and "leadership of Europe" were the most prominent themes, which parallels the arguments from the parliamentary debates and *The Guardian*.

Some articles that were against the euro presented Britain as "better" than European countries and/or Brussels, not in terms of its honourable history, but rather in the sense that the UK possesses superior people or political institutions, while Europeans and their political systems are supposedly rife with corruption. For example, "our honest and trusting habits . . . [mean] . . . our officials rigorously enforce Euro-laws while, in the rest of the Union, regulations are ignored through a mixture of corruption, sloth, and cynicism" (*Daily Express* 22/04/1998). Here,

Table 7.7 Reasons for support

Economic benefits	7
Leadership of Europe	10

Table 7.8 Percentage who are not satisfied with their national democracy.

	Britain	*Italy*
1999	28	70
2000	27	62
2001	27	59

Source: Eurobarometer.

we have a significant difference with Italy; in that country, when people talk about their political system, they often depict the country as some sort of banana republic. These differences in perception between the UK and Italy can be detected in the Eurobarometer data presented in Table 7.8.

Thus the British public displays a widespread scepticism suffused with variants of the idea of superiority – either moral or based on the idea of the quality of their people and institutions. It is this that helps to explain why most of the British masses do not see Europe as the solution to their problems, which was a significant difference with Italy, where many elites and non-elites believed that Europe would solve their 'backwardness' and/or marginalization in Europe. This helps to explain why the majority of the British masses opposed the euro even if they were totally uninformed about the currency. I asked Lord Howard Flight why the majority of British were opposed to the euro even though it was likely that most of them were not informed enough to objectively and independently evaluate the pro- and anti-euro arguments. He replied that

> It is a good point in the sense that most people do not understand the arguments [about the euro] that we have been discussing . . . I think the overwhelming consensus in the UK is that we don't like being bossed around by Brussels . . . when I studied medieval history at Cambridge there was a German professor and he said that in the UK there is the great Anglo-Saxon concept of power coming up from the people which goes back to the early Germanic tribes . . . where Europe still has the descending concept of power, either down from God or the Roman Emperor, and basically these two conceptions of power sit very unhappily together . . . very clearly the Commission has the descending concept of power and thinks that it is God; that, unconsciously, is one of the reasons that the British did not support the euro.

Differences and similarities

Chapter seven highlighted the intersections between the euro and perceptions of relative status in Italy. To wit: in Italy, adopting the euro was perceived to be some sort of solution to its relatively lower condition and status. In Britain, in contrast, many Europhiles believed that the euro would give Britain "leadership" of Europe. Students of Britain's role in the European project have recognized that this idea of "leadership" of Europe reflects traces of the imperial legacy (Deighton 2001; Haseler 1996; Gowland, Turner, & Wright 2010). In this narrative, Europe is a new platform through which Britain can reclaim its lost role of "great power."

For the eurosceptics, in contrast, adopting the euro would have been perceived as a lowering of status, influence, and national esteem. For some, it would have cemented the condition of equality of status between the UK and countries like France and especially Italy, which are perceived to be lower on the international pecking order. This has a long pedigree. As far back as 1959, the President of the Board of Trade, David Eccles, spoke of Europe as a "second class club" and of British membership as a "climbdown – the engineer's daughter when the general manager's said no" (Gowland, Turner, & Wright 2010, p 58). A comment of this nature would be unthinkable among Italy's mainstream elites. More likely is a comment that is found in chapter two and bears repeating: "Without Brussels, we [Italy] would be a larger version of Lebanon".

Britain's status-consciousness is influenced by the history of Empire, which gave a sense of esteem and superiority. Hugo Young, who was one of Britain's foremost commentators and writers on British politics, began his magnum opus on Britain-Europe relations with the following sentence:

> This is the story of fifty years in which Britain struggled to reconcile *the past she could not forget* with the future she could not avoid (emphasis mine).
>
> (Young 1998, p. 1)

There were even narratives, created in the Victorian era, about features of the British that supposedly made their global empire inevitable (Stephens 2004). The country had a difficult time adapting to the reality of the loss of empire. Near the end of the Second World War there was a denial of this painful reality, coupled with delusions of grandeur (Stephens 2004). This belief persisted until the Suez crisis, when the US forced Britain to withdrawal in a humiliating manner. It subsequently became painfully obvious to many that Britain had been relegated to the status of second-rate power at the global level. Not coincidentally, it was after this humiliating event that a serious debate began about the merits of joining the European project (Bache & Jordan 2006, p. 6). Even as late as 1964, when the reality of imperial decline was evident to most, the newly elected Labour leader Harold Wilson said, "We are a world power, and a world influence, or we are nothing" (Radici 1992, p 20). The country eventually accepted the reality of its second-rate status when it joined the European Community in 1973. This event, not coincidentally, was perceived as a lowering, not a raising, of the country's status and self-esteem (Jauregui 1999).

In Italy, in contrast, there is no recent history of empire comparable to Britain's that provided a sense of national esteem and superiority. Indeed, national status in Italy is perceived to be closely associated with how "European" the country is. In fact for many Italians the alternative to Europe is "Africa" (see chapter three) – a metaphor for "backwardness". Contrast this with Britain, where the alternative to

Europe is the "commonwealth" – a pretty prestigious club compared to "Africa". And so closer European integration for Italians was associated with higher collective esteem for the nation. It is partly for this reason that large sections of Italy's political class openly endorse a political/federal union. In addition, in the country's political and non-political discourse, adding the suffix "Europe" before an object implied that it is better than the alternative which is not "European" (as in a "European budget", a hospital of "European" quality, etc). This is because the meme "Europe" implied normality, progress, and modernization. Majorities feel "European" and have no conflict reconciling their national and European identities (Isernia 2005). This contrasts with the UK, where only a minority "feels" European (Worcester 2000, p. 59).

There are also some parallels between Italy and the UK. Many Labourites supported the euro because they hoped that closer ties with Europe would help to *Germanize* Britain. This belief was expressed in the Lords debates, which in many ways were more honest and frank than were the debates in the House of Commons:

> The noble Lord, Lord Heseltine, recently said that he had favoured the UK joining the euro because it would make us more like Germany. I believe that he was right, and he could still be right if the euro survives the present crisis.
>
> (Lord Monks, House of Lords Debate, 1 Dec 2011)

This level of frankness would be unlikely in the House of Commons because it would be politically damaging. It challenges the belief, held by many, in the UK's essential superiority vis-à-vis other European countries, including Germany. It also undermines the Blair government's narrative that joining the euro would give Britain "leadership" of Europe, for hoping that Britain would become more German is an admission of Britain's lower status compared to Germany. It would also challenge popular narratives held by the masses that equate Britain's relations with the EU with the struggles that took place in World War Two, when the UK was the free and democratic country that was fighting the evil Germany and its plans to rule the continent. For some pro-euro reformers, joining the EMU would make Britain more like Germany. In this sense, for some elements on the centre-left, Europe was a device to promote domestic ends. This attitude actually preceded the euro; many Conservatives in the sixties and seventies supported Europe because they believed it could help prevent some of the socialist reforms of Labour (Holmes 1996); meanwhile, many Labourites in the eighties supported Europe because they believed it would be an effective defence against some of the right-wing reforms being enacted by Thatcher (Philip 1992, p. 192; Haseler 2000).

This strategy was certainly present among some reformers in Italy in the run-up to the euro. Many supported the euro because, they hoped, Europe would promote their own domestic objectives. For instance, many hoped that the euro would help to Germanize Italy (see chapter one). Some on the left believed the euro would consolidate the social democratic model of political economy in the face of globalizing pressures. On the right, in contrast, there were (and are) elements who saw the EU as a defence and promotion of free trade (Della Porta & Caiani 2007), competitive and liberal (in the European sense) markets that would be potentially undermined by the left and their union supporters.

The problem for the reformers in both Italy and the UK who wanted to use Europe to promote their domestic ends is that the evidence shows that domestic structures are very resilient even in the face of Europeanizing pressures (Bache & Jordan 2006, p. 13; Baimbridge & Whyman 2008, p. 158; Featherstone 2011). This is particularly the case in Italy. Entering the EMU, many hoped, would transform the country. But despite being in the EMU for 15 years, the country continues to display many of the problems that have served to relegate it to second-class status in Europe: high levels of corruption and tax evasion, a divided and ineffective political class, low levels of productivity and innovation, low economic growth, low employment, and inefficient public services. The reason is that many interests have a stake in preserving the status quo, and they can use their political power, through the democratic process, to preserve their preferred political-economic structures.

Alternative explanations

Talani (2000) argues that one only has to look at the preferences of the City to understand why Britain did not join the common currency. According to Talani, the City risked losing its financial dominance if London was to be integrated into a common currency (2003). In a currency union, London would supposedly lose its comparative advantages and would be forced into tighter competition with Frankfurt and other financial capitals: as new financial instruments denominated in the new currency were created, other financial centres in Europe would be able to increase their market share (Talani 2003, p. 140). Talani adds that it is not a coincidence that one of the five tests was whether the euro would be beneficial to the financial industry; it shows that the government gave priority to the City over other interests in its decision on whether to enter (Talani 2003, p. 140).

There are both empirical and theoretical problems with this argument. First the former will be discussed. Throughout the text Talani repeatedly refers to the "City's" preferences. This assumes that the City is sufficiently homogenous to share the same "preference". But this is mistaken. The reality is that the City was divided on the euro, which is unsurprising given that the City is composed of different firms, which specialize in trading different securities, which creates different sets of cost-benefit analysis. Perhaps it is for this reason that Talani does not present any solid empirical evidence for her argument, such as a survey of City firms. Surveys that were taken, in fact, show that the *majority* of City firms were in favour of Britain entering the euro (KPMG poll, cited in House of Commons Debate, 1999). Even if one questions the representativeness of that sample, it still seems more likely, based on other evidence from British industry (Foreman-Peck 2004, p. 106; Barrell 2002, p. 63; Haseler 2000, p. 45), that the City was divided on the merits of entering. It follows that there were no "City" preferences.

There are also theoretical problems with her argument. First, the notion that the City would have lost its comparative advantages had it joined the common currency is unconvincing. London's comparative advantages include the English language, its common law system, its position in the middle of two time zones, and the cosmopolitanism of the city, advantages that other European capitals have a hard time reproducing. These advantages would have remained even had Britain entered EMU, and so even if we accept the dubious proposition that the City opposed entry because it would lose its comparative advantages, the argument flounders on the basis that London had other, arguably more important, comparative advantages that would not have been undermined had it entered EMU. Second, the fact that one of the five tests was whether EMU would be beneficial to the financial industry does not indicate that the government gave the City priority over other interests. Other tests included whether EMU would be beneficial for jobs and investment. Supposedly, these two tests refer to other British industries, as well as finance, suggesting that other sectors were also given importance. But this assumes that the government really intended the five tests to be the determining factor for British entry. Some researchers did attempt to determine whether the tests were met, using broad assumptions of "jobs" and "investment", and they determined that all the tests were met in 2002 (Barrell 2002). But this did not matter, because the tests were not what they were presented to be. They were a political strategy for a public which, polls showed, was overwhelmingly in favour of preserving the pound. The five tests were part of the government's strategy to present the decision on whether to enter as "essentially economic" when it was a political one par excellence. The opposition saw right through this strategy and accordingly pounded the government in parliament and the media, helping them to win the debate.

Another, in many ways more convincing, challenge to the arguments presented in this chapter come from public opinion data from Britain which suggests, according to some scholars, that British public opinion on the euro was nuanced, superficial, and malleable, and that Tony Blair could have won a referendum on British entry into the euro. In June 1992, polls showed that the British were marginally in favour of Maastricht (54% to 46%). But after the humiliating exit of Britain from the ERM, public opinion shifted to 68% opposed, 38% in favour (Worcester 2000, p. 55). What is more, in July 1998, polls showed that 33% were in favour of the euro, and 50% were against, but when the question was repeated with the condition that the government strongly urged Britain's joining, the gap fell to a mere 7% (Berrington & Hague 2001, p. 74). Finally, the experience of the 1975 referendum demonstrated that, when a decision has to be made about Europe, many in Britain will act in ways that defy prediction. Before the referendum, polls showed that a solid majority were opposed to Britain's entry into the EC. But the results of the referendum showed that views can suddenly shift, as two thirds voted in favour of staying. One reason is that both the major parties, most industry, and the media were solidly in favour, and this impacted public opinion. This suggests two things: first, that we should be sceptical of the many polls that support the notion of British euroscepticism. Second, that even if these polls accurately reflect a snapshot of the public's views, it does not follow that these views reflect an independent, coherent, and settled judgement (Berrington & Hague 2001, p. 69); often, these eurosceptic views are very superficial and can be shifted by governments and other elements of the ruling class.

This argument has many problems. For example, the few polls that showed large support for Maastricht and the euro would, I argue, have been different had the question added the condition that the euro was a federalist project that many hoped would lead to a political union. That is, the British display support for the economic dimensions of the euro, but there is little evidence that they would have displayed the same level of support for the political dimensions, which are more important. A thought experiment will help to show why. Imagine for the moment that Blair had successfully brought Britain into the common currency. Had he done so, he would have obtained a seat at the table; the topic of discussion at the table, however, would be transfers to uncompetitive Southern European countries, Eurobonds, a banking union with a centralized regulator, and the creation of a Eurozone minister with the power to override democracy and veto national budgets. Would the British consent to the euro had they been told that it could likely lead to these centralizing tendencies? Probably not. In fact the very idea of political union is unpalatable to most British citizens, even those who supposedly supported the euro. It follows that one must be sceptical of some of the pro-euro opinion polls cited in the previous paragraph, for the results of those polls would have been very different had the respondents been informed about the true political dimensions of the euro. Even the 1975 referendum must be understood in this context. The pro-EC arguments were exclusively about promoting free trade in Europe, not about the vision of political union that other member-states aspired to, and this is one of the reasons that most supported British membership in 1975 (Philip 1992, p 187; Personal Interview with Lord Flight).

Conclusions: the Eurozone debt crisis

This chapter has largely focused on Britain's approach to the euro, drawing on comparisons with Italy. Interestingly, in the past four years there has been a convergence between the two nations. The government of Matteo Renzi in Italy now speaks of Europe in terms of the national interest, red lines, and standing up to Brussels, which parallels Britain's approach very closely. At the mass level Italians are becoming, like their British counterparts, increasingly eurosceptic. Polls taken in May 2012 show that 40% of Italians want to return to the lira (*Telegraph* 30 May 2012), while more recent polls show that over half of Italians are now anti-euro (Paudice 2014). They blame the euro for many of the country's ills that have seemed to worsen in the past 15 years since the country entered.

Many British eurosceptics look at the troubles that Italians and other Southern European economies are facing and say "we told you so". And, in fact, reading the debates that took place in the nineties, they did indeed predict that the project would not succeed. As far back as 1991, MP Chris Gill foresaw that the euro would lead to

> responsibility resting with a body of people who do not have the authority to discharge that responsibility in full measure. This will result in public disillusionment with politicians and with the people's capacity to obtain satisfaction through their elected representatives. In the fullness of time that disillusionment will turn to frustration and anger, which will lead ultimately to the rejection of established political leadership, traditional party loyalties and the whole body politic.
>
> (Buller 2006, p. 209)

As the next chapter will show, that is a fairly accurate appraisal of what eventually transpired. The vindication is palpable in this British parliamentary debate:

> I would remind those people that the euroskeptics warned of the dangers of joining or having a single currency . . . we were told that if we did not join, we would be sidelined . . . indeed, people like me were called unpatriotic because we believed that it would be inimical to British interests to join the single currency . . . we have been vindicated by events.
>
> (House of Lords Debate, 3 Feb 2012, Lord Stoddart of Swindon)

In Britain this prescient scepticism helped to win the debate on the merits of the common currency and prevented the country from entering. These dynamics were present in the other countries that did not adopt the euro, Denmark and Sweden. Regarding the latter, similar to Britain, the pro-euro campaign was based largely on the supposed economic benefits of the common currency, with Prime Minister Goran Persson promising the euro would create 108,000 jobs (Ljungberg 2004, p. 22). Swedish Business was in favour; the powerful Confederation of Swedish Enterprise openly campaigned for the country to enter (ibid, p. 12). Respectable economic research also suggested that Sweden would benefit from joining.[1] Those opposed marshalled arguments that would be very familiar to eurosceptics in Britain. Echoing Thatcher and other realists, they argued that the euro was little more than a quid pro quo for France as the price for accepting German unification (Foreman-Peck 2004, p. 102), and this was not coterminous with Sweden's interests. It was also felt that the euro threatened the nation's parliament as the supreme source of sovereign legitimacy (Ljungberg 2004, p.21). Others argued that losing the tool of devaluation could lead to increases in unemployment (Vaubel 2004, p. 87). Lastly, unlike the Southern European countries, Sweden did not need "external pressures/impositions" to control public finances (Foreman-Peck 2004, p.103). In 2003, Sweden had a referendum on whether to join the euro, and the "no" side won 56.1% to 41.8%. Although in Sweden, unlike the UK, there is little talk of leaving the EU, opinion of the currency has dwindled to a miserly 9.6% in favour, with 82.3% opposed,[2] ensuring that the country will keep the Krona for the foreseeable future even though it is legally required to adopt the euro under the Treaty of Maastricht.

Denmark, like Britain, was able to obtain an opt-out, which *de jure* allows it more freedom on whether to join the Eurozone. Danish public opinion, like the British and Swedish, was and is also solidly opposed, as evidenced in their rejection of the euro in a referendum in 2000, with 53.2% voting against and 46.8% voting in favour. The results indicated that there was a significant difference between the public and the political/economic elite in Denmark. The two major parties, the Liberals and Conservatives, were solidly in favour, as were the industrial, banking, and union elite. The Danish central bank also actively campaigned in favour of the currency (Jesperson 2004, p. 57). Polls taken before the vote indicated a slight lead for the yes side, but this was undermined by a report released by the Danish Economic Council that concluded that the economic benefits from EMU would be small, and that the common currency could best be described as a political project (Marcussen & Zolner 2003). Since the vote, Danish support for the currency has plummeted, with recent polls showing that the euro's opponents are ahead by a margin of between 42% and 46% (Bloomberg 17/05/2013), although unlike Sweden, which allows the Krona to float freely, the Danish Krone is pegged to the euro.

Meanwhile, German support for the euro has increased with time. The crisis has also significantly altered the politics of the euro, making Germany the almost undisputed leader, at least in the economic sphere. The next chapter will explore this in more detail.

Notes

1 "Too much to Lose, or More to Gain? Should Sweden Join the Euro? Oxford University discussion paper, available at: www.economics.ox.ac.uk/research/WP/pdf/paper442.pdf
2 Polling data available at: http://investmentwatchblog.com/swedens-euro-hostility-hits-a-record/

References

"Analysis: Euro Tests," BBC News Radio 4. Aired on 12 December 2002. Available at: http://news.bbc.co.uk/2/shared/spl/hi/programmes/analysis/transcripts/02_12_12.txt.

Bache, I. and Jordan, A. (2006) The Europeanization of British Politics. In: I. Bache and A. Jordan (eds). *The Europeanization of British Politics*. New York: Palgrave Macmillan, pp. 265–279.

Bache, I. and Jordan, A. (2006) Britain in Europe and Europe in Britain. In: I. Bache and A. Jordan. (eds) *The Europeanization of British Politics*. New York: Palgrave Macmillan, pp. 3–33.

Barrell, R. (2002) The UK and EMU: Choosing the Regime. *National Institute Economic Review*, 180, pp. 54–70.

Berrington, H., and Hague, R. (2001) The Further off From England: British Public Opinion and Europe. In: A. Menon and V. Wright (eds). *From Nation State to Europe?* Oxford: Oxford University Press, pp 66–94.

Baimbridge, M. and Whyman, P. B. (2008) *Britain, the Euro, and Beyond*. Ashgate: Hampshire.

Buller, J. (2006) Monetary Policy. In: I. Bache and A. Jordan (eds). *The Europeanization of British Politics*. New York: Palgrave Macmillan, pp. 201–215.

Daily Express 22 April 1996.

Daily Express 22 April 1998.

Daily Express 28 May 2003.

Deighton, A. (2001) European Union Policy. In: A. Sheldon (ed.). *The Blair Effect*. London: Little, Brown, and Company, pp. 307–328.

Della Porta, D. and Caiani, M. (2007) Talking Europe in the Italian Public Sphere. *South European Society and Politics*, 12(1), March, pp.1–21.

Featherstone, K. (2011) The Greek Sovereign Debt Crisis and EMU: A Failing State in a Skewed Regime. *Journal of Common Market Studies*, 49(2), pp. 193–217.

Foreman-Peck, J. (2004) The UK and the Euro: Politics vs. Economics. In: J. Ljungberg (ed.). *The Price of the Euro*. New York: Palgrave Macmillan, 97–119.

Geddes, A. (2004) *The European Union and British Politics*. New York: Palgrave Macmillan.

Gowland, D., Turner, A., and Wright, A. (2010) *Britain and European Integration since 1945: On the Sidelines*. New York: Routledge.

Haseler, S. (1996) *The English Tribe. Identity, Nation, and Europe*. London: Macmillan Press.

Haseler, S. (2000) The Politics of the Euro. In: S. Haseler and J. Reland (eds). *Britain and Euroland: A Collection of Essays*. London: Federal Trust, pp. 25–52.

"Head to Head: Joining the Euro," BBC News, 28 April 2003. Available at: http://news.bbc.co.uk/2/hi/uk_news/politics/2981479.stm

Holmes, M. (1996) *The Euroskeptical Reader*, London: Macmillan.

House of Commons Debate, 'Euro.' 28 January 1999. *Hansard*.

House of Commons Debate, 'UK Role in Europe.' 13 January 1999. *Hansard*.

House of Commons Debate, 'Economic and Monetary Union.' 27 October 1997. *Hansard*.

House of Lords Debate, 'Eurozone Crisis.' 1 December 2011. *Hansard*.

House of Lords Debate, 'Eurozone Crisis.' 3 February 2012. *Hansard*.

House of Lords Debate, 'Eurozone Crisis.' 16 February 2012. *Hansard*.

Isernia, P. (2005) L'Europa Vista dagli Italiani: Vent'Anni Dopo, In: M. Cotta, P. Isernia, and L. Verzichelli (eds). *L'Europa In Italia*. Bologna: Il Mulino, pp. 223–277

Jauregui, P. (1999) National Pride and the Meaning of Europe: A Comparative Study of Britain and Spain. In: D. Smith and S. Wright (eds). *Whose Europe?* Oxford Blackwell, pp. 257–287.

Jesperson, J. (2004) The Stability Pact: An Economic Straightjacket. In: J. Ljungberg (ed.). *The Price of the Euro*. New York: Palgrave Macmillan, pp.45–57.

Levring, P. "Denmark Shelves Euro Goal Indefinitely as Crisis Scars Last," *Bloomberg* 17 May 2013.

Ludlow, P. (2002) Us or Them? The Meaning of Europe in British Political Discourse. In: M. Malborg and B. Strath (eds). *The Meaning of Europe*. Oxford: Berg, pp. 101–124.

Ljungberg, J. (2004) *The Price of the Euro*. New York: Palgrave Macmillan.

Marcussen, M. and Zolner, M. (2003) The Danish EMU Referendum 2000: Business as Usual. *Government and Opposition*, 36(3), pp. 379–402.

Paudice, C. (2014) Elezioni Europee 2014, Istituto Cattaneo: "L'Italia Paese in cui sono aumentati di più i cittadini sfavorevoli all'euro." Huffington Post. Available at: www.huffingtonpost.it/2014/05/22/europee-italiani-sfiducia-euro_n_5370827.html

Philip, A. B. (1992) Westminster Versus Brussels: The Last Crusade? In: M. Maclean and J. Howorth (eds). *Europeans on Europe*. London: Macmillan, pp 184–211.
Radici, G. (1992). *Offshore: Britain and the European Idea*. London: IB Tauris and Co.
Stephens, P. *Britain and Europe: An Unforgettable Past and an Unavoidable Future*. Hugo Young Memorial Lecture, 20 October 2004
Talani, L. S. (2000) *Betting For and Against EMU*. Aldershot, UK: Ashgate.
Talani, L. S. (2003) The Political Economy of Exchange Rate Commitments. In: M. Ryner and A. W. Cafruny (eds). *A Ruined Fortress? Neo-Liberal Hegemony and Transformation in Europe*. Oxford: Rowman & Littlefield, pp. 123–146.
Talani, L. S. (2011) The UK and the Euro in the Aftermath of the Global Financial Crisis. In: P. Della Posta and L. S. Talani (eds). *Europe and the Financial Crisis*. New York: Palgrave Macmillan, pp. 127–141.
The Express 02 December 1996.
The Express 14 December 1996.
The Express 30 April 2997.
TG2 Dossier Oggi Euro, Aired on RAI 1 May 1998.
"Union Leader Speaks Out Against Euro," BBC News 28 December 2002. Available at: http://news.bbc.co.uk/2/hi/uk_news/politics/2610817.stm
Vaubel, R. 2004. A Critical Analysis of EMU and of Sweden Joining it. In: J. Ljungberg. (eds) *The Price of the Euro*. New York: Palgrave Macmillan, pp. 87–96.
Warner, J. (2012) Only the ECB can Save the Euro Now, *The Telegraph*, 30 May 2012.
Worcester, R. (2000) The British: Reluctant Europeans. In: S. Haseler and J. Reland (eds). *Britain and Euroland: A Collection of Essays*. London: Federal Trust, pp. 53–72.
Young, H. (1998) *This Blessed Plot: Britain and Europe from Churchill to Blair*. London: Macmillan.

8 Germany and the future of the euro

When selling the euro to their publics, European policymakers tended to focus on the supposed economic benefits that would accrue to countries that adopted the currency. Most of their assertions were fallacious, but in light of the dynamics of contemporary democracies, it was also understandable. Politicians gain consent for their policies, however dubious, by framing them in terms of things that voters want: more growth, jobs, and opportunities. The average voter was perhaps less concerned about one of the main motivating factors of the euro: the wish to restrain a newly unified and powerful Germany (which might explain why this idea was less prominent in public discourse). The relatively lower salience of this view in politicians' political posturing does not make it any less important, however. Comments from the fathers of the monetary union (Marsh 2009, p. 75; Marsh 2013), as well as the confluence of historical circumstances that undergirded the euro, indicate that the fear of a powerful Germany, and the belief that only European institutions could restrain it, was a significant influence on many European elites, especially French ones.

The Eurozone crisis has shown just how spectacularly wrong this belief was. A deeper lesson is that, redolent of the Neapolitan proverb that the passage of time always reveals the truth,[1] power will eventually reveal itself despite attempts to disguise or repress it. Germany has risen from the Eurozone debacle as the country with the strongest and most robust economy, as the nation with the largest purse to finance the rescues of the countries of the periphery, and as the leader with the final say on the policies being put in place to save the currency. Partly as a consequence, some are asserting that only Germany has the power and resources to ensure the long term survival of the currency, and that, if it is unwilling to play the role of "benevolent hegemon" *à la* the USA during the 20th century, it should leave and allow the currency's present form to unravel (Soros 2012).

But this exaggerates the power of Germany; although few would dispute that it is Europe's unmatched leader, equally important for the long term survival of the euro are the dynamics of other Eurozone countries. Italy is strategically important in this regard. If it were unable to become competitive it could conceivably eventually need a bailout, and it is questionable that the ESM would have the resources to cover its huge debt. Alternatively, anti-euro political forces in Italy might continue to strengthen and prevent attempts to ensure that Italy remains a standing member of the currency. Both could potentially lead to its exit and begin an unravelling of the euro. France will also be decisive: the French-German duo has been the motor of European integration since its inception, and if it breaks down, there seems to be little hope for Europe in its current form. In this regard, trends are not encouraging. As this chapter will show, on numerous economic indicators, Germany's economy has performed well while France's has not, and this divergence is mirrored in the trajectory of public opinion towards a much more eurosceptic France (while Germany is increasingly Europhile).

Winners and losers

One of the more interesting features of the history of the euro is that Germans, although broadly pro-European, were relatively sceptical of the currency (Nordvig 2014, p. 27) from its inception even though they would eventually be one of the biggest beneficiaries of it. The reasons for the scepticism are multiple. One is shared with the UK: there was no widespread belief in an inferior political economy that could be fixed, or that needed to be constrained, by Brussels. There was also a deeply rooted emotional attachment to the deutschmark, which was a symbol of the country's wealth, prosperity, and ordo-liberal style of governance. What is more, the Bundesbank commanded a high level of devotion from across the political spectrum; as Jacques Delors said in 1992, "Not all Germans believe in God, but all believe in the Bundesbank". This, coupled with the fact that Southern Europeans were believed to be spendthrift and irresponsible, fuelled scepticism towards the idea of sharing a currency with them. German policymakers helped to make the euro palatable to the public by trying to institutionalize Germany's ordo-liberal system of governance across Europe as a whole. The Maastricht criteria (see chapter one) and the Stability and Growth Pact were tools to help "Germanize" Europe, although both were disregarded when it became politically convenient.

Regardless of this scepticism, the euro conferred a significant advantage to Germany because it is undervalued relative to what the value of a D-mark would be. This gives German exporters a competitive advantage. Correspondingly, the euro is overvalued compared to what the value of the currencies of Germany's competitors would be, such as the lira. Coupled with the inability to devalue in times of economic distress, this represents a significant disadvantage for countries in the periphery, especially Italy. This partly explains the significant divergence in the current accounts that began after the euro was introduced (see Figure 8.1).

What is remarkable about this data is that both France and Italy had surpluses or were close to balance in their current accounts before the euro was introduced, and subsequently became deficit countries. Meanwhile, Germany's current account has largely gone in the opposite direction. It was widely believed that in a currency union, these imbalances would not matter, since capital would be allocated efficiently and economies would converge. But, like so many other ideas promulgated by the pro-euro camp, this, too, has been shown to be wrong. The divergences in the capital account coincide with other indicators of economic strength.

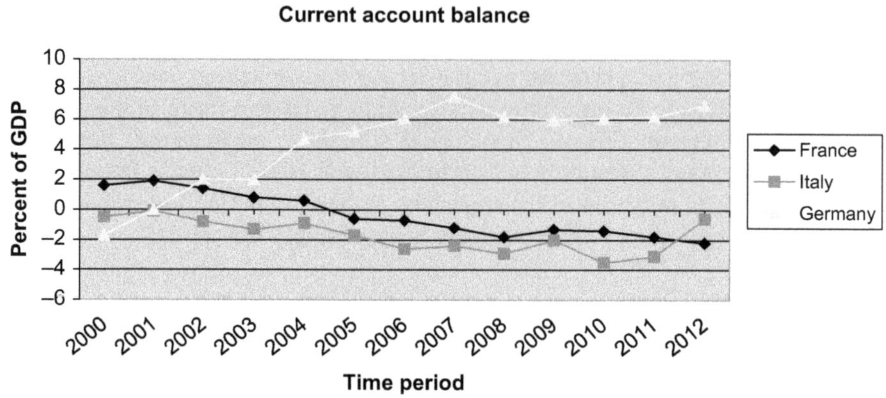

Figure 8.1 Current account balance

Source: OECD

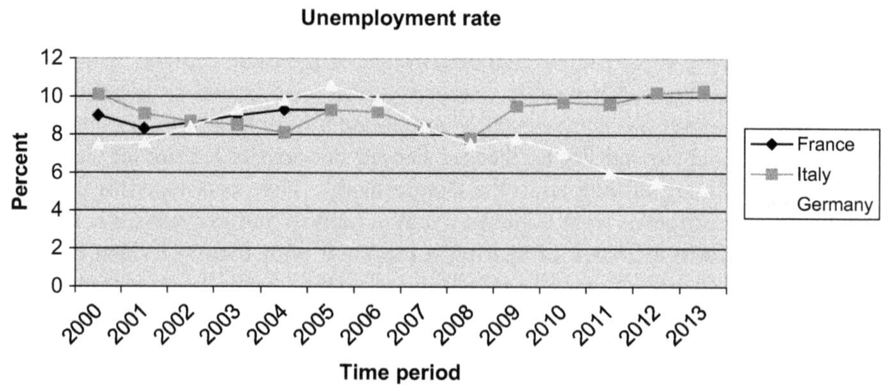

Figure 8.2 Unemployment rate

Source: OECD

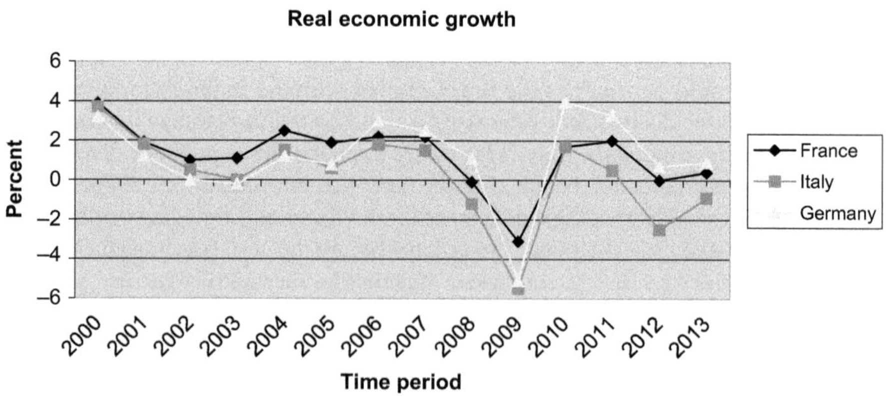

Figure 8.3 Real economic growth

Source: OECD

The data indicate divergences in some of the most important indicators of economic robustness. Of course, the distortionary effects of the euro do not explain all this change. Equally important for Germany's success are the Hartz reforms, undertaken by the SPD, which included tighter restrictions on unemployment benefits, collective wage restraint, and an emphasis on re-integration into the workforce through education and training (Younge & Semmler 2011). This helped to keep labour costs down in Germany relative to its competitors. Meanwhile, countries such as France and Italy failed to make the politically difficult decisions to make their economies more competitive. But the absence of the necessary structural reforms should not be exaggerated. The loss of the exchange rate and the lever of monetary policy to help smooth out imbalances played a major role, because it removed the capacity to make exports more competitive when deficits became too large. It also removed the price signal that under normal circumstances helps to coordinate the behaviours of domestic and international markets. When the current account is in deficit – when imports exceed exports – it indicates that credit-based consumption is too high. Under normal circumstances, investors start to demand higher interest rates, which reduces credit and consumption of imported goods, helping to balance the current account. Both France and Italy, as members of a common currency, lacked these signals, helping to delay the process of the needed rebalancing of their trade profiles.

These negative economic trends in Italy and France are the source of much misery and disillusionment, especially among youth, whose prospects are dismal. The effects have been toxic, from the rise of radical, populist parties (more on that below) to the exodus of thousands of educated youth to find work elsewhere. Millions of young people feel a sense of betrayal: they spent years studying only to find later that there was either no work or that the only work available was low-paid, short-term contracts in fields that they are over-qualified for. To be sure, this is not only a problem in Europe; many youth in North America also face a punishing job market even though that continent is in better economic health. But the data show that the youth unemployment situation is much worse in Europe than elsewhere in the OECD, especially in the periphery. Intermittent encouraging economic indicators in some countries, such as Italy, moreover, are not sufficient to address the scope of the problem. Job-generating growth that would help to make a real improvement in those numbers would need to be at least 3% a year. In Italy those kinds of numbers are nowhere to be seen, and the same is true for France, at least for the near future.

In light of these economic divergences, we should not be surprised that trends in public opinion between the countries have moved in different directions. Differences in attitudes towards Europe, especially between the North and the South, are not new; however, the Eurozone crisis has had a marked effect on popular beliefs.

The data show the divergences are significant. When we probe deeper, we find that the euro has become suffused with narratives that have brought to the fore many of the old stereotypes that Europeans have of each other, some of which have a sniff of racism and hostility (Rachman 2012). When the crisis reached a crescendo, many concluded that the cause was the "irresponsibility" and "corruption"

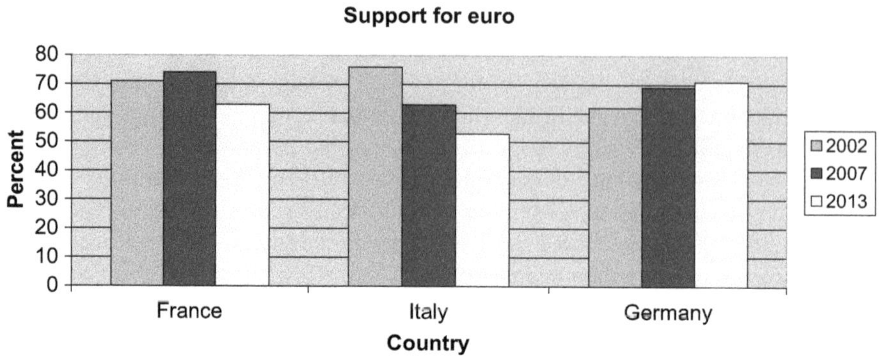

Figure 8.4 Support for euro

Source: Eurobarometer

of the countries in the South, especially Greece but also Portugal, Italy, and Spain (condescendingly referred to as the PIIGS). Meanwhile, tropes about Nazism and the German attempt to control or colonize the continent have become part of the political discourse of many parties, especially in France, Italy, and Greece. Both Italian and Greek newspapers have depicted Angela Merkel in a Nazi-style pose, causing justifiable outrage in Germany. One of the more important narratives, which resonates because it contains a grain of truth, is that the economic depression in some European countries is a consequence of German-imposed austerity.

The politics of austerity

The notion that fixing public finances was an essential cure to the crisis is fundamentally rooted in Germany's ordo-liberal philosophy that excessive debt is wrong in both the moral and economic sense, and that reducing debt through cutting spending and/or raising taxes is the essential medicine, however painful it may be in the short-term in terms of reduced output and higher unemployment. This philosophy rejects the Keynesian notion that deficit spending can and should be an instrument of economic growth. Rather, competitiveness is the result of keeping production costs and prices down, making labour markets flexible, and increasing investment in technology.

It was this philosophy that informed the Fiscal Pact (more on that below), and which guided the policies of important leaders like Mario Monti in Italy. The conditions on the bailouts of Portugal, Spain, Greece, Ireland, and Cyprus also all were in accordance with the set of ideas known as ordo-liberalism. With the exception of perhaps Ireland and Spain, the ordo-liberal policies put in place have not coincided with a rate of economic growth that would help to absorb the enormous number of unemployed workers, although other indicators are encouraging: bond market spreads between these countries and Germany are down, making their debts slightly less unaffordable.

Contra European populists everywhere, whether one calls these policies "austerity" or "ordo-liberal" it is only partly true that they are the result of the political preferences of Angela Merkel's government. A deeper cause is the structural character of the currency union itself, which represents the crystallization of German dominance and reflects its preferences. The legal and institutional architecture of the currency is an explicit rejection of Keynesian deficit spending in spirit and in letter. This constrained (even though it did not absolutely prevent) the capacity of policymakers to use deficit spending to increase aggregate demand during an economic slump.

But even more fundamentally, when the exchange rate ceases to be an instrument of making goods competitive on the international market, as is the case in a currency union without a redistributive political union, the only tool left is to reduce prices and wages, otherwise known as "internal devaluation" (Van Overtveldt 2011, p. 96). Reducing wages in the public sector requires reducing public spending and increasing layoffs; it also entails decreasing the benefits of many social welfare programs. In the private sector, reducing wages requires the consent of workers who are often unionized and unwilling to take pay cuts that are significantly below the wages that they agreed to and which were supposed to be protected in their contracts. Although in theory, in the long term this process of wage and price reduction could increase competitiveness, exports, and economic growth, in the short term it is economically painful: by suppressing the purchasing power of workers and beneficiaries of public spending, consumption is reduced, and since consumption is the other side of production, output decreases, too. This worsens the recession. As if it could not get any worse, the reduction in prices and wages makes debts relatively higher and hence harder to service: if a worker with an income of 35 thousand and a debt of 100 thousand faces a wage reduction of 20%, other things being equal, his debt has effectively increased by the same amount. This pain makes internal devaluation politically difficult, and few countries in the periphery, with the exception of perhaps Ireland and Spain, have been able to implement it across the board without difficulty. Greece has perhaps gone the farthest in implementing internal devaluation; wages, social benefits, and prices, on some estimates, have decreased between 25 and 30 per cent (Lundgreen 2013), but the price has been exorbitant: an economic depression, social conflict, the rise of radical neo-Nazism, and an increase in its debt levels even though it has already defaulted on loans to its private creditors.

The euro is similar to the gold standard – a historical comparison that provides little optimism. Both systems are based on fixed exchange rates that prevent the devaluation of the currency from being an instrument of economic adjustment, meaning that adjustment must happen internally. In the case of the gold standard, the internal devaluation and austerity that followed helped to create the political radicalism that helped to fuel World War Two (Sapir 2012). However, in an odd historical irony, the gold standard was more flexible than the euro because, with the former, a country still had its own national currency; if it needed to devalue, the said country could simply declare that its currency was no longer pegged to the precious metal. It could then stimulate demand through a cheaper exchange rate mechanism and the central bank's capacity to emit money and credit. Inflation often resulted, but for many this was an acceptable price to pay for the benefit of an economic adjustment that was relatively less socially and politically painful. This option is much more complicated and difficult with the euro. It would require an announcement that the old national currency would be introduced on a particular date, and that capital controls would be imposed to prevent capital flight. Contracts and debts would all have to be redenominated into the new currency, which would lead to endless litigation and, in many cases, defaults to both official and private creditors. Initially it would be chaotic and devastating, but eventually competitiveness would increase.

Another reason for the German-led austerity is that the alternative – a real transfer of resources from economically dynamic regions to those that are facing recession or depression – was and is not politically possible. This latter solution would have entailed the infamous "transfer union" that the rules of the Maastricht Treaty explicitly and unambiguously aimed to prevent. Germany, Holland, Austria, and other competitive and creditor countries would, in this scenario, try to stimulate demand in the depressed periphery by transferring resources to them. Alternatively, surplus countries could make the periphery more competitive by making themselves less competitive by, say, increasing their wages and prices rather than making (or forcing, depending on one's point of view) the South increase competitiveness by the painful adjustment that internal devaluation entails. It is not hard to see why this is politically impossible: no German leader, Merkel or otherwise, would have the legitimacy to either extract resources to transfer to the South or to force higher wages and prices. A policy of this nature would likely have led to a surge in support for the Alternative for Deutschland party in Germany, whose main agenda is to dismantle the euro while preserving the European Union.

European leaders understand these constraints, which is why many are calling for a real fiscal and political union which would theoretically be the pre-condition for the transferring of resources from economically dynamic to economically depressed regions of the continent. But it is not only surplus countries that would object to such a proposal; even in the Southern countries that could conceivably benefit from these transfers, there is fierce and obstreperous opposition to giving Brussels power over taxation and redistribution. When Wolfgang Schäuble suggested that, as the price for financial transfers, Brussels should have a veto over Greece's budget, there was collective outrage at the idea and papers presented it as a re-emergence of the Nazi attempt at domination of the continent. The same is true in most other countries. Very few voters would, if given the option, consent to more powers, especially those of taxation and redistribution, being transferred to Brussels. In fact, trends point to the opposite direction. In the EU budget negotiations of 2013, there were major disputes over a budget that amounts to less than 1% of European GDP, and leaders ultimately agreed to a reduction in spending (or to more "austerity"). A comparison with other currency unions illustrates the significance: central governments in both the US and Canada tax and redistribute between 20 and 24 per cent of their GDPs, amounts which most believe are essential to smooth out the inevitable economic divergences in such wide and diverse economies. This level of re-distribution is inconceivable in a Europe that struggles to agree on a budget that represents such a tiny fraction of its overall output.

In light of these very real structural and political constraints that prevent transfers from surplus to deficit countries, internal devaluation and austerity became almost inevitable. Thus the popular narrative that Angela Merkel's austerity policies are the cause of the periphery's woes is misleading; *any* German leader would likely have had to promote similar policies, even though, as the next section will show, many are ultimately unrealizable.

The Fiscal Pact

The fear of an imminent collapse of the euro that was a dominant theme of European and global politics between 2011 and 2013 has subsided. At the height of the panic, policymakers worked frantically to put in place a number of policy instruments to attempt to save the euro. Perhaps the most significant policy, and the one that most closely bears the stamp of Germany's ordo-liberal philosophy, is the Fiscal Pact, which includes the following rules:

- Balanced budget rule: government budgets shall be balanced or in surplus.
- Debt brake: governments with debts above 60% of GDP must reduce their debts at least 5% of the exceeded percentage points per year.
- Member states who are unable to satisfy these rules will face the "Automatic Correction Procedure".
- These rules must be embedded in domestic law and will be monitored by the Commission. If they are violated, the European Court of Justice will have the authority to sanction the non-compliant state 0.1% of GDP, and the funds will go to the European bailout funds or to the general European budget.

The Pact was impetuously ratified by the members of the Eurozone, often without an adequate consideration of the substantive implications. In this regard, Italy provides a case in point. When the national parliament voted for the pact, 498 out of 630 Parliamentarians were present, and 65 voted against, one of whom was Antonio Martino, the former foreign minister who was one of the few Italians to have predicted the actual effects of the euro for Italy. In this case, he and the others who voted against it seem to be the only ones who actually understood the implications of the Fiscal Pact for Italy. The country has the second highest debt in Europe, at 135% of GDP, and for Italy to actually comply with the Fiscal Pact, it would have to reduce spending by 45 billion euros every year for 20 years (Barbera & Feltri 2014, p. 106). It would be the height of understatement to say that this is unrealistic for a country like Italy, which experiences fissiparous social and political conflict while trying to reduce spending by a fraction of that. What is more, Italy *already has* a balanced budget rule in its constitution, and it has been ignored whenever it was politically convenient (Barbera & Feltri 2014).

The Fiscal Pact is also unrealistic for France. Although its debt is less than Italy's, it would still have to reduce spending by 30 billion euros every year for the next 20 years to satisfy the rules. For a country that has not had a balanced budget since 1974, this seems widely unrealistic. For both countries, the first test came in 2015, when the Commission provided its first assessment of whether their budgets were in accordance with the rules. In principle, the Commission has the authority to refer them to the European Court, which could sanction these states by imposing penalties. This represents not only a set of objectives that are almost impossible to reach, but it also potentially poses a threat to democracy, since budgets produced by democratically elected leaders can potentially be challenged and reversed by unelected judges in Strasbourg, whom most Europeans would not deem to be appropriate arbiters of decisions on how to spend public monies.

This is the theory, in any event. In practice, the Fiscal Pact was treated the way that other European rules have been when politically expedient: with irrelevance (Chorafas 2013). This already happened with the Stability and Growth Pact, which was supposed to prevent deficits from exceeding 3% amount of GDP. When it became politically convenient for France and Germany to violate it, they did so with the explicit consent of other European countries, like Italy, which also felt that one could or should be selective with the rules. The Fiscal Pact was also interpreted "flexibly" (Euro-speak for "ignored") because the rules were not possible for countries like France and Italy to meet.

There are other reasons why the Fiscal Pact will continue to be ignored. When Mario Draghi famously announced that he would do "whatever it takes" to save the euro, it was interpreted by observers to mean that the ECB would finally become a lender of last resort, making it a "normal" central bank. However, unlike other central banks, the ECB would also have the authority to impose structural reforms as the price for buying unlimited bonds; these reforms would include policies to make the countries more competitive and to fix public finances through spending cuts. The reason for this was to satisfy Germany, as Outright Monetary Transactions (OMT) are a blatant disregard of the original rule in the Maastricht treaty, which prohibited the monetization of government deficits, and the requirement that recipients implement structural reforms is essentially an attempt to satisfy Germany by applying the same logic that suffused the other instruments meant to save the euro, namely, Germany's ordo-liberal system of governance writ large across Europe. But I digress. Why would governments aim to apply the rigorous rules of the Fiscal Pact if they can now be bailed out by the Central Bank? One may reply that they would not want to be bailed out by the Central Bank because the imposition of the structural reforms would be a humiliating infringement on their sovereignty. But this exaggerates the capacity of the ECB to actually carry out this threat. Imagine for a moment that Italy required a bailout from the ECB. In theory, the ECB would make the policy conditional of the implement of structural reforms. And if Italy was unable to? Would the ECB actually turn off the taps if it meant that it would threaten an exit from the euro by one of the union's strategically important countries? This is unlikely, since the necessity of survival of the euro would probably trump all other considerations.

The OMT, then, if it is actually used, will probably be a paper tiger, and countries know this. They can therefore be confident that the ECB will bail them out while making noises about the need to implement structural reforms that will not need to be heeded. This potentially makes the Fiscal Pact essentially moot.

Nonetheless, it would be politically toxic in Germany if the rules were to be blatantly disregarded, which is why many leaders, especially Matteo Renzi, are making efforts to change the Fiscal Pact. Up to now, Merkel has responded with an unambiguous "nein", but there will be other ways to circumvent the rules. For a country to be referred to the court in Strasbourg will require a qualified majority vote. One can imagine a number of scenarios that prevent such an eventuality, such as the establishment of coalition led by highly indebted countries, such as France and Italy, to prevent, with the consent of other countries, any politically destabilizing decisions.

The backlash

For now, the survival of the euro, at least in the short term, is not in question, which is remarkable because there were many moments in 2012–2013 when it seemed to be on the precipice of collapse. European leaders may congratulate themselves on the way that they handled the crisis, but much of the public thinks differently. The EU-wide elections on 25 May 2014 represented a political earthquake. Polls showed that radical parties would take an unprecedented slice of the overall vote, and so the results were not a surprise, but they still did come as a shock. Populist or radical parties received the largest number of votes in many strategically important countries, and even where they did not come in first place, they increased their share of the vote, in some cases coming in second or third place behind mainstream parties. In the European Parliament they won around 30% of the seats, not enough to significantly impact legislation at the European level. But this does not mean that they will not be influential: their impact is already being felt at the national level, although it is unlikely that their policy proposals – exit from the euro and/or the EU, the erection of trade barriers and other protectionist measures, and the closing of borders to immigrants – will be realized, at least in the near term. A breakdown of their support highlights the scope of the results:

France: 24.9%
The UK: 27.9%
Italy: 27.3%
Greece: 39.5%
Germany: 9.4%
Denmark: 26.6%
Holland: 13.2%

Source: European Parliament

A number of conclusions could be inferred from these numbers. The countries where the results were most significant and where national politics will be most impacted by radical parties are France and the UK: in the former, Marine le Pen's National Front received almost 25%, and in the UK, the UKIP almost 28%, and, in both cases, mainstream parties received a proverbial pounding from large swathes of the electorate. The UK already will potentially leave the EU when it has a referendum on the question in 2017. In an ironic twist, Prime Minister David Cameron called the referendum, in part, to try to stem the tide of the UKIP, which he called a bunch of "fruit cakes, loonies, and closet racists". The results indicate that this strategy has failed, and that the UK is now closer than ever to leaving. This is the explicit objective of the UKIP, and evidently many Britons share that belief.

A British exit from Europe would have many negative implications for the EU, but the latter would likely survive the event. It is unlikely, as German Finance Minister Wolfgang Schäuble hyperbolically said in July 2014, that "the EU would be unimaginable without the UK". Rather, it would increase the power of statists and protectionists like Italy and France. In any event, it would survive, even though it would be a smaller and less influential version of its former self. The same is not true for France. Were it to leave, it would likely be the end of the euro and the EU. It is for this reason that the rise of Marine Le Pen's National Front (NF) is much more significant and deserves much closer attention. The influence of the NF is not new; its rise can be traced to the collapse of the Berlin wall and the subsequent triumph of neo-liberalism that characterized the national politics of the West and elsewhere, especially in the nineties (Berezin 2009). At the time, many centre-left parties that would have previously supported socialist policies accepted the orthodoxy of the inevitability and irreversibility of free markets and globalization. Consequently, many working class voters' interests were not represented in the platforms of the centre-left. Radical parties such as the NF filled the void by promising things that appealed to these voters: anti-globalization, anti-immigrant, and pro-nationalist policies. The de-industrialization of many Western countries that resulted from competition from low wage countries like China and India increased the economic insecurity of the working class and the support for parties like the NF. The Eurozone crisis has been a veritable boon for Marine le Pen. France's economic weakness cannot be entirely blamed on the euro, but there is no doubt that adoption of the currency has coincided with a worsening of the negative economic trends mentioned above. Marine Le Pen skilfully tapped into this increased anti-euro sentiment, and it is no coincidence that her support surged among those in the under-35s, the age group which has faced the brunt of the crisis.

In France the mainstream parties experienced a humiliating defeat, with Holland's ruling socialist party obtaining a paltry 14%; this is a scathing indictment of his handling of the crisis. He has only himself to blame. During his campaign for the presidency in 2012, he promised the French that he would promote growth by ending austerity at the European level. For the reasons adumbrated above, this was a chimera, and astute observers at the time knew it, but Holland nonetheless created big expectations that have not been met: austerity continues, and France's economic decline seems interminable. He is now viewed by large sections of the electorate, and especially voters of the NF, as part of the class of pro-Europe politicians who have created the very problems that they are trying to solve. If this sentiment remains and/or moves in the present trajectory, Marine Le Pen would have a decent shot at winning the Presidency in 2017. If that were to happen, we could expect that she would call a referendum on the euro and/or the EU. Previous referendums in France on Europe do not provide grounds for optimism that her initiative would be defeated.

The EU would likely not survive such an event. The Franco-German duo has been the motor of European integration; indeed, the raison d'etre of the EU was to end the destructive wars between these two countries. From the Treaty of Rome to the present, agreement between them was and is the *sine qua non* for all major integration initiatives. Their consent, financing, and political support are essential to everything from EU-wide policies on development and climate change to the policies that aim to save the currency. If this partnership were to break down, it is inconceivable that the rest of the structure would hold. Rather, we would probably see a dismantling, slow or rapid, of the institutions of the EU and the re-emergence of nationalism as a major factor in the politics of the continent – something that, in light of the 20th century, is not promising.

Can Italy replace France?

The victory of Matteo Renzi in Italy in the European elections of 2014, a mainstream centre-left, pro-European reformer who wants to, in his own words, "save" both Italy and Europe from the ravages of austerity, has warmed the hearts of many eurocrats and politicians in capitals from Berlin to Paris to Brussels. He represented an exception to the general radical trend, winning 40% of the vote, almost double the vote received by his populist rival, the M5S of Beppe Grillo. The result was also deemed to be significant because the previous elections indicated a trend towards radicalism. In the national elections of 2013 the M5S received an unprecedented quarter of the vote and became the second most important political party in the country. This happened, in part, because Italy has experienced some of the worst effects of the crisis: industrial production declined 25%, unemployment increased significantly, and a whole generation of youth has few prospects for stable and remunerative employment. In Italy the euro is widely blamed for this, which is why the M5S has called for a referendum on the currency. This anti-euro position, which is shared by other Italian parties, helped it to increase its share of the vote in the 2013 elections. Had the M5S won the European elections in May 2014, it would have been interpreted as another crack in the fragile chain that sustains the euro. But Renzi defeated it resoundingly, suggesting that Italians have woken up to the risk of the collapse of the currency and that they are willing to save it. The victory of Renzi was, as one prominent Italian put it, a signal that Italians want to finally implement the reforms that are needed to save the country (Reichlin 2014).

Perhaps. But a closer look at the numbers indicates that this optimistic interpretation is not well supported. First, voter turnout hit an all-time low in Italy; only about 58% of the electorate voted. Renzi's 40% of this vote represents only 25% of the electorate – hardly an indication that anywhere near a majority of Italians "voted for reform". Second, the MS5 is not the only party that opposes the euro; Lega Nord, Fratelli d'Italia, and some elements of Forza Italia also are not in favour or are very critical. If we add the votes received by these parties on to those won by the M5S, it indicates that over a third of the vote went to parties that oppose the euro; indeed, over half the MEPs elected are either extremely or moderately eurosceptic. Renzi will have to appeal to them to carry out his agenda, which is why he has changed the rhetoric on Europe. His PD party was often uncritically in favour of the European integration, while Renzi has begun to talk of Europe and the euro in terms of Italy's national interest, or with the language of aggressively confronting Brussels and fighting "austerity" (i.e., German) policies. On 2 July 2014, Italy assumed the presidency of the EU, and this new assertiveness of Italy's national interest and the need to promote expansionary policies at the EU level characterized Renzi's attempt to sell Italy's presidency to the public.

Renzi may very well succeed in softening the rules of the Fiscal Pact and allow the country to increase deficit spending over and above the 3% of GDP limit enshrined in the European rules. But whether this will, in Renzi's own words, "save" Europe is doubtful. It is unlikely that Renzi will be able to create the functional conditions of a currency union, i.e., a fiscal and political union that is the pre-condition for resource transfers from surplus to deficit countries. Where Renzi has an achievable opportunity is at the national level. He is aiming to implement a flurry of reforms to make the country more competitive, including increasing gender equality, making the legal and public administrative system more efficient and predictable, and introducing labour market reforms that address the huge amount of youth unemployment. These reforms could conceivably increase confidence and investment in Italy and halt or reverse the economic decline that the country has experienced in the last 20 years. The effect would surely be to decrease support for populist parties like the M5S and ensure Italy's standing as an effective and influential partner in the Eurozone. It is even remotely conceivable that, if France's decline were to continue, while Italy's reversed, the latter could replace the former as Germany's essential partner in the duopoly that leads Europe.

But if current trends are any indication, the odds of this happening are virtually nil. Although the spreads between German and Italian bonds have gone to pre-crisis levels, other indicators in Italy, such as employment levels and GDP growth, are dismal. What is more, both the IMF and the Commission predict sluggish growth in Italy for the near future, an amount which is certainly not enough to reverse the country's decline. This suggests that populist and/or anti-euro parties will remain a formidable force in Italian politics in the foreseeable future. It also suggests that Renzi will have serious opposition to his attempt to reform Italy, since many of these parties, such as Forza Italia, represent interests, like organized professionals, that will be harmed by Renzi's attempt to make the country more competitive. Intransigent interests are present in Renzi's own party, too, and past attempts of leaders to confront them have not been successful (see chapter five).

Thus the French-German leadership of Europe will remain, at least for now. The duo will probably muddle through, responding to crises in a way that saves the euro from collapse but that does not go far enough to actually create a functional and sustainable currency union. The banking union agreed to is a case in point. It gives the ECB authority over the health of nationally based banks, including the capacity to carry out stress tests, order re-capitalization, or to wind them down. There is even a fund at the European level to provide emergency capital to banks that may need it in times of stress. Optimists might say that this is evidence of the kind of political centralization that the euro needs. As ever, the devil is in the details. First, the fund to save banks is a paltry 55 billion euros – hardly enough to save *even one* of Europe's systemically important banks, never mind the entire system (Barbera & Feltri 2014). Second, the decision- making apparatus of the banking union is a byzantine mishmash of different bodies and committees, many of which will be staffed with appointees who must answer to national authorities – meaning the calculation of the national interest will probably still trump the European one. Even if this does not happen, the decisions will be too slow to respond to the immediate and unpredictable events that characterize financial crises. But most importantly, the banking union does not do what it was intended to: sever the link between weak national governments and weak banks. The reason is that the agreement does not include a *sine qua non* of a banking union: a deposit insurance scheme funded by central authorities to convince savers that a euro in a Greek bank has the same protection (and hence value) of a euro in a German bank. The bailout of Cyprus highlighted what can happen when that condition is absent: the unforeseen official expropriation of assets and capital controls that effectively make euros in the crisis country less valuable than those in the stable ones.

The official rhetoric from the French and German political class, as usual, will emphasize their "partnership" and "cooperation" and their unshakable "commitment" to the currency, but the underlying reality will be different: French weakness, German leadership, and a fundamental philosophical disagreement on the EU: France calling for "solidarity" (i.e. the backing of German taxpayers) and for industrial policy to increase competitiveness, while Germany continues to call for reforms consistent with its ordo-liberal system of governance. This deep philosophical disagreement reflects incompatible views about the organization of society. The French position is more statist and favourable to central planning, while Germany has embraced free markets and globalization even while it aims to preserve a significant social welfare system. The Eurozone crisis has only accentuated this dispute.

Cultural factors also matter for the future stability of the French-German partnership. There will need to be a change of mindset in both countries. France will need to accept that its statist prescriptions for economic growth are not viable in a Germany-dominated currency union and that adapting to the euro and to globalization may require a fundamental change in the way that it organizes its society. It may even have to make peace with that bogeyman of French politics: neo-liberalism. There is evidence that it is moving in that direction. President Holland recently announced a spate of pro-business policies, but he has little legitimacy for them, especially among his own socialist party, and this raises important questions on whether he will succeed. Germany, too, must come to terms with an unpalatable reality: the long term survival of the euro may require that it put its enormous industrial capacity and savings on the line to save the currency. It must accept the simple truth that a currency union, to survive in the long term, requires some degree of resource transfer from economically dynamic to economically depressed regions. Just as, say, taxpayers in New York do not protest or threaten secession when their tax dollars are used to pay federal benefits to poorer citizens in Wyoming, Germans will have to accept that some of their money will be used to transfer funds to Greece. Germany is justifiably reluctant, especially because its population is aging rapidly and the future liabilities of the German state to its aging citizens are huge, perhaps even unrealizable. Why should Germany be willing to fund, say, pensioners in France when it might not be able to fund its own senior citizens? Germans are also unwilling to provide these resources because they will be transferred with little accountability: the French may call for more "solidarity" but the French would never allow the Germans to have real authority in how the money is spent. Thus it is unlikely that the needed changes in collective beliefs will happen anytime soon. This is not a propitious foundation upon which to base the future of the euro.

Note

1 The proverb is: "A verita' e' figlia d' 'o tiempo". Italian translation: La verita e' la figlia del tempo.

References

Barbera, A. and Feltri, S. (2014) *La Lunga Notte Dell'Euro*. Milano: Rizzoli.

Berezin, M. (2009) *Illiberal Politics in Neoliberal Times*. Cambridge: Cambridge University Press.

Chorafas, D. (2013) *Breaking Up the Euro*. London: Palgrave Macmillan.

Lundgreen, P. (2013) The Looming Bankruptcy of Greece. *Caixin* Online, available at: http://english.caixin.com/2015-04-22/100802649.html

Marsh, D. (2009) The Euro: the Battle for the New Global Currency, New Haven, CT: Yale University Press.

Marsh, D. (2013) *Europe's Deadlock*. New Haven, CT. Yale University Press.

Nordvig, J. (2014) *The Fall of the Euro*. New York: McGraw-Hill.

Rachman, G. (2012) "Europe's Zero Sum Dilemma," *National Interest*, May/June Issue.

Reichlin, L. "Poche Illusioni Piedi Per Terra," *Corriere della Sera* 1 June 2014, available at: www.corriere.it/editoriali/14_giugno_01/poche-illusioni-piedi-terra-a9fe0a1a-e955-11e3-b53f-76c921903500.shtml

Sapir, J. (2012) *Bisogna Uscire Dall'Euro?* Verona: Ombre Corte.

Soros, G. (2012) The Tragedy of the European Union and How to Resolve It. *The New York Review of Books*, available at: www.nybooks.com/articles/archives/2012/sep/27/tragedy-european-union-and-how-resolve-it/

Van Overtveldt, J. (2011) *The End of the Euro*. Evanston: Ashgate.

Younge, B. and Semmler, W. (2011) The European Sovereign Debt Crisis. *German Politics and Society*, 97(29), pp. 2–21.

9 Conclusion

The international system is characterized by real inequalities of status and condition, which translate into power differentials that are objectively performed and that differentiate states into dominant and secondary, or "core" and "periphery". International relations theorists generally assume that economic size, military power, population, and technological sophistication are the main determinants of one's position in the inter-state pecking order. But in Europe, although these things matter, the qualitative dimensions of the economy also determine a country's place in the pecking order: levels of inequality, economic dynamism, social mobility, socio-political-bureaucratic organization, and the cultural beliefs of the nation. These elements, when taken individually, might not matter, but together they do and go a long way in explaining why some European states dominate the politics of the continent. European integration, from the beginning, was supposed to overcome that dynamic, which is another way of saying it was supposed to transcend the political implications of German dominance. Large but less powerful states, like France and Italy, have been particularly keen on integration precisely for this reason. But the evolution of the European project has only confirmed the realist insight that objective power, although it can be obscured, cannot be suppressed with good intentions and institutions. It will always reveal itself, in one form or another. Actors deal with this reality of hierarchy in a number of ways. Dominant states will act to preserve their leadership, sometimes by co-opting weaker states, other times by crystallizing their preferences in the institutions that emerge. But weaker states will aim to equalize their position in relation to the dominant state, although different actors have different ideas about how to achieve that objective. The Eurozone must be understood in that context: Germany saw it as an opportunity to expand its societal model to Europe as a whole, while lesser states, like Italy, believed that the euro would have an equalizing effect by enhancing their own position, weakening the position of Germany, or a combination of the two. The Eurozone crisis that began in 2007 has revealed how severely misguided this was, but what matters for understanding political behaviour is that it was believed and acted upon.

This framework provides a clue that helps to explain why Italy was predicted, accurately, to be one of the losers from EMU and yet the country, in the late nineties, enthusiastically embraced it: the euro was perceived through actors' aspirations rather than the reality of the currency union itself. Italians display the tendency to depict their nation as incorrigibly corrupt and backward. Like all compelling narratives, there is an element of truth to this idea, since on global rankings of indicators like corruption, tax evasion, economic equality, and public sector efficiency Italy does indeed score well below its peers. Most importantly, the nation is constructed on the basis of a comparison of a European ideal. When comparing themselves to "Europe", Italians, unconsciously or consciously, are largely comparing themselves to France and Germany. This construct is both analytic and normative, diagnosing the disease and the wish to cure it.

This construction of the nation and its relation to "Europe" took an imaginative flight of fancy in the late nineties when it was believed that entering EMU would correct the country's problems and raise the country's status and condition. The *vincolo esterno* (external pressure) of Europe could help Italy to fix its public finances. But it could not transform the country by, in the words of one euro-enthusiast, turning Italians into "mature and modern European citizens". Only Italians can do that, deciding by their own volition that they will now pay their taxes, and not pay bribes, and dismantle their cosseted firms and professions, and implement stronger cultural and legal mechanisms of accountability in every sphere of human activity – social, economic, and political.

On the surface, Britain in many ways was the polar opposite of Italy. The majority of Britons rejected the common currency. But below the surface there are similar dynamics. Like the Italians, the British idea of "Europe" largely refers to Germany and France, and this association is no less real when it is unconscious and latent. And as in Italy's discursive conception of Europe, these two countries, as constitutive elements of "Europe", are constructed in stereotypical ways. Entering Europe, for many Britons, meant being at the same level as these two countries. But this is where the similarity ends. The content of these constructions in the British political universe is very different, and to see why we must start with the way that many Britons construct their own imagined community. To start, with some small exceptions, there is no sense of inferiority with Europe; in fact, it is quite the opposite, as historical memories of empire, of being the "good guy" in World War Two, and of the association of parliamentary democracy and the common law with freedom give a sense of superiority compared to "Europe". When Margaret Thatcher said "I believe that Britain is the best country in Europe", it resonated with many Britons regardless of political ideology and social class. Had an Italian politician of Thatcher's stature said the same about contemporary Italy, very few Italians, perhaps with the exception of some fascists, would have taken him seriously. And so in Britain, with a few notable exceptions, there is little desire to obtain equality with Europe. In fact the idea of obtaining equality with Germany and France, both of which are associated in the popular imagination with war, absolutism, statism, and instability, would be deemed a lowering of the country's status and condition, not, as in Italy, a raising of these things.

The importance of cognition and affect

Most actors in the political communities under investigation could not analyze the complexity of the common currency. And so this lack of knowledge was replaced by cognitive schemes that contain memes such as hierarchy and equality, which characterize most inter-group relations. In Italy, the hope that the euro would help to equalize their inferior position in the European hierarchy became cognitively transformed into the theory that it would. These memes also had affective properties that produced approach tendencies, that motivated actors, and that helped make these ideas feel objectively real. In Britain, in contrast, the idea of being on equal terms with Europe was associated with negative affect, producing avoid tendencies. In other words, the memes "hierarchy" and "equality" had very different meanings and affective properties in Britain, which led to a very different outcome: the vast majority of Britons being opposed to entry into the common currency.

However, there is much variation in the cognitive schemes in Italy of a diverse range of actors, especially elites and non-elites. The findings were that elites display a stronger sense of identity than do non-elites; that is, they were more subject to non-rational influences, like feelings of belongingness, emotion, idealistic attachments, and abstract hopes. This seems to challenge conventional stereotypes of elites and non-elites: since the latter are patently less knowledgeable than the former, we might expect them to be more likely to be subject to non-rational influences. But this was not the case. Both, it bears repeating, interpreted EMU through the dominant discourses that were present in the late nineties, discourses that depicted the euro as some kind of solution to the country's problems and that only loosely, if at all, corresponded with the substantive content of the policy. But non-elites were less likely to have done so despite their lower level of knowledge.

The political discourses in Italy that surrounded the politics of EMU obscured the reality of the country's political situation, both internally and externally. Scholars elsewhere have highlighted that political identity often serves to hide painful truths (Hewstone 1986, Haseler 1996); the data that was collected for this project provides ample evidence for that astute observation. The narrative that the euro would fix Italy's problems, which have served to relegate it to second-class status in Europe, ignored the fact that only changes in Italians' behaviour, and not Europe, could do that. This narrative was reinforced by the German-level interest rates that Italy paid on its debt after it entered, which produced a false sense of security. These interest rates transmitted false information to policymakers because they were based, in part, on the belief that a Eurozone country could never default. The narrative through which the euro was understood also transmitted false information. By creating the impression that the euro would automatically be the solution to the country's problems, political agency was transferred to Europe, rather than to Italians themselves, where it properly belongs. It is partly for this reason that in the first 10 years of the euro, the structure of the political economy remained in place. Politicians who tried to implement the necessary reforms, like Cassese and Bersani, were forced to water them down because they were politically unpopular. The debt crisis that reached a crescendo in 2010 has shattered many illusions about what Italy must do to restore competitiveness and avoid default. The crisis also demonstrated the inadequacy of Italy's democratically elected governments, bringing in unelected technocrats, who tried, and failed, to transform the country.

Future research

There are findings in the preceding chapters that are valid for other European countries and which would be worth exploring. One of them is the role of associative evaluation in the construction of the nation: nationalized actors often define themselves on the basis of other social aggregates to which they belong rather than on the properties of their nation. These constructions are both descriptive and normative: they diagnose the disease and the prescriptions to cure it, which often entails some form of assimilation with the higher status or dominant state(s). The origins of this idea are in the discipline of sociology, where it has been observed, most notably by Elias, that individuals often define the properties of the self, not on the basis of the properties of themselves as individuals, but on the basis of the changing fortunes of the groups in which they belong. This project applied this idea to intergroup relations rather than individual-group relations, arguing that groups often describe their group status on the basis of their perceived assimilation, or lack thereof, with other groups. In Italy, for example, after entering the euro, many perceived that their status in the European inter-state pecking order had shifted because they were more "European", when, in fact, the structure of the political-economic and social relations remained unchanged. One can imagine that this dynamic was present even in other "periphery" European nations, which entered Europe because they believed that the latter would transform their country, and, after entering, believed they were more "European" and that their status had changed. Greece, Romania, Spain, and perhaps Bulgaria are good candidates for this framework. In Britain, in contrast, the euro was rejected, in part, because of the belief that assimilation with Europe would represent a reduction in the country's status and condition. In the intergroup context, this tendency to vicariously define status and condition on the basis of assimilation with other social aggregates certainly conditioned British attitudes to the euro, for the idea of being "equal" to Europe was associated with inferiority, not, as in Italy, with superiority.

This project relied mainly on three samples – interviews, newspapers, and TV clips – to examine their inter-textual congruence (the word text here refers to the constructivist conception of this word, as the surfaces upon which actors constitute political reality). These different texts were investigated to examine the presence and frequency of the cognitive and affective dynamics that condition a political community's approach to Europe. Further research could apply this inter-textual congruence method to other countries' relations with Europe to provide richly textured explanations of some of the variations that are observed in Europe. For instance, in the current Eurozone crisis, we are seeing the emergence of coalitions that are divided on the best way to preserve the euro: there are the creditor nations, led by Germany, who are calling for more rigour and austerity, and debtor nations, currently led by France, who are calling for more stimulus. On the surface, it appears that material dynamics, such as whether a country is a creditor or debtor, may best explain which coalition a country chooses to be in. But below the surface, it is plausible that nationally based narratives play a role. France's reluctance, for example, to surrender the kind of sovereignty that is implied in Germany's conception of a political union perhaps reflects the historical narratives, and their cognitive and affective salience, that have structured French-EU relations for decades. The same might be said about Ireland or Finland. The inter-textual congruence method would be an effective way to answer these questions.

Broader scholarly and political significance

One of the major criticisms of rational choice theory is that actors rarely have the knowledge to objectively evaluate complex policies. This is especially the case for the masses, most of whom could not identify the operations of a central bank that are used to control interest rates, much less a complex political structure like the euro. But the findings of this book highlight that more knowledge does not always equal more rationality. Most, perhaps all, of the highly intelligent elite members whom I interviewed in Italy for this project, who were almost uniformly enthusiastic about the euro, did not predict the grave difficulties that the euro has found itself in. What is more, most of the British who rejected the euro did so not because they predicted the current crisis. Many British eurosceptic elites predicted what has occurred. But the masses' opposition was based on more prosaic reasons: a belief in British superiority, or a sense that Britain did not belong in the euro because of essential difference with other (especially Southern) European countries, as evidenced by the following quote:

> Each [European country] is so different. France is completely different from Germany as is Italy. It is for this reason that I don't think that they would be compatible with one currency. It is wrong to impose one kind of monetary value on so many different economies.
>
> (*Sunday Express*, 18 November 2001, p. 9)

Compare that with this statement from former Italian Prime Minister and European Commissioner Romano Prodi:

> With the euro we will work a day less and earn as much as if we worked a day more.
>
> (Fragala 2013)

The juxtaposition of those quotes might make one wonder: who has the history of the euro shown to be right? To merely ask the question is to answer it, and this is all the more remarkable when we consider that the former quote was expressed by an average, barely adult British girl, while the latter comes from one of Europe's most illustrious leaders and technocrats, a professor of economics who has published widely and undoubtedly thought extensively about the euro that he helped to bring to Italy. And yet all this thought led him to the idealistic conclusion that the euro would somehow help Italians to work less and get paid more.

Britain has by no means escaped the effects of the crisis. But by not entering EMU, it has escaped some of the grindingly difficult choices that members of the common currency are being forced to make. It has preserved its autonomy to engage in the kind of large-scale quantitative easing that was very difficult and delayed in the Bundesbank-inspired ECB. It has not had to risk its credit rating by financing the Eurozone bailout funds that, were they to go sour, would threaten the credit even of economic behemoths like Germany. It has the option of staying out of the common currency, while other countries, even if they wanted to leave, could not without devastating economic consequences, at least initially. It could be argued, therefore, that Britain, by rejecting the euro, was more "rational". But this rationality, at least for most British citizens, did not emerge from a superior knowledge. It was rational in the sense that the consequences of the choice were better than the alternative. In this sense, *the idea*, but not the actor, was rational. And this suggests that an alternative definition of rationality might be based, not on the level of knowledge that the actor possesses, but on the consequences of the ideas that guide his behaviour. This would suggest that a time-lag is required before a decision or preference can be labelled "rational". The source of this rational idea may very well be nationally based narratives. In Britain, the sense that Britain did not belong in the euro because it was essentially better or different kept the country outside the euro, and in so doing protected Britain from many of the toxic effects of the Eurozone crisis. The euro debacle shows that the highly knowledgeable can make very irrational choices, while the unknowledgeable, unwashed masses can make very rational ones. Not because they could foresee the consequences of their choices. They couldn't. But rather because the ideas in their heads led to choices that produced favourable outcomes, at least compared to the alternatives at hand.

There are also important political implications, especially for Italy. The narrative that the euro would "save" Italy was widely held, but it was not invented by the masses. Like most other narratives that suffuse democratic practice, it was invented by elites. In the run-up to the euro, this narrative took many different forms; it was used to build support for the painful reforms that were enacted to satisfy the Maastricht criteria. It resonated with Italians because it seemed like a relatively painless way to escape their national nightmare. But the consequences of this narrative were harmful to the country's democracy. First, it obscured the fact that the true locus of agency is in Italy, not in Europe. In this sense, it reduced the sense of political accountability that is an essential element in healthy democratic practice. It also created exaggerated expectations about what the currency could do for the country. That these expectations were not met bred cynicism and has helped to fuel the widespread opposition to the euro that populist parties are exploiting. To some extent, this is a problem in all democracies. Politicians, to build support for their policies, make extravagant promises that exaggerate the benefits and ignore the true costs. In Italy, though, this has worsened the already preciously low levels of legitimacy that citizens ascribe to the political system. Living in Italy, and talking to Italians, one senses a deep and enduring malaise and cynicism. This is not a healthy condition, especially when the country needs the confidence and dynamism that are essential to restore economic growth and avoid a default. If this change does not occur, and the country continues to decline, then default on its debt would be only a matter of time.

Future possibilities

As the Eurozone crisis was reaching a crescendo, the President of the European Council, Herman Von Rompuy, astutely said that the "euro was like a drug" in the years before the crisis. The metaphor of a mind-altering and reality-obscuring narcotic is apt. Like the cocaine addict who, by snorting another line ignores the fact that his family, job, and health are deteriorating, many Europeans, stimulated by artificially low interest rates and unrealistic beliefs about the euro, ignored the very real structural weaknesses, at both the domestic and European levels, that created severe vulnerabilities that could only withstand crises with great difficulty and with very high political and economic costs.

Fearing the dangers that an unravelling of the currency might entail, European policymakers worked assiduously to save the euro by creating new institutions that aimed to centralize decision-making and perhaps create the pre-conditions for a real political union. On a positive reading, many of these ideas have succeeded. The outlines of a banking union have been accepted; a central fund, the European Stability Mechanism (ESM), has been agreed to, which will provide a high degree of economic firepower to assist economically distressed countries; and the ECB has finally agreed to be a lender of last resort. A closer look, however, does not council optimism. First, the proposed banking union still does not have a deposit insurance scheme, which is essential to sever the link between weak sovereigns and weak banks. Second, the ESM will not really transfer resources to economically distressed regions; rather, it will provide loans to national governments that have lost access to markets, which will only increase their external liabilities. This is not insignificant for countries, like Italy, whose debt exceeds 135% of GDP. Only a true fiscal union that gives a central authority taxing and spending powers can ultimately be the basis of a true political union with the power to transfer resources to regions that are either economically distressed or handicapped by the currency.

The euro will likely survive the near future, if only because the ECB will, in the final analysis, act as a lender of last resort and, in so doing, prevent a collapse. But this could lead to unexpected political consequences that might escape the control of even Europe's technocratic leaders. Although the ECB can now buy unlimited short term bonds from distressed governments, it comes with the conditions that they implement structural reforms that may or may not have democratic legitimacy (the Outright Monetary Transactions Program, or OMT). The German

Constitutional Court recently ruled that the OMT program violates European treaties, highlighting the fundamental disagreement between the ECB and one of Germany's most prestigious institutions. The major question, then, is whether Germans can be convinced that the OMT will not represent an illegal monetization of government debt. If not, the policy could lead to a strengthening of the Alternative for Deutschland party that wants Germany to leave the euro. In the elections of 25 May 2014, they received 7% of the vote, a significant increase from the 4% they received in the previous election. And in regional elections on 14 September 2014 their share of the vote was even higher: 9.8% in Saxony, 10.6% in Thuringia, and 12.2% in Brandenburg.

Other events could possibly lead to a destabilizing change in German public opinion. Up until now, Germany has been willing to loan (but not transfer) funds to economically distressed Eurozone countries. The capacity to do this has been possible because of the industrial and economic robustness of the country. But an economic downturn could potentially change that. Germany is now enjoying record levels of low unemployment and export competitiveness, but this could change if, say, another financial crisis were to lead to a credit contraction, a decrease in demand, and a loss of output. At that point, Germans might ask themselves: why should we save Southern Europeans when we are struggling? In addition, there are vulnerabilities in Germany, such as its rapidly aging population and fragilities in some parts of the banking system that could unexpectedly come to the fore and strain the country's public finances. This, too, would decrease its willingness to pay the costs of saving the euro. Lastly, one of the reasons that Germany was willing to help finance the bailouts to save the euro is that it has major trading relationships with other euro countries. This is changing, as trade within the Eurozone decreases even while it increases with non-Eurozone countries like China and Russia (Marsh 2013). If this trend were to continue, the incentive for bailing out other euro countries would decrease. After all, why protect markets that are becoming less important?

Many Germans believe that the only way for the euro to survive is for others to become more German: export powerhouses, fiscally prudent, and with an almost religious zeal for following rules. Many non-Germans, especially in Italy, agree, and they supported the euro precisely because they thought that it would impose German-style governance on a country that did not seem able to do the same for itself (or *vincolo esterno*, in Italian political discourse). In a sense, the Eurozone crisis gave Italians what they wanted: Mario Draghi and Mario Monti both used their levers of power to try to make Italy more like Germany. The result has been catastrophic, as now around half of Italians oppose the euro and many more resent policy being dictated by faceless bureaucrats in Brussels.

European integration, up till now, has largely been organized around the attempt to Germanize Europe in one way or another, and the Eurozone process has only accentuated this reality, but the blame cannot be placed solely on Berlin. Very important political forces in Eurozone countries are pursuing the same goal, including large sections of mainstream parties, and especially the centre-left, Europhile economists, and cultural elites in mainstream media outlets who tirelessly advocate German-style reforms. There are many reputable elites in peripheral countries who are challenging this form of integration by valorizing their own countries' particularities or advocating reforms that are appropriate for their own cultural contexts (an example in Italy is Ernesto Della Loggia, who expressed variants of this theme on the pages of *Corriere Della Sera* during the worst days of the Eurozone crisis). Unfortunately, most who are presenting alternatives are found on the radical sides of the political spectrum, and their legitimate criticisms of the euro are overshadowed by their shady and illiberal positions on other issues. Moreover, even when they have taken power, such as when Syriza won in Greece, other countries have rallied to Germany's side of the debate. This indicates that a change in the form that European integration has taken till now, namely, the attempt to Germanize Europe, is not forthcoming; that the ideological attraction of Germany's societal model, coupled with its material dominance, is the real motor and brake of Europe; and that other, weaker members must either submit or leave the union – with all the devastating consequences that will follow.

In light of these power dynamics, adjustment must happen internally/domestically. But this can be helped by the willingness of creditor countries to accept the dreaded transfer union in the form of the restructuring of debts of periphery countries like Italy. There is little hope, at least in the near term, that the country will produce the growth that is needed to absorb the masses of unemployed and to pay off its huge debt. Currently, just the interest on the country's debt costs 6% of GDP. These are resources that could be more usefully spent on investments that the country needs to increase its industrial potential. But as long as its debt remains high, those resources will be used to pay creditors. A controlled default that would make Italy's debt more manageable – say, that would bring it down to 80% of GDP – would create more breathing space for the country to use its resources to invest in the future. The same is true, *mutatis mutandis*, for other highly indebted countries in the euro's periphery. The political conditions for this policy are absent in creditor countries, but one can envisage that that might change. After all, nobody thought that Greece would be allowed to default on its private creditors, but it did, and although this did not solve the country's problems (it will need to default on its official creditors, too), it did temporarily increase confidence, at least until the next (predictable) crisis began after the election of Syriza.

Another crisis that was not existential in character would not necessarily be a bad thing. In fact, it could be salutary. Ever since Mario Draghi announced that he "would do whatever it takes" to save the euro, there has been a convergence of interest rates between the Germany and Italy. This may be rational from the point of view of investors – they are betting correctly that large countries like Italy will not be allowed to default – but it is not rational from the perspective of the common currency as a whole. It certainly does not reflect Italy's fundamentals; its low growth, high unemployment, and high debt do not provide grounds for the optimistic assumptions of investors who are willing to accept low yields on Italian bonds. But it is also not optimal because it takes pressures off governments to make politically painful reforms. Chapter seven mentioned the pattern that Italy is especially prone to: when the interest-rate spread between Italy and Germany increases, Italian governments panic and start implementing reforms. Then, mainly because of the actions of the ECB, the spread decreases, the panic is reduced, the pressure ceases, and Italian politics reverts to business as usual. This suggests that the ECB should, when the next crisis emerges, allow spreads to increase. This will create scaremongering about the existential threat to the euro, but the alternative – i.e. saving countries like Italy from the signals of markets – is the real threat to the long term stability of the currency. A fear of default, reflected in higher interest rates, would pressure Italian governments to overcome the societal interests that are using the democratic process to block the reforms that are necessary to create an attractive societal model that generates growth, employment, and confidence. An attractive societal model is the necessary condition for the enhancement of the country's status and prestige *regardless* of whether it is in a currency union or not, although the constraints of the euro make this objective harder than it otherwise would be.

References

Fragalà, G. "Dopo Monti, Prodi: ma gli italiani che hanno fatto di male per vivere con l'incubo dei Prof?" *Secolo d'Italia* 13 April 2013.

Haseler, S. (1996) *The English Tribe. Identity, Nation, and Europe*. London: Macmillan Press.

Hewstone, M. (1986) *Understanding Attitudes to the European Community: A Social Psychological Study in Four Member States*. Cambridge: Cambridge University Press.

Marsh, D. (2011) *The Euro: The Battle for the New Global Currency*. New Haven: Yale University Press

"My UK Values, by Eleanor," *Sunday Express* 18 November 2001: 9

Postscript

Greece shakes Europe to its core (again)

On 5 July 2015, the Eurozone saga took an unprecedented turn when a referendum was held in Greece. For the first time in the history of the common currency, the people were given the option of expressing their preference on the bailouts and austerity policies that, since 2010, have characterized the attempts to prevent the collapse of the Eurozone. This attempt to give a democratic element to the politics of the euro was not without comedy: the question that Greeks were asked to vote on – whether or not to accept the offer of Greece's creditors – had already been withdrawn, and hence, strictly speaking, they were voting for nothing. But leading countries, including Germany and France, solemnly declared that the referendum was about whether Greece wanted to remain in the Eurozone, and that a victory of "No" would mean exit. The stakes were therefore very high, and it was watched closely, especially by populists in other Eurozone countries, including Italy, that are working towards the same goal. In classical Greek fashion, the drama ended in tragedy: the No side won, an emotional roller-coaster of acrimonious negotiations ensued, expectations and uncertainty were high, and, ultimately, rather than leaving the currency, Greece remained in the Eurozone but at the very hefty price of accepting a set of austerity conditions that were worse than the ones originally on offer. This happened for a number of reasons, but the main ones are: the incompetence of the Greek government, the intervention of France in preventing Greece from crashing out of the euro, and the unwillingness of the majority of Greeks to voluntarily leave the currency even though this may be the least bad choice out of a number of unpalatable options.

One of the redeeming qualities of the dramatic weeks between the day of the referendum and the capitulation of the Greek government is that the true power structure of the euro was starkly revealed (again) in a way that left little doubt about its dynamics. The euro was supposed to lead to economic convergence and political unity that would help to realize the aspiration of the equality of its members. Instead, it has divided its members into creditors and debtors, accentuated the moral dichotomy between "virtuous" Northerners and "lazy" Southerners, and consolidated the hierarchical structure characterized by German leadership, French weakness, and other countries, including Italy, having little choice but to follow their dictates, at least on the most important matters in the governance of the currency. The sense of bitterness at this state of affairs is palpable in the public opinion data that show that the majority of Germans want Greece to leave the euro (Fahmy and Behrmann 2015), as well as the continued strength of eurosceptic parties in France, Italy, Finland, and other countries.

This chapter will trace the events that led to the Greek referendum and its aftermath. It aims to provide a tentative answer to one of the most puzzling questions of this saga: why would the majority of Greeks want to remain in the euro despite the economic devastation, as well as the humiliating political marginalization, that has accompanied their euro membership? My answer, based on journalistic investigations I conducted in Greece during the period from the day of the referendum until 10 July, is that the euro is perceived in political and cultural terms rather than on the basis of its concrete characteristics. As such, many Greeks ascribe non-monetary meanings to the euro that lead them to conclude that it would be best to remain in the currency, even though experts across the board feel that the euro is against the core interests of Greece. The chapter will conclude with some reflections on the proposals for political unification that have followed the Greek saga and argue that they are mostly chimerical.

The road to perdition

Greece's initial years in the euro coincided with a mini golden age. As credit flooded the country, debt and spending increased, leading to price rises and increased valuations that further fueled the country's speculative boom. One of the drivers of this bubble was its membership in the euro, which created a false sense of security that was reflected in the convergence of interest rates between Greece and its euro partners. The party came to a screeching halt after Greek Prime Minister Papandreou admitted that the country's fiscal accounting was the result of statistical chicanery and did not reflect the country's actual balance of payments; the real fiscal deficit was 12.5 percent rather than the 6 percent that was originally reported. This sparked a debt sell-off and skyrocketing interest rates, and closed off access to private capital markets.

At this point, European leaders had to decide whether to violate the Maastricht's Treaty no-bailout rule, or let Greece default. They subsequently violated the Treaty because it was feared that the alternative was a collapse of the banking system, which would spread contagion to other periphery countries and lead to a collapse of the currency. The first bailout, in 2010, consisted of 107.3 billion euros and included the memorandum of understanding (MOU) that stipulated a number of measures meant to put Greece on a sustainable path. It failed, mainly because its assumptions were unrealistic: the IMF projected a brief recession and a manageable rise in unemployment, and instead a dramatic decrease in output and significant increase in unemployment ensued. Despite this failure, creditors adopted the very same strategy for the second bailout in 2012 which, predictably, produced similar results.

The victory of the radical left-wing party Syriza in January 2015 cannot be understood without taking into account the economic failure of the two bailouts and, more importantly, the sense of humiliation and despair that they fueled. Syriza was a game-changer because it was the first time that a populist anti-austerity party took power in the Eurozone. It almost took power in 2012; pre-election polls suggested it could win, but its message of rejecting austerity was interpreted by many Greeks as a recipe that would have led to the ejection from the euro, and at the last minute many voters changed their minds and selected mainstream parties that continued the same policies of the previous years. The subsequent two years saw a worsening of Greece's condition and, hence, during the election campaign in 2014, many were willing to gamble Greece's euro membership by voting for Syriza, giving it a mandate to change the policies of bailouts and austerity.

The party's rhetoric was undoubtedly overblown. It promised Greeks that it would tear up bailout agreements, default on the country's debt, end austerity, promote socially inclusive growth through expansionary fiscal policy, and spark a change in the politics of the euro that would galvanize other populist, anti-austerity parties across Europe—and it would accomplish all this while remaining a member of the currency that was dominated by countries who did not share this vision. Syriza, in other words, conveniently ignored the most fundamental fact that has been emphasized in previous chapters, namely, that the real driver of Eurozone politics is an unequal power hierarchy with Germany on top (and with France as a lesser partner). Democratic majorities in peripheral countries, therefore, cannot change the politics of the euro without the consent of Germany, and there was little evidence that German leaders, or the German public, would accede to Syriza's demands. The question, then, was how long it would take Syriza to capitulate, or whether it was willing to take the logical step of staying true to its principles and leaving a monetary union governed by ordo-liberal principles that it nominally rejects.

It was under these conditions that the negotiations between the newly elected Syriza government and its Eurozone partners began in January 2015. The star of the show was the chiseled, motorcycle-driving Yanis Varoufakis, a British-trained economist and professor who, as Greece's newly minted finance minister, was the public face of the talks with Greece's creditors. Luckily, he has published detailed accounts of these negotiations in reputable media outlets (Varoufakis 2015a, Varoufakis 2015b, Parker 2015), and they are credible largely because they accord with the public statements of other Eurozone ministers as well as the agreement that was subsequently accepted by the Greek government.

The general outlines are the following: the newly elected Greek government felt that it had a democratic mandate to re-negotiate the MOU that had governed Greece's relationship to its creditors. The latter, in turn, made the reasonable assertion that the democratic will of Greece did not trump the democratic will of other Eurozone members. A blame-game ensued, with creditor countries blaming Greece for the country's dire situation, while Greece blamed the austerity conditions attached to the previous bailouts. Despite this toxic political climate, characterized by irreconcilable assumptions and highly unequal power dynamics, negotiations proceeded for three months and, at some points, there was even evidence for guarded optimism. According to Varoufakis, by April 2015 Greece was willing to accept 90 percent of the creditors' demands in return for some form of debt relief, but this was out of the question: Greece had to either submit entirely to the agreement or the negotiations would collapse, with all the dire implications that such an outcome implied. Syriza could not accept an offer that so blatantly violated its electoral mandate, and it was at that moment that Alexis Tsipras called the referendum so that Greeks could have a say.

Shortly after this announcement, the ECB decided to not provide further emergency liquidity to the Greek financial system, which was already hemorrhaging because of a bank run, until the status of Greece's euro membership was resolved. This led to the closing of the country's banks, and capital controls that included limits on the amount that could be withdrawn and transferred to foreign entities. Reasonable fears emerged that the country would not be able to purchase essential imports, like medicines and fuel, because importers could not withdraw sufficient funds to pay Greece's foreign suppliers. At this very dramatic point in the drama, Greeks were given a bitter taste of what an unmanaged exit from the euro would look like. During the same period, the mainstream media, in television and in print, inundated the country with apocalyptic scenarios that would supposedly transpire if the country reverted to the drachma, including untold impoverishment, civil war, utter collapse, and even foreign occupation.

It was in this context of a collapsing banking system and histrionic outbursts in the media that Greeks were asked to vote in a referendum that had the potential to determine whether they remained in the euro. Several polls taken the week before the vote suggested that it was too close to call; some reported a slight lead on the No side, while others reported that the Yes side was catching up. This further fueled speculation and shook the Eurozone to its core, dominating headlines and political discussion and creating faultiness across Europe between those who supported Greece's struggle, and those who blamed them for their plight.

On 5 July, 2015, Greeks voted. I was on an Aegean Airlines flight to Athens from Rome early that evening and, as the plane began its descent, the pilot announced the first exit polls that suggested a victory of the No side. In all my decades of regularly flying, it was the first time that I heard a pilot announce the results of a national vote. When the plane landed in Athens, more exit polls were being announced that confirmed that the No side won in a way that few predicted, with over 61 percent of the vote, and this despite the fear induced by closed banks, capital controls, the deluge of scare-stories in the mainstream newspapers and TV, and pre-referendum polls that showed that the country was almost evenly split on the question. I went straight from the airport to Syntagma square. As the phalanx of passengers exited Syntagma station and entered the square, there occurred a spontaneous chanting of "OXI OXI OXI" ("No" in Greek, pronounced Oi-hee). There was a sense of euphoria, as Greeks danced and sang and waved flags to celebrate the victory of the No side.

It was exciting but exaggerated, because the results of a referendum could not reverse the dynamics that characterized the Eurozone debacle in Greece up until then, namely, humiliating bailouts, economic depression, and the asymmetrical power relations between creditors and debtors that were the main driving force of these developments. Thus, unsurprisingly, this euphoria was short-lived, as the post-referendum negotiations proceeded with an air of drama and unreality that captivated the world. The major question that would have to be resolved remained: would Greece capitulate?

Post-referendum blues

Alexis Tsipras made an effort to show good faith when he replaced Yanis Varoufakis with the Oxford-trained Euclid Tsakalotos as the chief negotiator representing Greece in the talks with the country's creditors. He would bring, it was hoped, a softer, more conciliatory tone that contrasted with the perceived intransigence and arrogance of Varoufakis. Most informed pundits recognized that Greece's only possible trump card was the threat of leaving the euro and repudiating its debts, which would have entailed severe losses for creditor countries. It had a strong moral case for such a position, since most of the bailout money was surreptitiously used to save German and France banks that had helped to fuel Greece's speculative bubble.

Wolfgang Schäuble effectively neutralized Greece's only potential trump card when he called for Greece to leave the currency. This tactic was a master-stroke of strategy because it seemingly called Greece's bluff and undermined its only potential source of leverage. It also represented a major turning point in the history of the euro because it demonstrated that the currency is not irrevocable, as European elites believed. The statement also expressed the willingness of Germany to suffer major losses on its loans to Greece, which would inevitably happen in the event of a return to the drachma. Meanwhile, Alexis Tsipras said that he would do everything in his power to ensure Greece's continued euro membership. With these dynamics – Germany that wanted Greece to leave, and Greece that was unwilling to – the question was no longer *if* Greece would capitulate, but *when*, and with what conditions. The final deal included a third bailout of 86 billion euros, almost half of Greece's GDP, with conditions attached, such as the return to Athens of the hated "Troika" of international creditors to "supervise" spending cuts, tax increases, and privatizations. On 15 July 2015, we saw the sad spectacle of a radical left wing government authorize this deal in the Greek parliament. Even worse than this ideological *volte-face* is that it is continuing the policies of its predecessors, which have been catastrophic for the country.

Everybody unhappy in their own way

The deal satisfied nobody, and an indication of the sorry condition of the Eurozone's politics was that it was accepted by negotiators even though they manifestly did not want it. Fear of the alternative of Greece crashing out of the euro was the main driving force, despite the fact that many of the signatories perceived, accurately, the high probability that the third bailout will, like the first two, fail and, when it does, the country's euro membership will once again hang in the balance. Many blame Alexis Tsipras for the debacle, and when I was in Athens in mid-July of 2015 I observed many protests in front of the Parliament where cries of betrayal were expressed by voters who believed in, and voted for, Tsipras because they believed that he would get a better deal. There can be no doubt that he displayed a seriously incompetent negotiating strategy. His lack of a serious plan for a return to the drachma in the event of a collapse in the talks removed any potential leverage with which he could negotiate with other Eurozone countries. Moreover, creditor countries knew that an unplanned and unmanaged exit from the euro would be catastrophic for Greece, and that Tsipras would not go down in history as the Greek leader responsible for such an outcome. He therefore had to submit to their demands.

But it would be facile to only blame Alexis Tsipras. He did not have a democratic mandate for Greece to leave the euro, and to see why, we need to examine more closely that dynamics of Greek public opinion that constrained his actions. Polls repeatedly show that a large majority of Greeks are in favour of the country's continued membership in the euro. It was this that explained why, during the political campaign in late-2014, Syriza promised Greeks that it would not threaten the country's euro membership, even though most reasonable observers correctly recognized that this aspiration was irreconcilable with its other promises (restructuring Greece's debt, expelling the Troika, engaging in a Keynesian-style fiscal expansion). It also explains why, the week before the referendum on 5 July, 2015, Syriza campaigned for a "No" while re-affirming that it meant No *only* to austerity, *not* the euro.

This raises a question: why would Greeks continue to support membership in a currency that has manifestly been harmful to them? The reasons are complex, influenced as they are by many variables. One is class: socioeconomic and cultural elites are almost unanimous in their support for the euro. They tend to vote for the mainstream parties, like Pasok and New Democracy, which unquestionably support Greece's membership in the euro. Presumably, this is because these parties' supporters have something to lose in the event of a return to the drachma. But fears of economic losses only go so far in explaining this dynamic; there are other factors at play, as I discovered in my conversations with members of Greece's mainstream establishment. One person I interviewed, a professor of Political Economy at the University of Athens and a regular commentator on Greek television, told me he voted Yes in the referendum and is in favour of the euro, and said with a tone of conviction that the currency is in the best interests of Greece. But a little probing revealed a more complicated picture. He concedes that the austerity policies of the past five years have been a disaster and created a lot of social pain, and knows that the third bailout being negotiated will likely cause more of the same. He also recognized that the euro is a deeply flawed system: a currency union without the requisite political union that is a *sine qua non* for its proper functioning. I asked him how he reconciles these flaws with his pro-euro attitudes. He first told me that geographically Greece lives in an unstable neighborhood, and without the euro "it would be left alone". He also said that initially the euro coincided with a mini golden age in which standards of living rose for most. On the question of the lack of political union, he said that it might take 100 years, but it will happen.

Thus the euro for my interlocutor has meanings that are not strictly monetary, or not rooted in the concrete features of the currency. Rather, they are based on geopolitical fears, on memories of years of economic growth which coincided with the adoption of the currency, and on a faith – *faith* – that a political union will happen in the next 100 years.

The views of the masses on the euro are not dissimilar. My repeated conversations with Greeks of most political persuasions gave the impression of the widely held belief that without the euro, Greece will be "alone" in a dangerous geopolitical neighbourhood. This belief is held even though it is basically untrue: Greece's membership in NATO, as well as its strategically important location as a geographical bridge between the East and West would make any conflict with Turkey or in the Balkans a matter of crucial importance for European countries *regardless of whether Greece is in the euro.* For others, the euro is a symbol of their European identity in the sense of being "Western" and "modern", and exclusion from the currency union would, in their minds, undermine their sense of being "European". But this raises the question: who has decreed that the euro is essential for the possession of a European identity? The UK, Sweden, Poland, and Denmark are European despite not having the euro. The Swiss and Norway are not even in the EU, and yet both, by any reasonable standard, are "European".

This mix of sentiments reflects a trait that is observable in many other periphery countries that fundamentally reflects a sense – sometimes unspoken, but nonetheless present – of inferiority vis-à-vis Europe's "virtuous" countries; for others, it is indicative of the belief that Greece cannot become successful without being part of an ostensibly more advanced social aggregation like the EU. In this scheme, belonging to Europe is essential for the country's relative condition, status, and prestige, two elements that are highly valued for individuals as well as for nations. In this scheme, countries evaluate their relative position on the basis of association with groupings that are perceived to be prestigious. Chapter two of this book provided the theoretical basis for this idea of "Associative Evaluation" and showed how it characterized perceptions of the euro in Italy. Many in Greece also displayed it:

> It must be understood that for these [periphery] countries, EU membership signifies a certain modernity, both economic and political, an image of prosperity and power that the euro comes to validate at a symbolic level. [H]aving the common currency in their pockets, the Greeks symbolically reach the same level as the Germans or the French.
>
> (cited in Pettifor 2015)

In Athens, shortly after the referendum, I also interviewed someone who goes against the grain of Greece's establishment, even though he himself is part of their socioeconomic class. Like many other Greek elites, he was educated at universities in the English speaking world (McGill and the University of Chicago), and is a professor of finance and banking. Unlike most elites, he voted No in the referendum on 5 July 2015. Importantly, he unambiguously favours Grexit, and this makes him an iconoclast, since favouring a return to the drachma is associated with the extremist parties like the Golden Dawn. His views, I discovered, are devoid of the idealistic attachments, geopolitical fears, or symbolic associations that many others in the country express when they talk about the euro. For him, the currency is a matter of costs and benefits, and on this score, few would seriously challenge the assertion that it has been a disaster for Greece. In an interesting display of his heterodox views, he expressed to me that the transition from the euro to the drachma would not be the Armageddon that many predict would happen. Rather, with a bit of planning and good leadership, the change-over could happen in a matter of weeks, and any difficulties encountered in that period would be minor compared to the alternative of being shackled to the currency union. I then asked why the majority of Greeks don't feel like him. His response was that Greeks suffer from a minor form of Stockholm Syndrome, or Battered Wife Syndrome, both of which entail a pathological attachment to an entity that has harmed them. This may be somewhat hyperbolic but, then again, the saga that has characterized Greece's Eurozone membership has been, since 2009, one long painful sequence of events that, more than once, have raised questions about the degree of rationality of the actors involved.

Political repercussions

The Greek referendum reverberated across the continent and has significantly impacted European politics, although it remains to be seen how durable these changes will be. The most important outcome was that it revealed (again), beyond any reasonable doubt, the real power structure of the currency. The asymmetrical power relations were always there, but they were often cloaked with the rhetorical flair of European elites who would couch their decisions in the language of "partnership" and "unity". Now, they convince nobody. Germany is the leader, and has the final say on the major policies in the governance of the euro. France's weakness is no longer obscured behind the façade of the Franco-German motor. Italy's lower status is also before everyone's eyes. When Italian Prime Minister Matteo Renzi complained to Francois Holland about the dominance of France and Germany in the negotiations with Greece, he was expressing a widely felt sentiment in Italy, namely, the perceived unfairness of its relegation to the second-tier status.

It was not only the Italians who felt offended by this outcome. Europeans across the continent reacted very negatively to the third bailout. Ugly historical analogies that depicted Germany as bent on conquest gained prominence once again. Although they have been a staple of the politics of the euro, in form or another, since the debt crisis began, after the latest deal with Greece, there was a deluge of images on social media and in some newspapers that depicted images such as one with the German flag on top of the Acropolis. This evoked painful memories of the Nazi domination, including its conquest of Greece in 1941. Other examples include the trending hashtags of #thisisacoup and #boicottgermany. In addition, political alliances were overturned across the continent: on the one hand, we saw radical right-wing parties like the National Front in France and the Northern

League in Italy citing left-wing economists Paul Krugman and Joseph Stiglitz, both of whom condemned the treatment of Greece. On the other hand, some from the centre-left (for example, the social democrats in Germany) gave their consent to a deal that entailed austerity measures, like consumption tax rises and cuts to pensions, which would harm society's weakest. Meanwhile, those who were typically in favour of the EU, like the centre-left in Britain, became increasingly eurosceptic (Jones 2015).

Another effect was a renewed push to fix the design flaws of the currency to make it more sustainable. The outlines of the dispute, as expected, are between Germany and France. As always, here we must distinguish between what is publicly said by the elites from each country, and the underlying political realities that shape their respective preferences. Both agree that more centralization is required for the Eurozone, which presumably would entail a treasury and finance minister with an independent budget that could help to smooth out imbalances and ensure budget discipline. But this is where the similarities end. Germany wants these centralizing structures to be based on inter-governmental agreement. Meanwhile, France has proposed that an elected parliament is required to assure that this centralized treasury and finance minister are democratically accountable. This difference reflects the interests of the respective countries and will be difficult to bridge. A democratically elected Eurozone parliament of the kind proposed by France would mean that voters in that country would have a direct say in the budget largely funded by German taxpayers. It is not hard to see why this will not happen: German leaders do not have the mandate to fund a budget where the allocation of spending could theoretically be determined by voters in France and its allies in periphery countries like Italy, Portugal, and Spain. Evidence suggests that German leaders might be willing to agree to such an arrangement *only* after other countries converge with Germany in terms of competitiveness and economic output. But since this is unlikely in the foreseeable future, the French proposal will likely gather dust.

If centralization is to move forward, then, it is more plausible that it will bear the stamp of the German preference for an inter-governmental agreement, even though it is unlikely that France and other countries will agree to the establishment of a Eurozone treasury and finance minister that could intrude on their sovereignty. But this raises the question of whether the proposal will be sufficient to put the Eurozone on a sustainable footing, or at least on a path that will prevent another humiliating and demoralizing outcome similar to the one that transpired between Greece and its creditors in July 2015. It is hazardous to make predictions, given the flux of political events. The present conditions, including the widespread support for populist political parties and the euro's inadequate institutional architecture, suggest the road to salvation will be long and arduous.

Greece's future in the balance

The new bailout agreement which was bitterly swallowed by the negotiators includes strict conditions that would be difficult for any country to meet, and

Greece's current conditions are not favourable to such an outcome. Creditor countries will probably make noises about this being Greece's last chance, and that if it does not meet its obligations, external assistance will be cut, forcing a default and an exit from the euro. Equally plausible is that European leaders will demonstrate their continued talent in the art of muddling through by, say, fudging the numbers, or engaging in the usual diplomatic dance of calling multiple summits (with each one labeled as being the last chance to prevent catastrophe), creating new institutions, or delaying the day of reckoning by piling on new debts to pay for the old ones. But other events—such as a new financial crisis, or a new government in a strategically important country, or another referendum—could transpire to make Greece's euro membership hang in the balance. When one or several of these events occur, at a minimum the Greek government should have a serious "plan B" ready that would ease the transition to the drachma if the need arises. This would strengthen Greece's hand considerably, because it would signal to its creditors that it will not stay in the euro at any cost, and it would send a message to Greeks that the government is prepared for any eventuality. It would also send a message to the Greek people that the government would do its utmost to protect whatever savings Greeks had in the banks, and would ensure that the country had a sufficient stock of goods, like fuel and medicines, during the transition.

A controlled exit from the euro, while remaining a member of the EU, might be the least bad option for Greece. Although there is no formal legal mechanism for this option, policy is ultimately determined by its most powerful members (the bailouts, it is worth recalling, also had no legal basis, and yet they happened because Europe's leaders deemed them necessary). This means that if the will is present to keep Greece in the EU even though it reverts to the drachma, it will happen. And the evidence shows that the will is indeed there; in one of the many ironies of this saga, the man who is the personification of German cruelty in Athens, Wolfgang Schäuble, released a policy document on 12 July, 2015 that contained the most reasonable proposal: Greece could have a "time out" from the euro *while remaining a member of the EU*. This option would have allowed Greece to default on its unsustainable debt, now approaching 200 percent of GDP. Its competitiveness would have increased as well, perhaps leading to a boom in exports. Initially, the country would have difficulty paying for essential imports, but this problem would not be insurmountable, as Schäuble's proposal included the provision of humanitarian assistance that could have been used to ensure country had a sufficient stock of fuel and medicines. The fact that a developed, European country was receiving humanitarian aid would have been humiliating. But is that much worse than the policies that have been hitherto pursued, which have caused an interminable toxic cycle of crises, bailouts, austerity, and economic decline?

This suggests that the most difficult obstacle is psychological, not economic. First, some intellectual humility is required to admit that which most observers, publicly or privately, believe: it was a mistake for Greece to enter the euro. Second, Greeks must see the euro for what it is: an exchange-rate mechanism which, like the gold standard, constrains monetary independence. The main driving force of European elites was creating a political union, and each European country had their own reasons for pursuing this objective, which is why so many interpreted the euro, not on the basis of the rational costs and benefits, but through their aspirations. What is more, the euro, rather than unifying Europe, has divided it, and recent events point to further acrimony in the years ahead. Third, the euro it is not an essential element of European identity, which is at any rate an amorphous and subjective idea. Fourth, Greeks must begin to have faith in themselves as a people with the talents to solve their problems. This means discarding the widely held notion that it will become a third-world country outside the euro. A decent objective would be to obtain the status of Britain, Sweden, and Denmark, European countries that are members of the EU but not the Eurozone. This would not be a panacea, and it is likely that Greece, even outside the euro, would continue to suffer many of the malfunctions that characterize its political economy. Perhaps it would even become poorer outside the euro. But it would be free of the humiliating policies that have been implemented to preserve its tenuous membership in a currency union, and it would distance itself from the indignity of belonging to union where it is unwanted by the most powerful member.

References

Fahmy, D and E. Behrmann. "Germans Tired of Greek Demands Want Country to Exit Euro," *Bloomberg*, 15 March 2015. Available at: www.bloomberg.com/news/articles/2015-03-15/germans-tired-of-greek-demands-want-country-to-exit-euro

Jones, O. "The Left Must Put Britain's EU Withdrawal on the Agenda," *The Guardian* 14 July 2015. Available at: www.theguardian.com/commentisfree/2015/jul/14/left-reject-eu-greece-eurosceptic

Parker, I. "The Greek Warrior," *The New Yorker* 3 August 2015. Available at: www.newyorker.com/magazine/2015/08/03/the-greek-warrior

Pettifor, A. "The Euro, like the Gold Standard, is Doomed to Fail," *Project Syndicate*, + 31 July 2015. Available at: www.socialeurope.eu/2015/07/the-euro-like-the-gold-standard-is-doomed-to-fail/

Varoufakis, Y. "Germany Won't Spare Greek Pain: It Has an Interest in Breaking US," *The Guardian* 10 July 2015a. Available at: www.theguardian.com/commentisfree/2015/jul/10/germany-greek-pain-debt-relief-grexit

Varoufakis, Y. "The Defeat of Europe," *Counterpunch* 5 August 2015b. Available at: www.counterpunch.org/2015/08/05/the-defeat-of-europe/

Appendix

In the period from May 2010 to October 2010, I administered semi-structured interviews to 253 subjects in Italy, 69 of whom can be described as elites, and 184 as non-elites. Elites consist of politicians, both regional and national, professors from Italy's prestigious universities (Bocconi University, University of Trento, University of Bologna, etc), high-level bureaucrats, and managers of large firms. The composition of the elite part of the sample is the following: 13 are politicians, both regional (from Lombardy and Campania) and national, 12 are managers of large firms and banks, 36 are professors from Italy's elite universities, and 8 are economists at the Bank of Italy. The professors and managers were recruited through email and the snowball method. The economists from the Bank of Italy were interviewed at an international academic conference that took place in Rimini in June 2010. A close friend, who is a professor of economics in Toronto, graciously invited me to the conference and introduced me to the economists from the country's central bank, most of whom were there to present papers. Most of these elites are male, not surprisingly, since in Italy (as elsewhere) elite members continue to overwhelmingly be men.

The concept of elite is nebulous, and hence one may dispute the definition of elites outlined above. I argue that politicians, at the national and regional levels, constitute elite members because their decisions can potentially impact many, even if in practise their individual votes often count little in the creation of legislation. Professors, especially ones at elite universities, are opinion-makers and shapers and hence potentially very influential, even if some are much more influential than others. Managers of large firms also make decisions that can potentially have a significant impact. Moreover, Italy's central bank is one of the country's most prestigious, meritocratic bureaucracies. Scholars and economists who work there may not be decision-makers per se, but they produce the research upon which much political decision-making depends, and thus are arguably more "elite" than bureaucrats in other public bodies. All the categories represent a small sub-section of the population that is very influential, in relative terms, compared to the masses, and hence they can usefully be labelled "elite".

Non-elites were recruited using "purposeful sampling" (Dorofeev and Grant 2006, p. 42), which refers to the selection of subjects on the basis of criteria that restrict who can participate for reasons that have to do the objectives of the research. When selecting interview subjects in public places, the only criterion that restricted my selection was age: I only approached subjects who appeared to be past their late thirties/early forties. The reason is that some of the questions of the interview were focussed on the subject's attitudes in the mid- to late nineties, and I wanted to ensure that the subject was already politically mature in that period. As a result, most of the subjects are middle-aged. In any event, other scholars have discovered that age is not a significant predictor of attitudes towards Europe (Ammendola & Isernia 2005).

The non-elite part of the sample consists of 93 individuals from the South, and 91 from the North. Non-elites were recruited during the summer months of 2010 in public spaces where Italians tend to congregate during the warm summer evenings: piazzas, parks, commercial streets, etc. In the North, subjects were recruited in two cities: Milan and Trento. In the South, subjects were recruited in Naples, Salerno, and Bari. This method allowed me to obtain a sample that reflects Italy's regional and socioeconomic diversity. However, the distribution of categories of individuals in the sample does not correspond with the actual distribution in the country. For example, in the sample, almost one third are elites, while in the country, less than 5% are; in the sample, there are roughly equal numbers of Northerners and Southerners, but in the country, the population in the North is roughly 30% larger than that of the South. Women are also underrepresented, as they were less likely to consent to an interview than were men. The breakdown of the sample obtained in Italy can be seen in the following table:

Table XA Distribution of Sample (N = 253)

Elite membership	
Elite	69
Non-elite	184
Gender	
Male	184
Female	69
Region (non-elite)	
North	91
South	93
Occupation	
Professional	123
Commerce (self-employed)	28
White-collar worker	57
Blue-collar worker	32
No occupation (e.g. retired)	13

Sector of employment	
Public	113
Private	111
Unknown	16
No occupation	13
Political orientation	
Centre-right	25
Centre-left	76
Undetermined, no orientation	152

The total number of respondents, 253, was not part of the original plan. Initially, the intention was to interview a sample of between 100–150 people. But after beginning the process of recruiting actors, I discovered that it would be possible to interview many more than originally intended. Thus it was decided to continue the recruitment and interview of respondents until the end of the five- month period of my field work. The final result was 253 subjects.

This brings us to a potential dispute on the kinds of inferences that can be drawn from the sample. Some scholars would argue that, if the sample is not randomly selected, then inferences cannot be generalized to any actors outside the sample. This position, which is sometimes referred to as "pure probability theory", assumes that only in random samples do actors have equal probability of being selected independently of the researcher's biases or other influences; other samples – including quota sampling, purposeful sampling, etc. – reflect only the actors who were available at the particular time and place, or only those whom the researcher selects. These non-random samples, therefore, are not representative of the population and hence the findings cannot be generalized to a wider universe of actors (Nardi 2006).

Other scholars disagree with this position. First, they point out that random samples, too, are subject to availability bias. In many cases, only 30% of respondents are willing to consent to an interview, which requires another set of assumptions that may undermine the true representativeness of the sample (Dorofeev and Grant 2006). Second, if we were to take the pure probability theorist's argument at face value, it would negate the findings of much work in psychology and economics which is exclusively based on samples of university students; this seems questionable. Third, there are steps that can be used to minimize bias in non-random samples. One is called "deliberate sampling of heterogeneity" (Cook and Cambell 1979), which was utilized in the present work. For instance, in selecting professors as part of the elite sample, I initially went to the economics departments. But economists may share a similar world-view and/or ideology rooted in their training; and so I subsequently went to interview professors in the sociology department, a discipline which is often at odds with the economics profession in terms of world-view and ideology. This technique of deliberate sampling for heterogeneity was also applied regionally, since actors were selected from five different cities – two in the North, and three in the South.

Another way of reducing bias in non-random samples is to compare the results with those from representative samples. This is the approach that Hewstone (1986) takes. In his work on the social psychology of European integration, he relies on a sample of 545 university students, not randomly selected, roughly evenly drawn from the following countries: Germany, Italy, France, and the United Kingdom. His universe – that is, the unit he aims to generalize his findings to – is the "mass publics" in Europe, and he justifies his generalization to them on the fact that the statistical tests from his own sample are not that different from those of representative samples used by Eurobarometer polls. For instance, his results show that the British are the most eurosceptic, while Italians are the most euro-enthusiast, which is precisely what Eurobarometer polls taken in the same period indicate. The results from my sample, like Hewstone's, are not that different from the results of Eurobarometer research, and this further gives confidence that the argument from pure probability theorists – that non-random samples cannot be generalized to actors outside the sample – can be rejected. One of the reasons for this close correspondence between my sample and the results of Eurobarometer data is that the sample is to an extent "self-weighting" (Dorofeev & Grant 2006, p. 45), which means that under- or over-represented values partially offset each other. For instance, elites, who tend to be more supportive of the euro, are overrepresented in the sample by roughly 25%, while Southerners, who tend to be more eurosceptic, are overrepresented by roughly 30%. The overrepresentation of euro-enthusiast elites and the overrepresentation of eurosceptic Italian Southerners may offset each other, impacting the value of overall support for the euro in a way that renders the results more consistent with those of representative samples.

As mentioned, elites were selected with the snowball method, while non-elites were chosen with the purposive method. In order to determine whether the different sampling techniques impacted the distribution of values, the aggregate sample was statistically analyzed twice: once with elites, and once with only the non-elites but weighted to correct for the over-representation of eurosceptic Southerners. As was shown in chapter three, the results from the two samples are similar, giving further confidence that the results from the sample which includes elites (and which is self-weighting) are valid.

In summary, findings from non-random samples can be projected to a wider universe of actors, provided it is done with care and caution. This book uses three techniques to ensure that bias is reduced: the deliberate sampling for heterogeneity (with the exception of age), the comparison of some of my findings with the findings of representative samples from Eurobarometer, and limiting the universe of actors to whom the findings are projectable, namely, the middle aged.

The method utilized with the sample was the semi-structured interview (the questionnaire can be found below). The key elements within actors' cognitive frames that constitute the interpretive model mentioned above are the following: stereotypes, the hierarchy of European nations, Europe as a solution or fixer of this hierarchy, and the affect that is associated with these ideas. The interview questions were designed specifically to test for the presence and absence of these elements.

Subjects were encouraged to speak openly and freely about the reasons for support or opposition to the EMU; speaking about the "reasons" provided a richly textured account of actors' interpretations of EMU and Italy-Europe relations. Many actors, especially elites, responded with multiple reasons, and so I utilized the rule of "relative emphasis": I coded the reason that the actor placed the most emphasis on, which, I argue, is an indicator of the relatively stronger importance the subject ascribed to that reason. If the actor responded that the reason was European integration (as a majority in fact did), I then asked him or her why they thought that European integration was and is important for Italy. The responses to this question are a rich source of data on how the actor perceived Italy's relationship to Europe.

Subjects were also asked how they characterize Italy's image and position in relation to Europe's elite countries, both before and after entering EMU; if respondents replied that Italy was "inferior" to European countries, they were subsequently asked what were the causes of and the solutions to this state of affairs. The responses to these questions indicate how the subject places Italy in the hierarchy of European nations, the causes of this hierarchy, and the solutions to it. Level of knowledge on EMU was inferred with a question that asked the respondent if he or she was aware of any counterarguments to the euro, which, when coupled with the responses to the first set of questions (i.e., the "reasons" for their support or opposition to EMU), allowed me to determine with a relatively high degree of accuracy whether the subject was informed or not about EMU.

There were also questions posed that indirectly evoked some of the most interesting responses. For instance, one question was whether the majority of the subject's friends and relatives were in favour of EMU during the nineties, and, if so, the reasons for this support. The responses to this question often evoked the emotional and intellectual climate that the subject perceived. Another question asked respondents what it would mean for them if Italy was expelled from EMU, which evoked interesting responses that displayed how the actor constructed Italy's position in Europe, and Europe's role in Italy. Subjects were also asked whether and which country they felt Italy should emulate, which indirectly evoked the actors' feelings on Italy's perceived shortcomings vis-à-vis other European countries. Lastly, to determine how the actors' feelings and beliefs about Italy-Europe relations have changed through time, they were asked about their current attitudes towards EMU, and whether they have changed in the almost 10 years since it was introduced. These "indirect questions" evoked interesting responses that allowed me to determine the extent to which the actors' thinking on Europe was suffused with concreteness or abstract idealization, and whether they were sensitive to the concrete costs and benefits.

The responses to these questions also allowed me to code the political ideology of the subject while avoiding the problem of "social desirability bias". Scholars elsewhere have highlighted that many Italians are mostly unwilling to speak openly to researchers about their political ideology (Sani 1989, p. 282); I discovered this phenomenon was present especially among individuals on the centre-right, many of whom would not admit to a stranger that they voted for the party of Berlusconi.[1] Therefore, I coded political ideology on the basis of the ideological content of the responses to the questions above. For example, if the person responded that Italy was inferior because of the "communist magistrates", they were coded as centre-right; if in their responses they were fervently critical of capitalism and the Church, or if they said they had voted for Prodi and hence believed in his vision, they were coded as centre-left. There are some themes that cut across ideological lines and hence are ambiguous. For example, fear of immigrants is an important theme on the centre-right, but many individuals who might vote for the left also fear immigrants. Thus individuals whose responses were ambiguous were not coded as either left or right. I only coded those individuals whose responses gave me a high degree of confidence that their rhetoric matched their ideology (for example, it is unlikely that someone on the centre-left would tell me that Italy is infested with communist magistrates). Also, I only coded two categories, left and right, which excludes the variation in these ideological camps, such as the extreme left (SEL) and the extreme right (Lega). This method is not without its problems. But it is a valid way to circumvent the problem of social desirability bias that would have compromised the responses had I asked directly what their ideology was. Also, as a student of Italian politics, I am able to identify the rhetoric that is predominant on one or the other side of the ideological spectrum. I also had high standards – if there was ambiguity or uncertainty, the subject was not coded as either left or right. Consequently, less than half of the sample was coded: 101 actors out of 253, 76 of whom were on the left, 25 on the right.

Another source of potential bias is the fact that people generally have poor memories and hence asking them how they felt about, and perceived, the euro 13 years prior could evoke questionable responses. I argue this does not pose much of a problem, because entering the EMU was a significant event in the history of the country. The euro was part of the national conversation, especially in the late nineties, when entry was in doubt and policymakers worked frantically to ensure Italy met the Maastricht criteria by imposing austerity measures. Actors who watched the news or read the papers in that period, which would be most of them, would likely not forget how they felt about the prospect of adopting or being excluded from the euro, because it implicated their personal lives as well as the nation's place in Europe. In this sense, questions about the euro are qualitatively different from questions about other issues that are easy to forget about, such as events that happen regularly and that do not have implications for the entire nation. Thus the threat of memory availability bias, it seems, is minimal.

The interviews ranged from three minutes to two hours, but the average length was about 20 minutes. They were subsequently transcribed. During the process of transcribing, the tone of the language of the responses was also recorded in detail to give an indication of the emotional intensity that the subjects ascribe to ideas about Europe. This provided a richly textured transcribed account of all the interviews that were subsequently coded with a scheme designed by me to identify the presence or absence of the following key meanings: whether support was based on political or economic reasons, and on instrumentality or belongingness, the emotional intensity of the responses, whether and how the actor constructs the hierarchy of European nations, the causes and solutions to this hierarchy, and the extent to which the actor's thinking is suffused with concreteness or abstract idealization. All the variables are nominal, and hence basic chi-square tests were utilized to statistically test the differences between categories of individuals.

A note on the coding scheme is warranted. Readers will notice that in some of the graphs, newspaper articles and interviews were coded with the same categories, while in others, the categories are slightly different. The reason for the differences is that the newspaper articles imposed more constraints on which categories could be coded for. This was not the case with the interviews. As the interviewer asking the questions, I evoked responses that allowed for a greater variety of categories that could be coded. For instance, in Table 3.5, which displays the results of social comparison processes, interviews were coded for whether the respondent considered Italians to be *furbetti* (that is, cunning, deceitful, selfish, manipulative); this kind of language used to describe Italians is rarely found in high-brow publications like *La Repubblica* and *Corriere della Sera*, but in the interviews it was expressed sufficiently to warrant analysis.

The coding scheme raises legitimate questions about the findings, because many of the variables were coded, not on the basis of a fixed set of responses (as is done in the Eurobarometer research), but with the intent of "reading between the lines" of actors' responses, as it were. For example, I did not ask participants directly whether they were enthusiastic or not about the EMU, but I coded "enthusiasm" on the basis of the tone and language used to respond to the question of whether, and for what reason, they were in favour of the euro. In a similar vein, I did not ask participants whether they were on the centre-left or centre-right, but I was able to infer the ideology of many participants on the basis of their response to the question of what they believed were Italy's problems and the solutions to these problems; I also did not ask participants directly whether they believed that the EMU was the solution to Italy's problems, but I was able to infer whether they supported EMU for this reason on the basis of their responses to the other questions. This "reading between the lines" approach to survey research is not without its faults, but its advantages outweigh the risks because it allows us to probe deeper into the cognitive schemes of participants while mitigating the risks of social desirability bias. The coding scheme is available upon request for readers who would like more information.

The newspaper sample for Italy consists of 430 articles that were published between 1996 and 2004. Italy's two major national newspapers were selected, *La Repubblica* and *Corriere della Sera*: 209 of the articles are from the former, and 221 from the latter. Since the aim of the study is to identify how EMU was interpreted in terms of Italy's position in Europe, the only articles selected were those that discussed EMU or the Maastricht criteria in terms of their relationship to Italy and Italy-Europe relations. Therefore, the articles that discussed only the monetary, financial, and technical elements of EMU in a way that was divorced from Italy-Europe relations were excluded from the sample. The articles were coded with a scheme that aimed to identify the qualitative character of support for EMU, the way that Italy is conceived in terms of its relationship to Europe (in terms of hierarchy), and the presence or absence of counterarguments; the emotional content was identified by the tone of the language that was associated with EMU and Italy's chances of entering the former.

In order to analyze the way that EMU and Italy-Europe relations were represented in the TV news media, I went to the archives of the RAI (the RAI is Italian public television, a major news source for millions of Italians) in Rome and collected a sample of political talk shows and news reports that aired immediately before, during, and immediately after Italy entered EMU. Just like the sample of newspapers, TV shows that discussed the monetary, financial, and technical elements of EMU in a way that was divorced from Italy-Europe relations were excluded from the sample. As a result, the sample is relatively small: 19 clips. This small size made it doubtful that a content analysis – that is, counting the frequency and distribution of particular meanings – would be useful. Therefore, a more qualitative approach was needed. These news clips are a rich source of quotes and expressions that reveal elements of the intersubjective context in the period immediately before and immediately after Italy joined EMU.

The three sources that are analyzed – interviews, newspaper articles, and TV shows – can be conceived as three different texts, and highlighting the inter-textual congruence of these sources provides a rich account of the intersubjective context that is the subject of this book. This depends on certain assumptions about political and social reality, namely that it consists of narratives that are communicated through texts in the broadest sense of the term. That is, texts are not exclusively ideas written on paper, as the most common definition of the term conveys. Rather, human communication generally is understood to be composed of different texts which embody narratives that constitute social and political reality. As such, identifying the congruence between different texts is an effective way of constructing the building blocks of this intersubjective *reality as it is understood by the actors themselves*. Constructivist scholars elsewhere have testified to the utility of this method (Hopf 2009) and this book confirms that the inter-textual congruence method is indeed useful for scholars who focus on the ways in which political communities construct their worlds. Therefore, especially in chapters three and four, where the bulk of the empirical evidence is presented, the graphs and quotes should be understood holistically, that is, in relation to each other, as a kind of narrative that consists of the beliefs and meanings that actors ascribed to the EMU and Italy-Europe relations in the period 1996–2010.

Britain

The chapters on Italy were based on a set of data that took almost a year to collect, code, and statistically analyze. For reasons of time and resource constraints, a data set of that magnitude was not collected for the analysis of the

UK and the euro. This will limit the kinds of comparisons that can be made. For instance, interviewing 253 subjects in Italy allowed for a systematic comparison of the cognitive schemes of many categories of individuals, especially elites and non-elites. For the UK, to compare the cognitive schemes of elites and non-elites, I relied on interviews with three British elites and media and other sources that reflect elite's and non-elites views on the euro. For elites: Parliamentary debates, the BBC, and the Guardian. For non-elites: the tabloids and public opinion data from Eurobarometer. Although this more limited data from the UK restricts the inferences that can be made, it was nonetheless sufficient to investigate the patterns in the UK that highlight some of the key qualitative and quantitative differences with Italy.

Questionnaire:

1. Durante la fine degli anni novanta, lei ha sostenuto l'ingresso dell Italia nell'Euro? [if they respond yes] Quali furono le sue ragioni per questo sostegno?
2. Quali pensa siano le caratteristiche dell Italia, dalla fine degli anni 90 e attualmente, soprattutto a confronto con paese europei come Germania e Francia?

   If they outline list of problems, defects, etc, proceed to questions 3 and 4. If not, proceed to question 5.
3. Secondo lei, che e la soluzione per le problemi che lei abbia elencati? Italia abbia la capacita di risolvere questi problemi?
4. Chi o che cosa è responsabile per il fatto che l'Italia abbia queste caratteristiche?
5. Lei crede che l'Italia dovrà cercare di emulare I maggiori paesi europei? Perche?
6. Come pensa che l'Italia sia stata percepita dai maggiori paesi europei durante la metà e alla fine degli anni novanta? E attualmente?
7. Dopo che l'Italia e entrata a fare parte dell'euro, la sua valutazione dell'italia, rispetto agli altri paesi europei, era la stessa? Se si, in che modo ha cambiato la sua valutazione dell Italia dopo l'entrata nell'Euro?
8. Se l'Italia fosse espulsa dall'euro, come reagirebbe?
9. Per quanto riguarda la questione dell'ingresso dell'Italia nell'euro nel corso degli anni novanta, siete a conoscenza degli argomentazioni e controargomentazioni che sono state discusse negli anni Novanta? Si? Potete brevamente elencarli?
10. Nei dieci anni dall'introduzione dell'euro, il suo sostegno per l'euro è cambiato o è rimasto lo stesso? Quali sono le ragioni?
11. E a conoscenza se la maggior parte, tutti, o alcuni del suoi amici, la sua famiglia e i conoscenti hanno appoggiato l'entrata nell'euro negli? Se la risposta e si, quale e il motivo?
12. Qual e il suo mestiere, e il suo posto di lavoro?

Note

1 A revealing example is the following. I asked a person whom I befriended at the University of Trento who he voted for in the last election. Before replying, he looked around apprehensively to make sure that no one could hear, and then said that he voted for Berlusconi.

References

Ammendola, T. and Isernia, P. (2005) *L'Europa Vista Dagli Italiani: I Primi Vent' Anni.* In: M. Cotta, P. Isernia, and L. Verzichelli (eds). *L'Europa in Italia.* Bologna: Il Mulino.

Cook, D. C. and Cambell, D. T. (1979) *Quasi-experimentation: Design and Analysis Issues for Field Settings.* Boston: Houghton-Mifflin.

Dorofeev, S. and Grant, P. (2006) *Statistics for Real Life Sample Surveys.* Cambridge: Cambridge University Press.

Hewstone, M. (1986) *Understanding Attitudes to the European Community: A Social Psychological Study in Four Member States.* Cambridge: Cambridge University Press.

Hopf, T. (2009) Identity Relations and the Sino-Soviet Split. In: R. Abdelal, Y. M. Herrera, A. Johnson, and R. McDermot (eds). *Measuring Identity: A Guide for Social Scientists.* Cambridge: Cambridge University Press, pp. 279–314.

King, G., Keohane, R. O., and Verba, S. (2001) *Designing Social Inquiry.* Princeton, NJ: Princeton University Press.

Nardi, P. (2006) *Doing Survey Research: A Guide to Quantitative Methods.* Boston, MA: Pearson.

Sani, G. (1989) The Political Culture of Italy: Continuity and Change. In: S. Verba and G. Almond (eds). *The Civic Culture Revisited.* Newbury Park, CA: Sage Publications, pp. 273–318 .

Index

Note: Page numbers with *f* indicate figures; those with *t* indicate tables.

Alberti, L. B. 26–7
amoral familism framework 69, 70
Associative Evaluation 4, 17–22, 144, 157
austerity, politics of 3, 8, 130–3; Berlin Consensus and 67; France and 136–7; Greece and 151, 153, 156; internal devaluation and 69; Renzi and 137, 138

Babele Euro (TV programme) 43
backwardness: causes/solutions to Italy's 81–2, 81*t*; EMU as reason for 82, 82*t*; EMU as solution to Italy's 43, 51*t*, 109; equality principally and 15; Europe as equalizer of Italy's 40, 52; of Franco era in Spain 18, 87; Italian 26–7, 38*t*, 39, 41, 59, 65; Lebanon 17; socioeconomic, in Italy 23
Bastasin, C. 68, 71, 77
BBC, European Monetary Union and 109–10
Beach, D. 14
belongingness 43
Berlusconi, S. 67
Bersani, P. L. 74
Bertinotti, F. 40, 44
Blady, S. 91
Blair, T. 120
bottom-up discourses 19–20
Britain, European Monetary Union and: alternative views of 119–21; BBC views of 109–10; *Daily Express* views of 114–16; elite level views of 106–8; Europhiles/eurosceptics views of 116–19; Eurozone debt crisis and 121–3; exchange rate mechanism and 105–6; *Guardian* views of 110–13; mass views of 113; overview of 104–5
Brogi, A. 22–3
Brown, G. 106–7, 110
business, Italy's decline and 74–5
Buttiglione, R. 97

Cameron, D. 136
Casini, P. 67
Cassese, S. 24
causal attribution theory 16
causal schematas 16
Cavani, M. 40
Centorrino, M. 41
Chevallard, G. 23
Child, J. 14
civic culture 69–70
Club Med country 25–6, 92, 101
Cobianchi, M. 74
coding scheme 169
cognition: diversity and 48, 61–2*t*, 63; euro support in Italy and 34–46; hierarchy and 14–17; identity *versus* rationality logic at level of 49; importance of, and affect 143–4
Cole, A. 97
Converse, P. 21
core, periphery and 13–14
Corriere della Sera 45
corrupt European countries 99*t*
cultural explanations, for Italy's decline 69–70

Daily Express 105; EMU views in Britain 114–16, 114*t*
D'Alema, M. 27
deliberate sampling of heterogeneity 165–6
Delors, J. 127
Der Spiegel 67
Dini, L. 44

discourses, as interpretive schemes 11–13; bottom-up 19–20; top-down 19
diversity, cognition and 48
Draghi, M. 67, 134, 148

ECB *see* European Central Bank (ECB)
Eccles, D. 117
Elias, N. 17, 18
elite status: in Britain, EMU views of 106–8; cognitive schemes of 21–2; EMU knowledge and 60–2*t*, 62–5; euro and 3; makeup of, interviews 163
Ellman, L. 107
EMU *see* European Monetary Union (EMU)
entatitivity 15
ERM *see* exchange rate mechanism (ERM)
ESM *see* European Stability Mechanism (ESM)
euro: and Italy's decline 78–84; cognition, affect, support for 34–46; criticism of 42–3; disincentivized reform caused by 78–84; elites and 3; future research for 144–5; Germany and (*see* Germany, euro and); Greece and 79–80; humour and 91–2; Italy and 2–3, 23–4; relative status and (*see* relative status, euro and); social devastation of 3; theoretical overview (*see* euro, national politics and)
euro, national politics and 10–28; Associative Evaluation and 17–22; cognition and 14–17; hierarchy and 13–14, 24–8; ideas, beliefs and 11–13; Italy and 22–4; overview of 10–11
Europe, hierarchy and 13–14, 24–8
European Central Bank (ECB) 67
European integration 37–8*t*
European Monetary Union (EMU) 1; attitudes towards 35*t*; counterarguments of 41*f*; emotional content and 43–5, 44*f*; European integration and 37–8*t*; Europe-as-equalizer idea and 40–1; joining, mental map of hierarchy and 27–8; knowledge of (*see* European Monetary Union (EMU), knowledge of); losers from 11; scholarship on 10, 12–13; social comparison processes 38*t*; to solve Italy's problems 39*t*; support of, reasons for 36–7, 36*t*, 37*t*; *TG2 Dossier Oggi Euro* dialogue 36
European Monetary Union (EMU), knowledge of 42, 42*t*; by gender 51–2*t*, 52–3; by political orientation 56–8*t*, 58–9; by region 53–4*t*, 54–6; by status 60–2*t*, 62–5
European Stability Mechanism (ESM) 147
Europe-as-equalizer, European Monetary Union and 40–1
Europhile label 3, 5, 7, 70, 71, 75, 106, 108, 110, 148–9
eurosceptic label 3, 34, 43, 104, 111, 117, 121–2, 166
exchange rate mechanism (ERM) 105–6

family-oriented capitalism 74
Fazio, A. 43, 45, 64
Fearon, J. 10
Ferrera, M. 73, 79
Financial Times 105, 115
Fiscal Pact 133–5
Five Star Movement 78
Flight, H. 105, 108
France: current account balance 128*f*; ease of doing business ranking 101*t*; Fiscal Pact for 133–4; real economic growth 128*f*; Rule of Law Index ranking 101*t*; unemployment rate 128*f*
Frattini, F. 97
Friedman, A. 40, 43, 91, 110
Friedman, M. 11
furbetti 39, 59, 81–2, 169

gender, Italy's decline and 72–3
Germany: current account balance 128*f*; ease of doing business ranking 101*t*; euro and (*see* Germany, euro and); real economic growth 128*f*; reunification of 1; Rule of Law Index ranking 101*t*; unemployment rate 128*f*
Germany, euro and 28, 126–40; austerity and 130–3; Fiscal Pact and 133–5; future possibilities for 147–9; Italy replacing France and 137–40; overview of 126–7; political backlash from 135–7; scepticism of 127; winners and losers from 127–30
Giannini, M. 45
Gill, C. 122
Greece, referendum in 151–61; bailouts and 152–3; future of Greece and 159–61; initial years in euro and 152; overview of 151–2; political repercussions of 158–9; post-referendum issues 155; support of euro, reasons for 156; Syriza party elections and 152–3; Tsipras and 155–6; Varoufakis and 153–4; voting results 154–5
Gualmini, E. 79

Guardian, The 105; articles on Britain and Euro, number of 111*f*; EMU views and 110–13; euro support/opposition in 112–13, 112*t*

habitus concept 17–18
Heath, E. 108
Hewstone, M. 166
hierarchy: Associative Evaluation and 17–22; cognition and 14–17; dimensions of 4; Europe and 13–14; ideas and Europe's 14; Italian elites and perceptions of 25–6; Italy's place in 22–4; mental maps of 24–8
Hitchens, P. 114
Hix, S. 101
Holland, F. 158
humour, euro and 91–2
Huysseune, M. 22

identity index 49
identity logic: *versus* rationality logic 49–50; strong, meanings/feelings associated with 49; weak, meanings/feelings associated with 49–50
Il Sole 24 Ore (newspaper) 44
immaturity thesis 77–8
integration initiatives 15; intergroup comparisons and 15–16
internal devaluation 131
international structure, euro and 69
interviews, sample distribution of 164–5*t*
Isernia, P. 63
Italy: backwardness of 26–7, 38*t*, 39, 41, 59, 65; capitalism model of, described 74; copying Europe's major countries 92*t*; corruption and, perceptions of 100*f*; current account balance 128*f*; decline in (*see* Italy's decline, acceleration of); ease of doing business ranking 101*t*; elites and perceptions of hierarchy in 25–6; euro and 2–3, 23–4; female participation in labour force 72–3; Fiscal Pact for 133; hierarchy of 22–4; Maastricht criteria and 1–2; national income share in 100*f*; perceptions of Europe 22; political economy of 68–9; productivity in 100*f*; real economic growth 128*f*; relative status and 88–95, 93*f*; Rule of Law Index ranking 101*t*; study conclusions about 141–2; tax evasion in 75–6; unemployment rate 128*f*
Italy, European Monetary Union and: BBC views of 109–10; exchange rate mechanism and 105–6; *La Repubblica* views of 111–13
Italy's decline, acceleration of 67–84; business and 74–5; cultural explanations for 69–70; euro and 78–84; gender and 72–3; immaturity as cause for 77–8; overview of 67–9; professions and 73–4; public sector and 77; state-level explanations for 70–2; structural explanations for 69; tax evasion and 75–6

Jabko, N. 12
Jaruegui, P. 18

Kinnock, N. 109
Krugman, P. 11, 159

language, properties of 48
Lapalombara, J. 75
Leaderless Europe (Hayward) 96–7
Lebanon backwardness 17
legal costs, of tax evasion 76
Letta, E. 99
Lippman, W. 21
Loggia, D. 27

Maastricht, Netherlands 1
Maastricht criteria 1, 25, 55, 67, 79; Italy and 1–3
Maastricht Italia (TV programme) 40, 43–4, 110
Maastricht treaty 1, 19, 79; German policy and 69, 97, 132; Greece and 152; Italy's place in Europe and 92, 92*t*; Outright Monetary Transactions and 134; purposes of 1; United Kingdom and 122–3
Marr, A. 114
Martino, A. 42, 133
Marzano, A. 44
Mazucelli, C. 14
McNamara, K. 12
memorandum of understanding (MOU) 152
Merkel, A. 130, 131, 133
Mister Euro (TV programme) 40–1, 44
Monti, M. 76, 78, 148
moral costs, of tax evasion 76
MOU *see* memorandum of understanding (MOU)

National Front (NF) 136
newspaper samples 169–70
non-elite status: cognitive schemes of 21–2; described 163–4; EMU knowledge and 60–2*t*, 62–5

OMT *see* Outright Monetary Transactions (OMT)
Optimum Currency Area (OCA) 11, 42
ordo-liberal policies 131
Ottinger, G. 99
Outright Monetary Transactions (OMT) 134–5, 147–8

Pederson, T. 14
periphery countries: core *versus* 13–14; external pressure of Europe and 68; Germany as bailout financer of 8, 11, 126; hierarchy and 24; immaturity of 77; international structure of, euro and 69; Italy as 97, 127
Persson, G. 122
political community, identity within: analysis framework 49–50; data/commentary of results 50; elite/non-elite status and 60–2*t*, 62–5; gender and 51–2*t*, 52–3; language and 48; overview of 48–9; political orientation and 56–8*t*, 58–9; region and 53–4*t*, 54–6; study analysis 65
Prodi, R. 74, 91, 112, 145
professionals, as pro-European groups 73–4
professions, Italy's decline and 73–4
public sector, Italy's decline and 77
pure probability theory 165
Puri Purini, A. 17
purposeful sampling 163–5
purposive method 166

raccomandazioni 65
Radice, G. 104
rational choice theory, criticisms of 145
rationality: *versus* identity logic 49–50; models of 10–11
Redwood, J. 109
relative status, euro and 87–102; discourse and misperception of 89; identity and 87–8; Italy case study 88–95; overview of 87; perceptions of, in Italian newspapers 93*f*; perception *versus* reality of 95–102
Renzi, M. 73, 121, 135, 137, 138, 158
Repubblica, La 45, 111; euro support/opposition in 112–13, 112*t*
Risse, T. 12
Rotfeld, A. 98

sample distribution of interviews 164–5*t*
Savona, P. 43, 109
Schäuble, W. 110, 132, 136, 155, 160
Scheff, T. 18
Scotson, J. 18
second tier status 7, 17, 88, 95, 96, 98, 102, 158
semi-structured interview method 166–7
Single European Act (SEA) 1
snowball method 166
social comparison processes 38*t*
Spain backwardness 18, 87
Stability and Growth Pact 134
state-level explanations for Italy's decline 70–2
Stephens, P. 105
Stiglitz, J. 159
structural explanations for Italy's decline 69

Talani, L. S. 119–20
Tangentopoli scandal 71–2
tax evasion: Italy's decline and 75–6; legal costs of 76; moral costs of 76
TG2 Dossier Oggi Euro dialogue 36
Thatcher, M. 28
thick version, of rational choice 10, 11
thin version, of rational choice 10
top-down discourses 19
transfer union 132
Trichet, J-C. 67
Tsakalotos, E. 155
Tsipras, A. 154, 155–6
Tullio-Altan, C. 23, 26, 27, 71–2

United Kingdom (UK): "Big Three" and 97, 99; Brown's five tests and 107–8; ease of doing business ranking 101*t*; Eurozone debate of 5, 104–5; exchange rate mechanism and 105–6; Rule of Law Index ranking 101*t*

Varoufakis, Y. 153–4, 155
Veltroni, W. 91
Venturini, F. 45
Von Rompuy, H. 147

Wendt, A. 10, 14
Willis, F. R. 22
Wilson, H. 117
World Economic Forum 2010 Global Gender Gap Report 72

Young, H. 117
Young, J. 114

Zaller, J. 34

For Product Safety Concerns and Information please contact our EU
representative GPSR@taylorandfrancis.com
Taylor & Francis Verlag GmbH, Kaufingerstraße 24, 80331 München, Germany

www.ingramcontent.com/pod-product-compliance
Ingram Content Group UK Ltd.
Pitfield, Milton Keynes, MK11 3LW, UK
UKHW022126190926
475702UK00013B/1666

* 9 7 8 0 8 1 5 3 7 1 0 7 6 *